2001

2001

R 2001

2003

2003

27 APR

-5 MAY

2 a MAR 2

Culture, Politics, and Television in Hong Kong

Until the mid-1980s, when it became clear that Hong Kong would return to China, Hongkongers tended to identify themselves as something other than mainland Chinese. Now that Hong Kong is again a part of China, the local population have had to come to terms with their previously suppressed Chinese identity.

This book is concerned with how the identity categories of Hongkongers and mainlanders have changed in the 1990s. The analysis focuses on the role, in this process, of the popular media in general and of television in particular. The author looks specifically at the relationship between 'television ideologies' and 'cultural identities', and explores the role of television in the process of identity formation and maintenance as illustrated by the case of Hong Kong television.

Eric Kit-wai Ma is Assistant Professor of Communication at the Chinese University of Hong Kong. He is the author of several books written in Chinese on the popular culture of Hong Kong.

Culture and Communication in Asia
Edited by David Birch
Deakin University, Australia

Trajectories: Inter-Asia Cultural Studies
Edited by Kuan-Hsing Chen

The Politics of Chinese Language and Culture
The art of reading dragons
Bob Hodge and Kam Lovie

Constructing 'Post-Colonial' India
National character and the Doon School
Sanjay Srivastava

Culture, Politics, and Television in Hong Kong
Eric Kit-wai Ma

Culture, Politics, and Television in Hong Kong

Eric Kit-wai Ma

London and New York

First published 1999
by Routledge
11 New Fetter Lane, London EC4P 4EE

Simultaneously published in the USA and Canada
by Routledge
29 West 35th Street, New York, NY 10001

Typeset in Baskerville by
Keystroke, Jacaranda Lodge, Wolverhampton
Printed and bound in Great Britain by
Mackays of Chatham plc, Chatham, Kent

British Library Cataloguing in Publication Data
A catalogue record for this book is available from the
British Library

Library of Congress Cataloging in Publication Data
A catalogue record for this book has been requested

ISBN 0–415–17998–X

For L.

Contents

Series editor's preface

Critical scholarship in cultural and communication studies worldwide has resulted in an increased awareness of the need to reconsider some of the more traditional research practices and theoretical/analytic domains of arts, humanities, and social science disciplines, towards a recognition of the differing imperatives of what critical studies of culture and communication might look like in an Asian context. The demand for research materials, undergraduate textbooks and postgraduate monographs continues to grow in line with this increased critical awareness, while developments across the world continue to recognise the need to situate work in communication and cultural studies on and in Asia within a more global framework.

This series is designed to contribute to those demands and recognition. It aims to look in detail at cultural and communication studies from critical perspectives that take into account different 'Asian' imperatives. In particular, it focuses on work written by scholars either living in or working on the region, who have specific interests in opening up new agendas for what constitutes critical communication and cultural studies within and about Asia. The overall aims of the series are to present new work, new paradigms, new theoretical positions, and new analytic practices of what might often be traditional and well-established communication and cultural activities and discourses.

The theoretical direction of the series is principally targeted at establishing these new agendas and by critically reflecting upon the appropriateness, or otherwise, of theories and methodologies already well established, or developing, in cultural and communication studies across the world. Having said this, however, the series is not aimed at producing a monolithic blueprint for what constitutes critical cultural and communication studies in or about Asia. Nor is there a specific agenda for what the series might consider to be an appropriate critical cultural and communication studies for Asia.

The series is not, therefore, designed to create an orthodoxy for 'Asian' communication and cultural studies, but to open up new ways of thinking and rethinking contemporary cultural and communication practice and analysis in the arts, humanities, and social sciences. The series is aimed to counter, as much as possible, those essentialising processes of colonialisation, marginalisation, and erasure, which have taken place in the past by the unproblematised imposition of Western theory upon cultures, societies, and practices within, and on behalf of, Asia.

Many of the books in this series may not necessarily fit comfortably into traditional disciplines and paradigms of Asian studies of cultural and communication studies; nor are they intended to. The main aim of the series is for all of its books to argue for a diversification and opening up of existing theoretical positions and specific discourses across a wide range of texts, practices, and cultures. All of the books in the series will be positioned to argue persuasively for the development of studies in culture and communication that are able to frame critical commentary through theoretical and analytic practices informed first and foremost by a concern with Asian cultures and discourse.

The series has as its fundamental premise a position that argues that analysts can no longer operate as neutral, disinterested observers of some 'reality' which supposedly pre-exists the discourses that they are analysing. To be critical necessarily means to be self-reflexive. In that sense, then, the series is designed to position cultural and communication studies in and about Asia as critical disciplines which require, within their own practices, an approach to developing some sort of praxis that enables the work that we do as analysts significantly to contribute to political, social and cultural discourses and awareness, at local, regional and global levels.

Series Editor: David Birch, Deakin University, Australia

Editorial Advisors
Ien Ang, Murdoch University, Australia
Tony Bennett, Griffith University, Australia
Kuan-Hsing Chen, National Tsing Hwa University, Taiwan
Jae-Woong Choe, Korea University, Korea
Chua Beng Huat, National University of Singapore, Singapore
Lawrence Grossberg, University of North Carolina, Chapel Hill, USA
Sneja Gunew, University of Victoria, Canada

Annette Hamilton, Macquarie University, Australia
Ariel Heryanto, Universitas Kristen Satya Wacana, Indonesia
Masao Miyoshi, University of California, San Diego, USA
Yoshinobu Ota, University of Kyushu, Japan
Gyanendra Pandey, University of Delhi, India
Ubonrat Siriyuvasak, Chulalongkorn University, Thailand
Panuti Sudjiman, University of Indonesia, Indonesia
Trinh T Minh-ha, University of California, Berkeley, USA
Yao Souchou, Institute of Southeast Asian Studies, Singapore
Robert Young, Wadham College, Oxford, UK

Tables and figures

Tables

Figures

Acknowledgements

Very special thanks are due to Professor James Curran, my supervisor at Goldsmiths College, University of London, for his insightful suggestions and intellectual inspiration. I am also grateful to Professor Joseph Chan, who gave me continued intellectual guidance in the years when I was a student at the Chinese University of Hong Kong. Kindest thanks to Professor Michael Curtin for his detailed comments on the manuscript. His substantive criticisms improved the book immeasurably. Professor John Eldridge and Professor Richard Collins read the manuscript with great care, their comments were particularly helpful at the early stage of this project. I am very grateful to Professor David Birch, the general editor of this series, and the reviewers of this book for their invaluable recommendations.

The case studies in this book relied on archival materials, programme schedules, video tapes, and shooting scripts, which are inaccessible to academic researchers. I am indebted to Professor Ng Ho for helping me gain access to the materials I needed. The organisational analysis in chapter 7 is based on interviews with 20 Hong Kong TV producers, scriptwriters and senior executives. They were generous in giving me their time for the long interviews. This book is a very small part of a project entitled 'Mass Media and Political Transition in Hong Kong', which was supported with funds from the Hong Kong Universities Grants Committee. I would like to thank Professor Chin-Chuan Lee, the principal investigator, for including me in his ambitious project. Thanks also go to Victoria Smith and Goober Fox at Routledge for their editorial support, and to Denise Lam for managing the manuscript.

I am grateful to my daughter Natalie and my wife Louisa, for tolerating the late nights, and for their day-to-day encouragement and support. The completion of this book is testimony to their understanding and companionship.

Abbreviations

ATV	Asia Television Limited
BLR	*Below the Lion Rock*
CUHK	Chinese University of Hong Kong
GBU	*The Good, the Bad, and the Ugly*
GIS	Government Information Service
GT	*Great Times*
HA	Hongkonger/Ah Chian (identity categories)
HKL	Hong Kong Legend
MCD	Membership Categorisation Device
RTHK	Radio Television Hong Kong
RTV	Rediffusion Television
TVB	Television Broadcast Limited

Chapter 1

Identity, culture, and the media

Hong Kong is now part of China. The people of Hong Kong, both in legal elucidation and in historical exegesis, are now citizens of the People's Republic of China. While their political identity seems rather settled, their cultural identity continues to undergo complex and contradictory processes of transformation (Abbas, 1997; Cheng, 1996; Ma and Fung, 1997). In retrospect, the formation of a distinctive local identity has only taken root since the late 1970s, when the new-found Hong Kong identity was largely constructed by foregrounding cultural differences between Hongkongers and mainland Chinese. The majority of Hong Kong people are ethnic Chinese like the people in mainland China, but in the mass media, mainlanders were stigmatised as 'uncivilised' outsiders against which modern, cosmopolitan Hongkongers could define themselves. This de-sinicisation produced an ambivalent and sometimes contradictory Sino-Hong Kong identity. On the one hand, Hong Kong people identified with traditional Chinese culture in an abstract and detached sense, but on the other hand, they discriminated against particular cultural practices which were seen as affiliated with the communist regime on the mainland.

Since the news of the inevitable return of Hong Kong to China broke in the mid-1980s, Hong Kong people have had to face again their once-suppressed Chinese identity. No longer can one see the unrestrained stigmatisation of mainlanders in the vivid social imagination of the popular media of the 1970s and the early 1980s. The Hong Kong media have recently turned their attention to the historical 'roots' of Chinese culture, and mainlanders have been represented in more favourable terms. This remapping of identity boundaries involves complex and dynamic struggles among institutions and actors, which engenders the selective processes of remembering and forgetting.

What this book tries to do is to chart these mediated processes of de-sinicisation and re-sinicisation of the Hong Kong identity from the 1970s to the 1990s. I shall focus on the highly visible, but shifting, identity boundaries between mainlanders and Hongkongers, asking when, how, and why the new mainland immigrants of the 1970s were differentiated as 'non-Hongkongers' by the people of Hong Kong, who were themselves previous Chinese immigrants or their descendants. I shall also ask how these identity categories of Hongkongers and mainlanders changed in the 1990s, as China was first conceived and then subsequently became the new political master. Analyses will focus on popular media in general and television in particular.

Thus, the specific questions that I am going to answer in this book are twofold: First, what are the persistent identity categories constructed in media texts and circulated among the general public of Hong Kong? How do these categories change in response to socio-political changes? How different is the Hong Kong identity constructed in the television programmes produced by different organisations during different historical periods? Second, if there are obvious differences in the programmes produced in different organisational and historical contexts, what contributes to these differences? What are the relation-ships between texts and contexts? What are the mechanisms that shape and influence the various forms of televisual discourses? The first set of questions involves *locating* those identity categories in televisual texts and in social practices. The second set of questions involves *explaining* the continuity and changes, and the similarities and differences of identity categories by way of organisational and historical comparison. These questions, which concern the specific case of Hong Kong identity, underlie the more general aim of the book, which is to examine the ideological character of television.

Television and identity

By presenting the Hong Kong case, this book specifically explores the relationship between *television ideologies* and *cultural identities*. Both concepts are among the central problematics of current television studies.[1] In critical media studies, television has traditionally been conceived as carry-ing dominant ideologies in service of the status quo; but this conception, in both its crudest and most refined forms, has been strongly contested by the recent emphasis on textual fragmentation and audience reception. On the other hand, the issue of cultural identities has been of pressing concern, both in public discussion and academic discourse. Since the end of the Cold War, many parts of the world have been experiencing an upsurge of nationalism which is muddled with the fevered activities of identity confirmation and exclusion. Repeated attempts in academic discourse to deconstruct ahistorical identities have been unsuccessful in silencing essentialist identity claims. In addition to this, when the issue of television ideologies and cultural identities are put together, the relationship becomes even more confusing. The relationship between the two is often conceived under a plethora of claims, ranging from the strong identity-conferring ability of the television medium, to the relativist position of limited television influence on nomadic identities. This book attempts to clear up some of these confusions and explore the role of television in the process of identity formation and maintenance, as illustrated in the case of Hong Kong television.

Although this book is about Hong Kong television, it also touches on the symbiotic relation between television and film in Hong Kong. Both media show strong institutional ties with each other and articulate dominant identity representations in much the same way. Together they contribute to the vitality of local culture despite their strong market-led mode of operation. Right now there is a tremendous amount of interest in Hong Kong movies. This book serves to introduce Hong Kong television into the discussion and help international readers to understand the broad cultural base from which Hong Kong film and television have developed a distinctive visual aesthetic and indigenous culture.

The structure of this book is built around case comparisons of different periods and between television organisations. Before going into specific case studies, chapters 2 and 3 first present socio-historical analyses of the role of television in the formation of local cultural identities in post-war Hong Kong. By contrasting the socio-political contexts of the 1970s (chapter 2) and the 1990s (chapter 3), the variances of television ideologies in these two periods will bring to light the dynamics between televisual texts and their contextual influences. In the 1970s, when Hong Kong was politically separated from China, and the resentment against immigrants from mainland China was widespread, television melodrama serials and other popular films strongly reinforced the stigmatisation of outsiders and the consolidation of an indigenous cultural identity for the established Hongkongers. But in the 1990s, as China regained sovereignty over the colony, there emerged a crisis of identity transformation, and television dramas from different television organisations differentially drew upon the cleavages of dominant social discourses. This macro overview will provide the socio-historical context for the case studies in subsequent chapters.

Chapter 4 is an in-depth case study of a television serial produced in the 1970s. The analytical focus is on the articulation between textual and social discourses. The serial highlights the conflicts between mainlanders and Hongkongers in the late 1970s. Shortly after the serial was released, mainlanders in the territory were being addressed after the name of a mainland character in this particular serial. The negative textual representation became a source of social stigma for the new immigrants. Textual and contextual analysis will demonstrate how this television serial, in textual and social discourses, constructed cultural identities both for established Hongkongers and for new immigrants from mainland China.

Chapter 5 compares this case study of the 1970s with two television programmes produced in the 1990s. I shall argue that the multiplicity and stability of televisual meaning are subjected to the structuring of dominant powers in their socio-historical contexts. In the 1970s, there was a set of relatively stable identity categories of 'Hongkonger' and 'mainlander'. In the early 1990s, when China was regaining sovereignty over the colony and political powers were intrusive in media politics, the identity categories of Hongkonger and mainlander, as inscribed in televisual discourse, became unstable and polysemic. These polysemic categorisations are not ahistorical and idiosyncratic, but are over-determined by the cleavages of dominant discourse in the larger social context.

Chapters 6 and 7 provide a case comparison of two television dramas produced by two different television institutions in the 1990s. Chapter 6 is a textual comparison of the two dramas produced respectively by commercial and public television. The textual analysis shows that the two dramas have different ideological and polysemic patterns. The ideological diversity of the two dramas suggests the deferential effects of institutional dispersion of the respective organisations on televisual discourses. Chapter 7 is an institutional analysis of the production process of the two selected dramas and will trace the organisational source of the ideological diversity identified in chapter 6. The analysis will explore how television ideologies and polysemies are articulated in the inter-play of socio-political and institutional influences. It is a refinement of the concept of overdetermination by highlighting the dispersion effect of different television institutions. In sum, chapters 4, 5, 6 and 7 are case comparisons across different times and institutions.

Chapter 8 draws this book to a close by summarising the main theoretical arguments and empirical findings in three broad general-isations: First, television ideologies exist in a field of domination with variable forms and patterns. Second, specific ideological forms depend on the interplay between contextual and organisational definers. Third, television has a variable ideological impact, which is most effective in reinforcing social hierarchies.

Transgressing the bounds of media analysis

Having briefly set up the specific signposts for this book, I want to sketch out in this introduction a more general approach that underlies the case studies that occur in following chapters. This book attempts to answer the recurrent call from divergent traditions to break the compartmentalisation of media studies and work out a multi-dimensional and contextual approach to media analysis (Corner, 1995; Curran, 1991a, 1990a; Golding and Murdock, 1991; Gripsrud, 1995; Hall, 1989; Kellner, 1995; Murdock, 1989a, 1989b, 1995; Peterson, 1994; Stevenson, 1995; Thompson, 1990; van Dijk, 1994). My attempt is a multi-faceted study of Hong Kong television grounded in their organisational, social, and historical contexts. A justification for this kind of contextual approach can be given in a quite straightforward argument: mass media, as a central cultural institution of modern society, is deeply embedded in its socio-political contexts within which media texts are produced and consumed. The tripartite instances of text, production, and reception each have a distinct logic of their own which cannot be determined by, or dissolved into each other, yet they are tied together in such a complicated dynamic that concentrating on each of the individual instances risks distorting the whole of the communicative process. Analysis of individual instances can be of value when generalisations are made within the reasonable limits allowed by the empirical data. For example, audience ethnographic studies can enhance our understanding of the discursive practices of television reception within everyday activities. Textual analysis can enrich our understanding of the formal aspects of media texts. However, problems arise when the analysis of any single instance is carried out with the implicit or explicit aim of making a generalisation applicable to the whole institution of the television medium. Textual analyses which conceptualise the nature of film and television through textual properties alone, risk falling into the fallacy of textual determinism. Audience studies, which claim that the whole system of televisual meaning is idiosyncratic, risk *detextualising*[2] the television medium, and dismissing altogether the moments of determination brought about by the political economy of televisual texts.

Indeed, compartmentalising television studies may lead to theoretical distortions, while a multi-dimensional approach can foster a much more comprehensive understanding of the mass communicative processes. However, this is easier said than done. Despite growing cross-disciplinary initiatives, the relation between those who work respectively on text, reception, and production remains, at worst, hostile, and at best, suspicious.[3] I think part of the reason is that a contextual approach inevitably means 'transgression' (Gripsrud, 1995) of established borders between research traditions, and that these traditions have long been separated by prestige-bound methods and theories. A contextual analysis often requires the analyst to venture into unfamiliar terrain and to defend himself or herself armed with unfamiliar concepts and tools. But the reward is worth the effort. A context-sensitive approach can modulate the pendulum swing between extreme forms of media determinism and unrestrained relativism which have been common in media research for the past few decades. Contextualising media studies within the specificity of the socio-historical context implies the relativising of the media determinacy in grand media theories, and, at the same time, fixing the complex yet patterned media phenomena in their immediate contexts and saving media analysis from the solipsism of the 'post-mass-mediated world'.[4]

This book is such an attempt. It is intended to be a multi-dimensional exploration of Hong Kong television programmes, regarded as complex media and cultural phenomena, comprising their socio-historical contexts, the actual televisual texts, their production processes, and some significant aspects of the audience's appropriation. The emphasis is to contextualise the tripartite instances of text, production, and reception of television programmes, by placing them in wider circles of relevant organisational, social, and historical circumstances (see Gripsrud, 1995: 1–5). In doing so, I am steering a winding course between a number of seemingly opposing ideas and methods, which have been deployed to analyse the television medium in different research traditions. These traditions, concepts, and tools will recur in different ways in the following chapters. Here, by way of introducing the overall design of the book, I shall mention some of them, in simple but overlapping dichotomies, signalling the markers that will enable me to negotiate a third route. The third route I propose is unoriginal and revisionist, with winding trails, fuzzy edges, and overlapping boundaries; it is not intended to be another neat theory with rigid parameters, but hopefully, when taken as a whole, it will give a more balanced understanding of the television medium and its relationship to the formation and maintenance of cultural identities.

Political economy and cultural studies

The first pair of dichotomous terms into which I shall attempt to find an inroad is between political economy and cultural studies. British media studies has been roughly divided into the tradition of political economy on the one hand and cultural studies on the other (see Curran *et al.*, 1996; Ferguson and Golding, 1997).[5] The former is materialist in its theoretical approach, has a research agenda which concentrates on media ownership, media economy, and media organisation, and more readily uses methods of mainstream sociological and organisational analysis. The latter is culturalist in its perspective, works mostly on textual analysis and audience research, and reveals a preference for qualitative and ethnographic methods. Of course these distinctions are highly general and undifferentiating,[6] but they do represent prestige-bound preferences across the divide which have persisted for years. The inadequacies of either side are quite obvious: the mass media are characterised by the duality of the material and the discursive, the economic and the symbolic, and the industrial and the cultural. However, quite a number of academics acknowledge this duality but continue to concentrate on one side and pay scant attention to the other, leaving what Murdock (1989a; 1997) calls a 'missing link' at the heart of media studies. This missing link is partly responsible for some of the weaknesses in the works of both traditions.

On the part of the political economists, there is a central problem of economism and reductionism. Some forms of the political economy argument have 'no conception of the struggle for meaning' at all (Hall, 1989:50). The symbolic is usually reduced to the economic order. Acknowledging this criticism, Garnham (1995, 1997) refuses to engage the question of struggle and articulation and maintains that the determining moment rests at the economic end of media processes. However, recent audience studies have shown the complicated cultural logic and the diverse fields of articulations within and between texts and audiences. Although economic practices determine the distribution of cultural practices, they cannot explain and determine the complex patterns of meaning articulated within the limits of that distribution (Grossberg, 1995). Faced with these multiple cultural articulations (see Slack, 1996), a one-to-one relationship between the economic and the cultural seems to be highly inadequate. These criticisms of economism and reductionism are familiar arguments that need detain us no longer. Yet it is interesting to note that the objection is well taken by one of the leading political economists Graham Murdock, who holds himself partly responsible for that wrong perception (1989a). He admits that in some of his early assertions, the mode of production 'determines in the last instance'. The term 'last instance' implies that no matter how far the analyses go, they always come back to the economic; this unbreakable, one-to-one, and unidirectional relation between the economic and the symbolic is reductionistic and needs to be revised. Thus he proposes moving 'from last to first', seeing the economic as the necessary starting point for analysis but not the destination. This means that

> economic dynamics play a crucial role in structuring social spaces within which communicative activity takes place, but that within these spaces the symbolic sphere operates according to its own rules, which establish their own independent determinatons.
>
> (Murdock, 1989b:230)

On the part of the culturalists, the missing link between the symbolic and the economic renders the elevation of the cultural aspect as an independent mode of analysis. Thus Fiske (1987) celebrates the independence of the 'cultural economy' from the 'fiscal economy' and sets free audience activities from the structure of power and inequality in which the audiences are embedded. This is why Fiske argues that there is no need to worry about the limited diversity of mainstream television programming, since in the cultural economy, the skilful audiences can produce polysemic cultural meanings from the limited televisual discourses offered to them. He is challenged by culturalists and political economists alike for being too affirmative to the establishment (e.g. Golding, 1990; Morley, 1993). Perhaps it is quite misleading to single out Fiske as a representative of the culturalist tradition, because within the tradition there are numerous researchers who are critical of his unrestrained populism. More recently, there has been a tendency to institutionalise cultural studies behind the walls of universities and hence dilute its critical edge in cultural intervention (Gitlin, 1997). Culturalists are accused of paying too little attention to the political economy of cultural production. But ignoring the economics does not necessarily mean that all culturalists are celebrating the popular and bypassing the issue of domination. There are those in critical cultural studies who have long been engaged in the critical project of exposing different forms of domination. Within this *critical* fraction of the culturalist camp, there has been a strong emphasis on the complicated articulation between dominant cultural patterns and the media output. This emphasis, which remains one of the greatest strengths of British cultural studies, should benefit materialists' research by explaining domination via the cultural link as well as the economic link.

What all this amounts to is the need for 'a new synthesis combining political economy and culturalist insights' (Curran, 1990a:133; Kellner, 1997). As Murdock (1995, 1997) contends, critical political economy is at its strongest in explaining who gets to speak to whom, and what forms these symbolic encounters take in the major spaces of public culture. He also contends that cultural studies, at its best, has much to say about how dominant and popular discourse and imagery are organised in complex and shifting patterns of meanings, and how these meanings are reproduced, negotiated, and disputed in the ebb and flow of everyday life. Hopefully, this book can bring together the strengths of both traditions.

Essentialism and constructionism

The key subject of enquiry of this book is that of cultural identity. The historical, shifting, and constructionistic nature of cultural identities has of late attracted a good deal of attention (see Hall and du Gay, 1996; Preston, 1997). Cultural identities are in constant contestation and revision (Schlesinger, 1991). The elaboration of cultural identity is a chronic process in which histories, traditions, and social memories are invented and revised according to political and economic needs (Brett, 1996; Hobsbawm and Ranger, 1983; Samuel and Thompson, 1990). This constructionist perspective challenges the modernist concept that identity is given biologically or produced by acts of individual will. It also challenges the widespread belief that there are ahistorical cultural identities that have to be defended and protected.

While acknowledging the fluidity of identities, I would like to argue, with equal emphasis, that the urge for a stable identity is a persistent and recurrent drive in social and cultural practices. Despite various attempts at deconstructing ahistorical identity claims, essentialist identities are still very popular among a wide variety of social and ethnic groups. Simply showing the process of identity construction fails 'to grapple with the real, present-day political and other reasons why essentialist identities continue to be invoked and are often deeply felt' (Calhoun, 1994:14). The discussions in the following chapters try not to dismiss this essentialist tendency by simply 'proving' the historical nature of cultural identity. Instead, I want to account for the dual tendency of essentialism and constructionism that revolves around the social practices of identity formation and maintenance.

The case of Hong Kong identity presented in this book illustrates, in a dramatic way, how the Chinese identity faded out under the colonial rule of the British government, and began to re-emerge as China regained her sovereignty in 1997. The nationalistic Chinese identity, the historical identity, the colonial identity, and the cultural identities of the Chinese mainlanders and local Hongkongers all come into play, with varying degrees of force at different historical moments of time (Ma and Fung, 1997). Against this historical and thus shifting identity de-marcation, it is quite revealing to see the strong tendency of essentialist identity being claimed by the local Hongkongers. Their strongly felt need for identity confirmation casts a reasonable doubt on the kind of soft relativism that glorifies individual choice and suggests that all identity claims have the same standing in social practices and cultural representations. In the case of Hong Kong, the constructionist view can be deployed positively to see the identity formation process as a 'project', highlighting the collective will to foster a local and indigenous cultural identity. It is a historically constructed identity which is claiming an ahistorical status.

As Larrain (1994) observes, and the Hong Kong case demonstrates, identity confirmation processes may easily become ideological when some versions of identity are concealing the cultural diversity in the interests of an established group. The ideological aspect of identity assertion can be further amplified by the mediation of television. I shall argue that television is offering narratives, myths, icons, themes, and membership categories from which cultural identities can be constructed. The identity boundaries of them/us, good/bad, inclusion/exclusion are not presented in polysemic array but are structured ideologically in hierarchies and inequalities, or to coin Massey's (1991) term, in power geometry. Identities are historically invented and revised, but they are often celebrated or suppressed in ahistorical, essentialist, and ideological forms.

Media-centricity and the marginalisation of media influences

This book is about television ideologies and cultural identities. The primary aim is to explore the role of television in identity formation and maintenance. When we talk about the relationship between the two issues, we enter into a murky field populated with diverse and contra-dictory claims about the identity-conferring ability of television. Debates on the subject are often mixed with taken-for-granted assumptions which are confusing and questionable. One of the most common assumptions is a media-centric view of society, in which 'the media are firmly placed as central and attributed with a high degree of political, social, and cultural power' (Corner, 1995:4). This tendency can be seen in recent media studies[7] which consider the media alone as the central and causal factor in social and cultural analyses. As media studies institutionalised, it is hard for media researchers not to let the importance of the study get out of proportion. This kind of media-centricity also emerges out of the academic circles into public discussion. Perhaps because television penetrates modern societies at a rapid and conspicuous rate,[8] media policy-makers and laymen alike often assume that television is most influential to the cultural identity of a population. Domestic television production and distribution are assumed to be of paramount importance in cultural defence (against foreign media imports) and nation building (inventing or consolidating national identity). Schlesinger (1993) describes this as the 'fallacy of distribution': domestic media products are often believed to have an innate identity-conferring ability once they are distributed via the media.

While there is a tendency towards media-centricity, there is also a tendency towards marginalising the media, especially in the anthropological and historical studies of identity and nationalism. These studies helpfully highlight the historical and social contingencies of nations and nationalism (Anderson, 1983; Gellner, 1983; Hobsbawm, 1992; Smith, 1991), but most of them surprisingly neglect an analysis of the role of the mass media in identity formation. There is scant discussion of how the spread of popular print media was related to the rise of nationalism in the eighteenth century (e.g. Anderson, 1983). Thompson (1990) rightly argues that 'mediazation' has become the central process of modern culture. Martin-Barbero (1993) shows how Latin Americans had their first taste of nationhood with the advent of the mass media. Popular media is not the only factor in the construction of cultural identity, but it remains an influential one. As Corner puts it,

> [whilst] media-centricity can result in a disabling overestimation of media influence, it would be prudent not to push television too far into the wings of modern social analysis, since it is, on any estimate, one of the defining institutions of modern society.
>
> (Corner 1995:5)

In this book, I shall try to analyse the role of television in the process of identity formation in a context-sensitive way. I shall illustrate, using

Hong Kong as an example, that identity formation is a social process that involves both media and non-media related factors. Socio-historic factors may reinforce and/or oppose other media factors in the process of identity formation and maintenance. The media may have powerful[9] or limited[10] effects in different socio-historical circumstances. Media researchers and media policy-makers who fixate on the power of the media will easily lose sight of the larger contextual forces at work. Anthropological and historical accounts that ignore the influence of the mass media may also miss one of the major building-blocks of modern cultural identity. Only when the compartmentalised research traditions are surpassed can we understand more fully the dynamic interplay between the mass media and other social agents. The general argument of this book, therefore, is that the mass media, and television in particular, has a strong reinforcing effect on identity formation and maintenance if it works in congruence with other socio-political factors. In other words, the more compatible the media and non-media factors, the greater the reinforcing effects, and vice versa.

Contingency and determinacy

A full appreciation of the interplay between media and non-media factors in specific historical contexts inevitably introduces the notion of contingency. 'Contingency' has been helpful in restoring *differences* from the totalitarianism of grand narratives in modernity. Ideology in the grand theories of modernity (such as Marxism, classical political economy, and Weberian theories) tends to be universalistic, to disregard difference, and to reduce the specific to the general (Larrain, 1994). Most of these grand theories have an essentialist view of identity. The discourse of a coherent self is often distinctively modern, and modernity is distinctively linked to the discourse of a moral and rational self (Calhoun, 1994). However, when the mono-discursive society of modernity gradually evolves into the multi-discursive society in most late capitalist nations (Fiske, 1994; Kellner, 1995), ideology dissolves into a diffused discursive power, and identity becomes nomadic. In multi-discursive societies, it is quite difficult for analyses of contemporary media culture *not* to take account of the multiplicity and differences in discursive relations and discursive practices.

As Corner (1995) discerns, there is a general shift away from the general theories about influence in both social scientific and critical/ideological studies. Media researchers have become more sensitive to the occurrence of variables, the causes of which cannot be directly explained, nor the consequences neatly generalised. Television studies has become more contextualised in the specific instances of television viewing (e.g. Ang, 1996; Petrie and Willis, 1995; Silverstone, 1994). Localised contexts are taken more seriously even in the research that deals with globalisation and international media influences (e.g. Liebes and Katz, 1990; Sreberny-Mohammadi, 1991) and historical perspectives have been adopted to situate media influences more fully in their political and social contexts (e.g. Curran *et al.*, 1987; Robins, 1996).

The notion of contingency is even more immediate because of the widespread use of case studies in television research. Researchers working on cases are regularly confronted with the notion of contingency every time generalisations are made. In this book, contingency is taken as a positive notion. I maintain that the notion enriches our understanding of the multifarious media phenomena of the present day by encouraging the appreciation of specificity and historicity.

While this is a comparative case study which fully registers contingent factors, it does not easily discard the notion of determinacy. The danger of contextualised studies is to see total contingency, indeterminacy, and randomness as inevitable and necessary outcomes.[11] The cost of total contingency for social science is very high because 'it ultimately reduces society to a random arrangement of floating antagonisms between various forms of power and resistance to power' (Larrain, 1994:104). Television ideologies and cultural identity are contingent, yet I shall argue in the following chapters that they are overdetermined by multiple contextual forces. The contingencies can be loosely fixed within the limits imposed by concrete organisational, socio-political, and historical contexts. I shall employ the Gramscian concept of hegemony and Hall's articulation theory (Morley and Chen, 1996) in steering an analytical path between total contingency and reductionistic determinacy. The hegemonic articulations between dominant interests and television ideologies are always linked together under certain historical conditions, at specific conjunctures, to certain political subjects. They are linkages which are not necessary, determined, and essential for all time; but 'no simple correspondence' does not negate the existence of 'no necessary non-correspondence' (Hall, 1985; 1996). Hegemony is sensitive to historic contingencies and pragmatic political strategies. Shoring up popular demands, the dominant groups are shifting along with complicated social alliances to promote 'hybridised' dominant ideologies and articulate them on to the popular media. Thus contingent ideologies and identities should not be disconnected from the power hierarchies of the wider social context. I shall demonstrate these complex yet loosely patterned articulations in the case of Hong Kong television. As Corner observes,

> contingency points to complexities of interrelationship which may finally evade analysis, but to install it too firmly as an idea rsks giving up on television studies as social investigation, just as not admitting it at all risks theoretical self-delusion and analytic insensitivity.
>
> (Corner 1995:6)

Ideological influence and emotive interpretation

The question of television ideology and determinacy immediately raises the issue of media influences. The notion of media influence, whether behavioural or ideological, has been quite unfashionable in the past decade. The criticisms levelled at behavioural media effect research, such as its simplistic stimulus–response model, its overly individualistic orientation, and its methodological reductionism, are frequently raised and need no further delineation. On the other hand, in the research on media ideology, influences mean masking and reproducing dominant social relations in the interests of the status quo. But in recent debates, not only have the grandiose and deterministic claims of ideological effects been refuted, those more subtle ideological analyses which recognise the complexities of textual forms and audience negotiation have also been strongly contested. In fact, the very concept of 'ideology' has greatly lost its currency in recent academic discourse. More media researchers shift away from the study of media ideology and effects to the areas of audience interpretation and everyday consumption of media products. It is almost a cliché now to say that different audiences come up with different interpretations of media texts at different moments and in different situations, and that the multiplicity of media interpretation defies any claim of powerful media impact and influence. Television viewing is always viewing-in-contexts and, as Ang (1994) notes, contexts are indefinite; subculture settings, demographic differences, and class or group affiliations have differential influences upon the audience. While fully agreeing with the complexity of interpretative activities, I shall argue that the concept of influence is still indispensable in the study of television. Curran *et al.* open their anthology on media impacts with this assertion: 'It is almost impossible to make any statement about the media of communication without offering an implied model or theory of how information exercises influence' (1987:1).

'Interpretation' is not an escape route to avoid the unfashionable issue of media influences. As Corner insightfully argues, influence and inter-pretation are interconnected; and the core of that interconnection is the production of meaning. He recognises that 'most, if not all, of the kinds of influence imputed to television require that, at some point, mean-ings . . . are generated in viewers' heads' (Corner, 1995:135). As argued above, meanings, interpretations, and influences are contingent; but contingency does not negate the possibility of media power. Rather, contingency of interpretation and influence requires the differentiation of the various forms and contexts of media effects. Although it is no longer acceptable to view the media as a 'free-floating, independent satellite beaming down influences on the mass publics' (Curran *et al.*, 1987:2), it is still possible to relocate media influences in the context of competing social forces that determine the trajectory of media influences. Instead of asking whether there is influence or not, or refuting the very concept of influence by claiming polysemic interpretation, it is more fruitful to pose the following questions: What kind of televisual texts are involved? What cluster of meanings are invoked? What kind of influences are possible? How is influence exerted, in what direction, in which contexts? And what specific issues are under scrutiny (Corner, 1995; McLeod *et al.*, 1991)?

Accordingly, I shall confine myself to the specific issue of the influence of television on the formation and maintenance of cultural identity. I shall try to break down the analytical boundary of interpretation and influence by arguing, with the support of the findings in the book, that television is very influential *in providing interpretative categories of identities* and *setting up strong emotional barriers* between these categories of identity. Television is polysemic, but polysemic interpretation does not lessen its ideological influence (Lewis, 1991). The commonly taken-for-granted but deeply flawed argument that polysemy implies powerless television needs to be explicitly debunked. Old-fashioned theories of strong ideological effects implicitly assume that media power rests upon the unproblematic decoding of coherent textual meanings. With this assumption, polysemic texts and polysemic interpretations logically imply a limited ideological influence. I suggest that the logic of this argument should be reversed. Indeed, multiplicity is, beyond doubt, one of the major characteristics of the mass media environment in late capitalism. We can even accept polysemy as the 'essential property' of the mass media in general and fictional television in particular. But it is precisely within the polysemic media environment that television reveals its true power in identity formation and maintenance. We can look for those myths, icons, categories, stereotypes, and narratives that persist in popular television and refuse to be dissipated into polysemic texts and idiosyncratic interpretation. If these identity categories stubbornly resist change to such an extent that they suppress diversity, stigmatise outsiders, and confirm the established, then they become agents for fixing the uneven distribution of meaning (interpretation) and thus exert an ideological influence. The more stable these categories are in the flow of television polysemies, then the more power they can exert as ideological influences.

Furthermore, theories about television influences, such as the dominant ideology thesis, seem to carry a bias towards the cognitive side of interpretation and influence. However, the power of television centres more on the emotive, associative, and categorisational aspects which evade the flux of cognitive meanings. Audience can make polysemic readings in the cognitive sense, but still cling on to relatively stable membership categories in their idiosyncratic sense making, and can still be strongly influenced by emotive valorisations such as prestige, disgrace, charisma, and contempt attached to such categories. Scheff (1994) points out that discussions on national and cultural identity – for instance, Anderson's (1983) concept of imagined community – are mostly cognitive and say little about feelings and emotions, which, Scheff maintains, are important components of the very concept of cultural identity. A similar argument is put forward by Barbalet (1993), who argues that theories of citizenship have largely left out emotional issues such as inequality and resentment. Social memory is maintained through popular narratives which largely work in the affective mode (Fentress and Wickham, 1992). The emotive aspect of the ideological influence of television on identity formation is an under-researched area which I shall highlight in the case studies that follow. The case studies will show that television constructs and reinforces membership categories (especially the category of outsider), and is capable of imbuing these categories with delimited activities and emotions. Case studies will show that both influence and interpretation are interconnected with emotionally loaded meanings, which are regulated within relatively stable identity categories. A note of caution: the ideological influence of emotive interpretation should always be analysed within specific circumstances. As argued above, the strength of the effect varies in different socio-historical contexts. I shall explain these variations with the aid of Corner's (1995) notion of the cenripetal/centrifugal interplay of television and society.

Centripetal consolidation and centrifugal reinforcement

The argument in this book, concerning the influence of television on the specific issue of identity, is basically that of the *reinforcement effect* of television. Identity categorisations and category-bound emotions are not imposed on to the public from without; television simply draws towards itself the publicly felt sentiments of in-group pride and out-group contempt, objectifying and consolidating them into the televisual texts as membership categories. These objectified categories then amplify and reinforce group affiliation and antagonism among the audience. Here, Corner's (1995) notion of the centripetal/centrifugal interplay is most useful. He maintains that television is having both a centripetal and a centrifugal relationship to culture and society. In its centripetal mode, television has a powerful ability to draw towards itself and incorporate broader aspects of the culture; it is a capacity for cultural ingestion, in which much of the culture is routing via television, whether consciously or not. In the centrifugal moments, television seems to project its images, character types, catch-phrases, and social stigmas to the widest edges of the culture, permeating if not dominating the conduct of other cultural affairs. This interplay of centripetal consolidation and centrifugal reinforcement can be shown more clearly by comparing the role of television in the identity formation processes in different socio-historical contexts. The reinforcement effect is exerted most strongly when it works together in the same direction with other contextual factors.

The comparative study in this book shows that in the 1970s, when Hong Kong was politically and culturally separated from China, the need for a localised identity was strongly felt, and resentment against legal and illegal immigrants from China was widespread. Melodramatic serials at that time exerted a powerful effect of centripetal consolidation and centrifugal reinforcement, through which the established Hong-kongers confirmed their in-group prestige and stigmatised the main-landers as outsiders of lesser human worth. Television centripetally drew on to itself the public antagonisms against the outsiders, constructed a social stigma for them, and projected it centrifugally into social discourses and practices. But since the early 1990s, mainlanders have been gathering political power, and there has been a deeply felt identity crisis and resentment against the 'invasion' of the mainlanders. Television absorbs these crises and cleavages, resulting in different forms of polysemic texts and interpretations – the insider/outsider identity categories persist in televisual discourses, but with more contradictions, and less reinforcement effects.

The overlapping dichotomies discussed above represent some of the core ideas of this book. They are singled out from the very start because they signal the compartmentalised knowledge which I want to open up. These seemingly antithetical dichotomies are partly responsible for some of the one-sided and reactionary arguments in media studies. Existing concepts and methods do not precisely fit the discursive space left between these dichotomies (for example, influence vs. interpretation; quantitative vs. qualitative, etc.), resulting in the push and pull of academic discourse. Obviously, I am trying to find a third alternative somewhere in between. The analyses in the following chapters will run in different directions and with different emphases, tracking and resting here and there in between the signposts mapped above. I agree with Kellner (1995) that the more theories one has at one's disposal, the more tasks one can perform. The theoretical concepts and methodological tools presented in this book are not intended to be neat theoretical models, they are adopted for pragmatic reasons. My preference for theoretical and methodological pluralism reflects my reservations towards the mosaic atomism of some extreme forms of 'historicist theories' (Larrain, 1994), and also towards the ontological commitment of grand universalistic theories. I am going for mid-range fuzzy theories which have the flexibility of accommodating historical contingencies and at the same time allow for the fixing of cultural patterns and tendencies in specific socio-historic contexts. As Kellner puts it,

> theories are seen to be either useful or deficient through their application and effects. Contextual pragmatist and 'multiperspectival' approaches thus work together to open up theoretical inquiry to a multiplicity of discourses and methods. Theories and discourses are more or less useful, depending on the issue under question, the specific application of the theory in the theorist's hand, and the goals intended.
>
> (Kellner, 1995:27)

Thus this project necessarily adopts an interdisciplinary approach. As Murdock suggests, it 'requires us to build bridges between specialisations that have been separated within mainstream research and bring together a range of expertise, ranging from social psychology and socio-linguistics, to textual analysis, political economy, and cultural history' (Murdock, 1989b:246). The analytical strategy of this book will travel the winding path in between the dichotomies mapped above.

Chapter 2

Mediating Hong Kong identity (I): De-sinicisation

Since the collapse of the communist East, the West has lost an imaginary boundary for maintaining cultural identities. Brett (1996) elaborates on the global trend of aestheticising histories for touristic consumption. Kammen (1993) talks of a 'heritage syndrome' in America, where the public is historicising the present by adapting past heritage for identity confirmation. Picht (1993) speaks of a 'fevered search of identity' and Hoffmann (1993, 1994) of an 'identity crisis' associated with social integration, mutations, and transformations in Europe. In Asian countries, the question of identity is often related to the discursive strategy of essentialising Asian traditions and defending these traditions against Westernisation (Wang, M.L., 1991; Yao, 1994). The case of Hong Kong was further complicated by, in Abbas's (1997) words, 'the cultural politics of disappearance' in the run-up to 1997. In this and the next chapter, I shall present a socio-historical analysis of the role of television in the formation of local cultural identities in post-war Hong Kong.

Behind the plethora of labels and slogans that characterise recent discussions of cultural identity, Schlesinger (1991) discerns some widespread conceptions and assumptions that are confusing and questionable. In public discussion, cultural identity tends to assume an essentialist and ahistorical nature which has to be protected and defended. However, against the popular notion of nations existing from time immemorial, academic writings have emphasised the contingency and historicity of cultural identity (Anderson, 1983; Gellner, 1983; Hobsbawm, 1992; Smith, 1991).[1] Another area of confusion is related to the role of the mass media in identity formation and maintenance. Historical and anthropological analyses have the merit of highlighting the historicity of national and cultural identity, but most of them seem surprisingly to neglect a discussion of the role of mass media in the process.

Contrary to the scant attention paid by historians and anthropologists to media factors, media policy-makers often assume them to be the most influential in determining the cultural identity of a population. Domestic media production and distribution are assumed to be of paramount importance in cultural defence (against foreign media imports) and in nation-building (inventing or consolidating national identity). The 'fallacy of media-centredness' (Lodziak, 1986) and the 'fallacy of distribution' (Schlesinger, 1993) are evident in policy documents such as *Television without Frontiers* produced by the European Communities (EC, 1984), in which domestic media products are assumed to have identity-conferring powers. Similarly, many Asian countries are very conscious of the capacity of television to foster national culture and identity. It may be done in the name of maintaining traditional cultural heritage, but, more often than not, it also serves the implicit purpose of political consolidation (see Heidt, 1987; Katz and Wedell, 1977; Lent, 1982; Reeves, 1993; Wheen, 1985).

Research on the impact of the media on identity paints an inconclusive picture. In the Malaysian case, Karthigesu (1988) shows that those Malaysian television programmes which are directed towards nation-building have proven to be unsatisfactory to the local audience. In a study on the relationship between television and national identity in Singapore, Heidt (1987) carried out quantitative and qualitative analyses of Singapore television programmes in a constructed week and concludes that the assumption about the central role of television in national culture is a case where 'rhetoric far exceeds evidence'. Even in a country like Singapore, which stresses social planning, market imperatives work against official directives to bring in a high percentage of entertainment programmes. Collins (1990) reaches a similar conclusion from a more extensive discussion of Canadian television. Despite the fact that a considerable proportion of Canadian viewers watch American entertainment shows, Canadian identity is still in robust health. There seems to be only a weak link between polity and culture. From the Canadian case, Collins challenges the assumption of the necessary congruence between sense of citizenship and symbolic culture. He argues that symbolic culture, especially television culture, is neither a sufficient nor a necessary agent for the formation of national identity. A sense of citizenship can rest on a healthy political institution without a commonly shared national symbolic culture.

The studies by Collins and others contest the notion that television has a powerful identity-conferring ability. However, I shall argue, in the light of the Hong Kong case, that these studies can only reach the conclusion that television is not an effective agent for realising cultural imperatives when imposed from above; they do not have enough evidence to undermine the role of television in cultivating, reinforcing, and objectifying the collective identity that evolves from *within* social practices. Like Canada in some respects, Hong Kong does demonstrate a weak link between polity and culture.[2] But unlike Canada, Hong Kong does not have a democratic political institution. Due to the deficiency of the Hong Kong polity as a representative structure, and also because of other social factors that will be discussed in a moment, television culture plays a central role in identity formation in post-war Hong Kong. Simply saying that television has a powerful or a limited effect on identity formation is of little value unless it is related to concrete historical contexts. Instead of asking whether it has an influence or not, or refuting the very concept of media influence on identity formation, it is more fruitful to relocate media influences in the contexts of competing social forces that determine the trajectory of media influences (Curran *et al.*, 1987). In this and the next chapter, I shall illustrate, by examining the Hong Kong case, that identity formation is a complicated social process that involves the interplay between media and non-media processes. The media can have powerful[3] or limited[4] effects depending upon different historical circumstances. Media researchers and media policy-makers who fixate on the power of the media will easily lose sight of the larger contextual forces at work. Anthropological and historical accounts that neglect the influence of the mass media, may also miss one of the major building-blocks of modern cultural identity. Thus this chapter is an attempt to explore the relaionship between social power and media representation in identity formation.

As recent studies (e.g. Robins, 1996; Wang, 1994) have shown, identities manifest themselves primarily in the differentiation of the us/them boundary. My main argument is that in-group/out-group identities are sustained by social powers, which are translated into, and in turn reinforced by, media representation. As a manifestation of social imagination, the media is the site in which the boundary of the imagined community is constructed and reconstructed along the shifting power geometry of the larger society. In Corner's (1995) words, this circulatory process is a 'centripetal and centrifugal interplay' – television draws on to itself publicly felt sentiments, consolidating them into identity categories. These objectified categories are then 'projected' centrifugally into social practices, reinforcing the public sentiments in turn. These centripetal consolidation and centrifugal reinforcement processes are often compli-cated by other social processes. Hence the role of television in identity formation and maintenance needs to be generalised in a more context-sensitive way.

In the following socio-historical analysis, I shall identify some of the contextual factors that have shaped the television ideologies and cultural identities in Hong Kong. Accordingly, the analysis in this and the next chapter deals with the specific circumstances of Hong Kong. To some, the discussion might seem 'local', but as Gripsrud (1995) points out when he analyses the Norwegian case, media studies in the Western world have long been working on American and British phenomena which are 'local' and 'exotic' to outsiders. It is worth pointing out that, at the present juncture where international academic discourses have become more frequent, learning localised media processes outside the Anglo-American world can enrich the theorising activities of international media studies. As I go from the specific to the general, the localities of the Hong Kong case will be more immediately accessible, and the arguments of the 'local' will meet the common theoretical concerns of international readers.

Historical backdrop

In the years before and after the reversion to Chinese sovereignty in 1997,[5] Hong Kong experienced an upsurge of nostalgia. Popular icons from the past were re-erected and received with enthusiasm. Hong Kong-made commercial products that had proved successful in the past were repackaged in new chain stores. Television talk shows and magazine specials began to feed on social memories and traditional artefacts. Nostalgia has always been a favourite item in popular culture, but it is often a strategy of identity confirmation in times of crises and change (Furedi, 1992; Kammen 1993); this has been especially true in the case of Hong Kong. As the geo-social boundaries of Hong Kong and China were undergoing significant change, the symbolic expressions of a distinct Hong Kong community started to become important to the people of the territory (Cohen, 1985). A large-scale exhibition entitled 'The Hong Kong Story' is a concrete example. It was installed in the Hong Kong Museum on permanent display. The exhibition comprises different corridors packed with anthropological accounts of the territory. At the end of the history corridor, a multi-media show summarises the social history of the past 30 years in a succinct array of sight and sound. The songs that are threaded into the narrative of the show trigger collective memories and a strong emotive response from the local audience. In fact, they are theme songs from popular television drama serials of the

1970s and the 1980s; but in some respects, these secular songs have the consolidating effect of a national anthem.

As a Chinese society under British colonial rule, Hong Kong had no national anthem before 1997. The collectivism of the Chinese anthem was incompatible with the individualistic and competitive ethos of Hong Kong. The British anthem 'God Save the Queen', which in the 1970s and the early 1980s was the standard item on the television screen at the end of a broadcast day, had long been relegated to jingles on street corners and on comedy shows. Hong Kong had no official symbol to which the indigenous culture could anchor itself.

Looking back at the colonial years, the colonial government had adopted an economic *laissez-faire* and social non-interventionist policy. No official attempt had been made to promote a collective identity for the colony. Hong Kong had been a British colony since 1842,[6] but from 1842 up to the Second World War, one hundred years after British rule, Hong Kong's population was still very small[7] and the residents maintained close ties with the mainland (Agassi, 1969; Fok, 1990). There was a relatively free movement of population between Hong Kong and neighbouring Guangzhou province. This was radically changed in the 1950s. The communist take-over of China in 1949 heralded a new era in the history of China as well as of Hong Kong. Waves of refugees from China poured into Hong Kong.[8] In the 1950s, the colony had nearly 2 million newcomers representing about two-thirds of the population. From the perspective of population structure, one could argue that modern Hong Kong was born in the 1950s, not in 1842.[9]

From that time Hong Kong rapidly changed from an entrepot to an international financial centre. Culturally, Chinese traditionalism was smoothly replaced by a secular indigenous culture. This indigenous culture may have been highly Westernised, but remained at root deeply Chinese (Agassi and Jarvie, 1969). It comprised Chinese traditions which were Anglicised with Western professional concepts and romanticised terms.[10] The colonial government had shown great restraint in not intervening in the local culture. It even discouraged the promotion of a Hong Kong identity among the younger generations. The reason was that Britain sought to maintain the fiction that Hong Kong was only a commercial entrepot in order to avoid antagonising the Chinese government, which also wanted temporarily to maintain a commercial and apolitical territory for economic and diplomatic reasons. Although a substantial proportion of the population harboured pro-China or pro-Taiwan nationalist sentiments and were hostile to the communists, the colonial government was quick to suppress and eliminate decisively these political forces whenever they surfaced into the public arena. Concerned primarily with sustaining economic and social order, the colonial administration sought to distance itself from identity politics. Schools and other government institutions did not narrate a history of national or political identification. There was no coherent historical narrative for the younger generation to make sense of their socio-historical world.

Popular media then easily took up this cultural space. Without any state-imposed shackles, popular media, film, and television culture in particular, had evolved to become a cradle of indigenous cultural identity. The simple term 'Hongkonger' gathered weight and meaning in films, television serials, and Cantonese pop songs. However, this indigenous culture took an obvious turn during the mid-1980s. After the signing of the 1984 Sino-British Declaration, which declared the inevitable return of the colony to China, the people of Hong Kong experienced a rapid process of politicisation, and the middle class increasingly demanded a voice of their own in social and political debates.

In the late 1980s and early 1990s, Hong Kong's behaviour surprised the Chinese leaders, which saw Hong Kong as being apolitical and concerned only with the accumulation of wealth. Tightened control followed when China realised the growing localism in the territory. Fuelled by the new-found pride in its economic vitality, China is promoting a brand of nationalism that claims its proprietorship over a unique Chinese culture.[11] It is repeatedly claimed that Hongkongers are the 'sacred and inalienable' members of the Chinese community. An ahistorical Chinese identity is created to foster patriotism and political commitment.[12] The aim of this and the next chapter is to use Hong Kong as a case to examine how these changing social, political, and cultural forces are articulated within the television medium through the formation and maintenance of cultural identity. This socio-historical analysis will then set the stage for the case studies of the subsequent chapters.

The historical analysis in this and the next chapter will respectively deal with the social circumstances of Hong Kong before and after the mid-1980s. Contrasting the two periods reveals a contextualised understanding of the interplay between media and social factors. In this chapter, I shall concentrate on the historical context of Hong Kong before the mid-1980s. In this period, the newly emergent indigenous culture of Hong Kong was closely related to the development of the local television industry. Television's central role in this consolidation process was a result of the convergence of at least four historical contingencies, namely:

- the social and cultural severance from China,
- the coming of age of the locally born generation,
- the non-interventionist policy of the colonial government, and
- the rapid expansion of a persistently surplus television economy.

De-sinicisation: the social and cultural severance from China

In the post-war decades, Hong Kong experienced a de-sinicisation process which gradually separated Hong Kong socially, politically, and culturally from mainland China. Hong Kong was already an immigrant society before the massive influx of mainland refugees after the Chinese Communist Party came to power in 1949. Among the refugees of the late 1940s were experienced entrepreneurs, particularly the Shanghainese entrepreneurs, who brought with them capital and technical know-how (Wong, S.L., 1988). There was also a large number of unskilled refugees who became a plentiful source of cheap labour. Both groups were vital to the economic take-off of post-war Hong Kong. Since a considerable proportion of these sojourners treated Hong Kong as a temporary refuge, their primary concerns were daily survival and the accumulation of enough earnings to return to their home country (Agassi, 1969). However, the economic ties between Hong Kong and China started to weaken during the Korean War and the beginning of the Cold War in the early 1950s. China and Hong Kong were separated in the ensuing East–West divide. China sided with North Korea, while Hong Kong, as a British colony, was required to honour a United Nations trade embargo against China (Lane, 1990). Although some kind of economic relations between Hong Kong and China[13] continued after the Korean War, the two started to develop along radically different paths. For 30 years (1949–1979), hostile external conditions and self-imposed isolation left China largely outside the rise of Eastern Asia; while the century-old entrepot trade of Hong Kong was abruptly and largely brought to an end. China was no longer a partner in the two-way transit trade. In order to survive, Hong Kong had to develop an export-oriented industrial economy, and has since then developed into a financial hub for Eastern Asia.

The separation from China was also reflected in the cultural realm, but the separation was at a slower and intermittent pace. The scant literature of the time captured the paradoxical psyche of the then sojourners in Hong Kong: they longed for an idealised traditional society on the mainland and at the same time abhorred the turbulent political reality in the North.[14] The print media were mostly run by intellectuals fleeing to the colony from mainland China. Their cultural frames of reference were predominantly anchored in the traditional culture of the northern mainland. To these northern writers, Hong Kong was a 'cultural desert'. Newspapers were mainly focused on developments on the mainland and local news was less than sketchy (Kuan and Lau, 1988). This cultural bias is deeply rooted in a Chinese elite culture which considers the mainland as the political and cultural centre while Hong Kong is seen as the barbaric periphery (Wong *et al.*, 1997).

In the 1950s, Hong Kong already had a flourishing Cantonese dialect film industry with an annual output of some 150 films (Leung and Chan, 1997). The films reflected a national (China) and regional (Southern China/Cantonese) culture; local Hong Kong culture had yet to be crystallised on the screen (Choi, 1990b). Cantonese[15] films produced at that time suggest a curious exclusion of local social reality. There was virtually no Hong Kong film that dealt with modern Chinese history (Jarvie, 1977). Located in nowhere places without specific references, the characters were exposed to all kind of conflicts, diseases, and tragedies. Solutions always went back to the traditional virtues of forbearance, the safety net of familial and ethnic ties, and in particular, filial piety, deference to patriarchal authority, female chastity, and even loyalty to the ruling government (Choi, 1990b; Kwan, 1990; Law, 1986). Hong Kong films were characterised more by pretextual means rather than by portraying slices-of-life; by abstract thinking rather than clear practical experiences; and by expressionism rather than realism. Local social conditions were not explored by the film-makers – especially those who produced films in the 1950s and the early 1960s. The explanation of such social detachment may well be the refugee mentality of the producers who exercised self-restraint in order to avoid possible political trouble. There was also a commercial reason: localism was to be avoided because these films were exported to markets outside Hong Kong. Jarvie (1977) also suggests that the social detachment of the films actually reflects a society that had lost its bearings. As a result, the cultural base of traditionalism in Cantonese films in the 1950s had increasingly become obsolete and irrelevant to the local audience of that time; the market was rapidly lost. The annual production of Cantonese films dropped from around 200 films in the early 1960s to 35 in 1970; there was not even one produced in 1972 (Choi, 199b).

This brief analysis of the media culture in the 1950s depicts the ambivalence felt by Hongkongers about adopting an indigenous identity while at the same time it indicates that they were undergoing a gradual severance from traditional mainland culture. To the people in post-war Hong Kong, Chinese nationality increasingly existed only in imaginary abstraction. Under communist rule, mainland China went through drastic social changes that the people in Hong Kong found difficult to identify with. Traditional culture did not have a political and social reality to which it could anchor itself. It could no longer be recalled at first hand, except in the retold oral tradition of refugee parents. Traditional values lost their social relevance in the highly urbanised setting of Hong Kong. Hong Kong was modernising by incorporating Western lifestyles; it was attuned to a hybrid, cosmopolitan cultural environment which was increasingly receptive to imported cultural products such as Hollywood movies. In contrast to the virtuous Chinese men in Cantonese films of the 1950s, popular screen heroes included the 'individualistic, hedonistic, and womanising secret agent James Bond, and later the unscrupulous, pecuniary, and manipulative bounty-hunter in Clint Eastwood's spaghetti westerns' (Leung, B. K. P., 1996:65).

Hong Kong's separation from China took its final step in the 1960s, when the romantic-turned-violent Cultural Revolution in mainland China spilled over to Hong Kong. In 1966 and 1967, politically motivated riots and social confrontations filled the streets of the colony. The riot revealed a two-fold message: First, it showed that some of the Hong Kong people were beginning to take local affairs seriously. The riot was initiated by young men who had been brought up in Hong Kong and were clearly unhappy with the Star Ferry Company's decision to raise fares (Young, 1994). Second, the riot acted as a catalyst which speeded up the process of separation between Hong Kong and China. The locally initiated riot soon turned political. During the first few months of 1967, Hong Kong experienced an influx of Maoist propaganda and an increase in labour disputes. Hong Kong leftists seized the opportunity to turn labour demands into political demands and to call for an end to the British oppression. The demonstrations became more and more violent, resulting in 51 deaths, 800 injuries, and 5,000 arrests (Lane, 1990). It was unclear whether the violence was provoked by Chinese revolutionaries or the local police. The complicity of the event was quickly reduced to a political disorder associated with the Cultural Revolution on the mainland. As the riot was seen to be primarily communist-instigated, the Hong Kong population lent its support to the British Hong Kong government. In addition, the serious damage of the revolution in China became apparent to the people of Hong Kong as news of widespread famine on the mainland was reported in the news media and through familial networks. The dead bodies of 'revolutionaries' and 'counter-revolutionaries' were discovered floating along the South China Sea into Hong Kong waters. Hundreds of thousands of desperate refugees fled over the border into Hong Kong. Even local left-wing followers lost faith in the cause of the Chinese Communist Party. Socially and culturally, Hong Kong further detached itself from the influence of mainland China. The sojourner generation gave up hope of returning to China and started to consider Hong Kong as a permanent home.

The local generation

Commercial terrestrial television was first introduced in 1967, just after the riots and civic disturbances of the same year. In the late 1960s, of the total 4,000,000 population, nearly one-third of them had emigrated from China after the communist take-over. There had also been a persistently high birth rate from the late 1940s through the 1950s. Therefore, in the late 1960s, when commercial terrestrial television was launched, 43 per cent of the population fell in the 10–35 age-group, and the proportion of the population born locally surpassed 50 per cent for the first time. To the generation that was born or brought up in Hong Kong, the traditional culture of rural China was, what Raymond Williams called, a residue culture; because of the cultural severance from China, the new generation had only a remote knowledge of the neighbouring mainland. It was not uncommon to find university students who did not know the names of prominent leaders in China. The Hong Kong generation was brought up in a social environment very different from that on the mainland. The shift in the economy of labour-intensive to information-intensive, the rise of Hong Kong as one of the largest financial centres in the world, and the initiatives of the Hong Kong government in welfare, public housing, education, and transportation had provided the urbanised setting for the 'emergence of a Hong Kong Man' who is very different from the Chinese of the mainland (Baker, 1983). These contextual factors, which became the material base of a new cultural identity,[16] can be summarised under four general rubrics:

1   Anglicised educational system;
2   social preconditions (e.g. government-subsidised housing, trans-portation);
3   economic opportunities;
4   influx of new Chinese immigrants.

Anglicised educational system

The Anglicised education system had weakened the Chinese identity of the local students. While connections with the Chinese hinterland were greatly reduced, and the population more stabilised, it became possible for Hong Kong to develop its own school system which suited the needs of both the colonial rulers and local Chinese students (Luk, 1989). The system trained and certified teachers, set standards for examinations, made up syllabuses, published textbooks, and established English as the prestigious language – since ability in the language guaranteed highly paid jobs both in the civil service and in the commercial sector. In 1953, English secondary schools outnumbered Chinese language secondary schools for the first time and quickly became the mainstream (Choi, 1991). This had an enormous psychological impact on the de-sinicisation of the local Chinese, because language is a major medium of identi-fication. On the other hand, the government was extremely careful about the school syllabus of Chinese studies. In a report on Chinese studies published in 1953, there was no mention of cultivating a sense of national identity, as one would be likely to find in a national curriculum document (Luk, 1989). The curriculum aimed at a Chinese identity in the abstract, but did not relate that Chineseness to either contemporary China or the local Hong Kong landscape. In schools, students learnt little about China and Hong Kong, and particularly little about modern Chinese history and development. The British government had always stressed the economic value of Hong Kong as a middleman in Sino-British trade (Lane, 1994; Sweeting, 1992; Tang, 1994). The colonial government did not want to produce colonial subjects loyal to the British government; it aimed at making a Hong Kong Chinese who was able to speak the language of the dual centres of China and Britain, but without any strong identification with either country.[17]

Local history was deliberately ignored to prevent the development of collective political efforts independent from the Sino-British dualistic political structure. History was not deployed to narrate a nation for political identification. As a result, local history had never been incorporated into the general school curriculum; only recently have there been some modifications after the handover. To the general public, local history was not given a strong discursive expression. The education system deliberately avoided any nationalistic sentiment; this produced a vacuum of cultural identification which was then easily filled up by the local popular media. The local generation grew up, acquiring a territorial identity that was drastically different from the pre-war Chinese and the Chinese under communist rule. The native-born Hongkongers went in search of an identity from the popular media in part because their education failed to provide them with a coherent historical narrative to explain their place in the world.

Social preconditions

The government was responsible for securing the necessary pre-conditions, like housing and transportation, which made it possible for the Hong Kong people to call Hong Kong home. In the 1950s, the collective experiences of mobility and resettlement occupied an important part in the social memory of the Hong Kong people. Crossing the border into the territory, many settled themselves in illegal huts on roof-tops and on the edges of mountains. After a great fire in one squatter area in 1953, the government started a large-scale resettlement project. By the end of the 1970s, close to 50 per cent of Hong Kong's total population was housed in government or government-subsidised dwellings (Young, 1994). The resettlement process was often portrayed in the popular media: children running along corridors of these govern-ment estates; parents coming back from work; residents watching tele-vision together after dinner. These became familiar images on television dramas and government-produced documentaries. The public housing project provided a materialistic basis for the formation of a 'home in Hong Kong' mentality (Lui, 1988a). The government also undertook colossal public projects such as large-scale reclamation and the building of large reservoirs, road networks, and mass transit systems. The city 'grew up' with the people and the local generation witnessed a process of community building which not only improved their quality of life but also created a sense of pride and belonging to the territory once seen as only a temporary refuge.

Economic opportunities

The post-war economic take-off provided unprecedented opportunities for upward mobility. The number of registered factories increased from 3,000 in the 1950s to 10,000 in the 1960s. Registered foreign companies increased from 300 to 600 (Young, 1994). Despite the ups and downs of the global economy, Hong Kong experienced sustained economic growth all through the post-war decades until the recession in 1998. Economic transformation and the sudden population increase led to a truncation of whatever class structure had existed previously (Leung,

B. K. P., 1996). Working-class families were relatively less restricted to their class positions because of the structural changes wrought by industrialisation and technological advancement. The miraculous growth rate not only improved the living standards of grassroots workers, but also created a new generation of middle-class managers, technicians, accountants, social workers, doctors, lawyers, professors, and administrators (So and Kwitko, 1990; Cheung and Louie, 1991). Prompted by Hong Kong's hasty and compressed process of urbanisation, the erosion of traditionalism took place at a much faster rate here than in other countries. The local young people were quickly absorbed by mushrooming factories and offices, where they were confronted by competitive and highly individualistic social relations. Traditional values, which weighed the collective good against personal gain, and which stressed sacrifice, submission, obedience, and harmony, were less applicable in the commercialised setting of Hong Kong.

Some have labelled the elite of this local generation the new middle class and argue that they played an important role in the democracy movement in Hong Kong (Cheung, 1988). How to define this new middle-class group remains problematic (Lui, 1988b), but the emergence of a distinct local generation in the late 1970s and early 1980s is undeniable. In a survey taken in the early 1980s, 65 per cent of the respondents considered their roots to be in Hong Kong, while only 24 per cent, mostly the elderly, said their roots were in China (Cheng, 1984). In another survey in 1985, about 60 per cent of the local respondents chose 'Hongkonger' over 'Chinese' as their identity (Lau and Kuan, 1988). Lau and Kuan also found that the higher the education and the younger the age of the respondents, the more they chose 'Hongkonger' as their identity. This means that the local generation, especially among the educated middle class, had developed a strong identification with the territory. The truncation of social classes and the keen sense of a common fate led to the emergence of a collective identity that embraced all social classes. How far this perception matched reality is arguable, but it was celebrated in the popular media and was perceived as 'natural', at least by the local generation of the time. I shall come back to the ideological aspects of this Hong Kong dream in chapter 4.

Influx of new Chinese immigrants

Lastly, the local identity of Hong Kong was further strengthened by the massive influx of Chinese new immigrants in the 1970s. Waves of new immigrants crossed over the border in the 1970s for political and

economic reasons.[18] Although the people of Hong Kong were themselves
Chinese refugees or their descendants, they started to become aware of
the different way of life on the mainland and differentiated themselves
from the new immigrants. As many have noted, identity boundaries
are established primarily through inclusion and exclusion (Jenkins, 1994;
Robins, 1996; Schlesinger, 1993), and the experience of the 'us' is
strengthened by the presence of the 'them' (Cohen, 1985; Wang, G.,
1991). The tensions and conflicts between the newcomers and the local
Hongkongers of the time solidified into the concrete social practices of
identity formation and consolidation. Social surveys in the early 1980s
showed that Hong Kong people generally felt that the newcomers were
responsible for the decrease in wages and an increase in violent crime.[19]
The new immigrants were singled out as a distinct social category and
had negative images heaped upon them.

Interestingly, while Hong Kong experienced abundant mobility
opportunities in the 1970s and saw itself as a classless society, economic
identities were being displaced by the socio-cultural identities of both the
Hongkongers and the mainlanders. Most mainlanders of the 1970s were
confined to the working class and were faced with formidable obstacles
in attaining economic and social mobility. Doubtless, there were also
Hongkongers who remained in the underprivileged working class. However, the 'detainment' of the mainlanders in a distinct social, economic,
and cultural group strengthened the cultural identity of the established
Hongkongers, and at the same time prevented social conflicts in
the 1970s and the 1980s (whether between or within the social groups
of Hongkongers and mainlanders) from emerging in the form of
class conflicts. I shall return to this in some detail in chapter 4. What I
want to stress here is that the socio-cultural differentiation between
Hongkongers and mainlanders, or the 'othering' of mainland Chinese,
was a benchmark against which Hong Kong people could consider
themselves as different and distinct. Hong Kong people are always ethnic
Chinese, but starting from the 1970s, they were, in their own eyes, *Hong
Kong Chinese*, in dramatic contrast to the mainland Chinese. Given these
contextual factors in the post-war years:

> something unique has been emerging from Hong Kong's cities: it is
> the Hong Kong Man. He is go-getting and highly competitive,
> tough for survival, quick-thinking and flexible. He wears western
> clothes, speaks English or expects his children to do so, drinks
> western alcohol, has sophisticated tastes in cars and household
> gadgetry, and expects life to provide a constant stream of excitement

and new openings. But he is not British or western (merely westernised). At the same he is not Chinese in the same way that the citizens of the People's Republic of China are Chinese.

(Baker, 1983:478)

Television and identity formation

The above discussion has delineated the material basis for the emergence of a new cultural identity in Hong Kong. Television played a critical role in this process of identity formation. To concentrate on television does not mean other media are irrelevant to identity formation; however television is dominant among all media in reaching the public on a regular basis and in a domestic setting. It is the domestic myth-maker which incorporates motifs and imagery from all other forms of popular media (Umphlett, 1983). The dominant role of television was particularly evident in Hong Kong in the 1970s.

Locally broadcast television was introduced in 1967 by the Television Broadcast Ltd (TVB), following by Rediffusion Television (RTV) in 1973. TVB's Cantonese channel,[20] TVB Jade, has dominated the local television screen since its introduction. For more than two decades, TVB Jade has secured more than 70 per cent, and sometimes as much as 90 per cent of prime-time rating *share*. Similar to the experience of many countries, the new medium achieved quick penetration, snatched a major audience share from other media, and has become the predominant mass medium of Hong Kong.[21] Just a few years after the introduction of television broadcasting, the Cantonese film industry ground to a disastrous halt.[22] Some cinemas closed down, while others started screening foreign and Mandarin films. While in the late 1960s there were arguably internal financial problems within the film industry which were responsible for this decline, the popularity of television exacerbated the speed of the demise (Leung and Chan, 1997). The official television monitoring organisation, the Hong Kong Television Advisory Board, acknowledged in its report of 1974 that television viewing had replaced cinema going and had become the principal leisure activity in Hong Kong.[23] However, as I shall discuss in a moment, this confrontation between film and television quickly evolved into a reconciliatory and symbiotic relationship in the 1970s.

With reference to the fact that Hong Kong people in the late 1960s and early 1970s did not have a firm cultural bearing, it was not surprising that the fast-growing television medium had quickly become a cradle of collective identity and a cultural resource that unified popular tastes

(Kung and Yueai, 1984). I have already pointed out that Cantonese films in the 1950s and 1960s were rooted in a Chinese tradition largely irrelevant to the local situation, and that the printed media were mostly focusing on China. In contrast, television had quickly become a major producer of highly localised media texts and cultural symbols of the times (Chan, K. C., 1990, 1991; Chan and Lee, 1990, 1992). Television news, which remained in the top ten television programmes throughout the 1970s, devoted a considerable proportion of its time to local issues. For the first time, the people in Hong Kong started receiving a daily diet of television images of the city. Through the screen, the literal, much-ignored notion of 'Hong Kong society' was knitted into visual news narratives. The abstract 'city of Hong Kong' was able, at least as represented in the news programmes, to incarnate itself into concrete, integrative, and localised social events. The 'local', instead of the 'remote' China, started to become the point of reference for the public. As argued by Anderson (1983), the boundaries of a community exist in the minds of their beholders; collectivity is necessarily imagined since members of even the smallest nation will never know most of their fellow-members. Yet in the mind of each person, there is the image of their community. This 'imaginary' and symbolic nature of identity boundaries renders television an influential symbolic source of identity formation. The people of Hong Kong 'saw' Hong Kong for the first time through the daily broadcast of television news. Television provides a sense of co-presence and collectivity. As Hallin (1993) notes, news creates a 'sphere of consensus' by addressing the public as if everyone shares the same values.

Of all the television programmes on the air at that time, melodramatic serials were one of the most consolidating cultural resources. As in most Asian countries, dramas attracted addictive viewing when television was first introduced. From the 1970s to the early 1980s, prime-time melo-dramas persistently attracted 2 to 3 million Hong Kong viewers (half to sometimes two-thirds of the population). It was not unusual for the final episode of major serials to achieve ratings of 60 to 70 per cent, which meant it could empty streets and restaurants.[24] These television dramas featured domestic stories located in concrete social situations and stood in stark contrast to the social exclusion characteristic of Cantonese films of the 1950s and the 1960s (Chan, K. C., 1990; Kwan, 1990). The kind of people depicted in these fictional worlds manifested distinctive outlooks, aspirations, and lifestyles, and shared a highly localised language pattern. There was little trace of Chinese traditionalism. Moral norms were ambiguous, and personal survival was much more important than the collective good. The uncompromising secularism and non-commitment were markedly different from the moralistic outlook of Chinese culture. Fictional characters in these dramas were easily identifiable and instantly became household names.

Hong Kong melodramatic serials quickly gained the cultural prestige that was difficult to acquire in Western countries where television in general, and soap operas in particular, were rejected as degrading cultural forms.[25] Partly because Hong Kong did not have a hegemonic high culture, the newly established television quickly absorbed writers, artists, intellectuals, and university graduates into the industry and became a dominant cultural form in Hong Kong. The cultural charisma of Hong Kong television melodramas of the 1970s and their impact on local culture was very much parallel to the situation in Latin America, where acclaimed artists joined the industry to produce *telenovelas* which dealt with national life and culture using refreshing artistic styles (Martin-Barbero, 1995).

A significant but often neglected effect of Hong Kong television on identity formation is that of the categorisation of mainland Chinese as non-Hongkongers. The differentiation of Hongkongers from mainlanders in the 1970s was sociolinguistically related to the television serial *The Good, the Bad, and the Ugly* (the serial will be discussed in detail in chapter 4). In the serial a character named Ah Chian became a very popular figure once he made his debut. A refugee from China, and industrious by nature, he was portrayed as an incongruous figure in the fast-paced life of Hong Kong, and became a comic as well as tragic character. The name Ah Chian, which is discriminatory and has a contemptuous ring to it, has since been used widely by the people of Hong Kong to refer to the new immigrants from China. The nick-naming becomes a kind of a 'speech act' which illustrates vividly how a name/character that originated in a melodramatic serial can carry over to other media and indeed to concrete social practices. When the serial was released, the cultural differences between the local people and newcomers were already felt in social interactions, but the television serials objectified and dramatised the differences, gave the non-Hongkonger a name, and created, in popular memory, an outside group against which Hongkongers could define themselves. Ah Chian was depicted as stupid, slow on the uptake, backward, poor, and a shallow country hick. In contrast, the Hong Kong Man, seen in the mirror of Ah Chian, was clever, savvy, progressive, rich, and modern (Cheng Yu, 1990). Thus the serial has, in Sacks's terms, enacted a 'membership categorisation device'[26] which sets Ah Chian the mainlander against the local Hongkongers. To the newcomers, this stereotyping and stigmatising process became social domination, but to the locals, the negative image of the Chinese immigrant became a cultural resource for identity confirmation. The Hongkongers saw their own identity from the vantage point of the mainlanders and drew boundaries to differentiate against them. Here we see a dual process of exclusion and confirmation, an inherent process which is often found in identity formation and maintenance.[27]

As Roger Silverstone (1981, 1988) observes, television discourse performs for the contemporary society the mythic function of spatial and moral ordering of experience. Through its fictional and factual contents, confusing and discrete social practices are objectified in totemic symbols and mythic narratives to become anchor points and reference frames for everyday experience. This collective sense-making was much needed by Hong Kong's local generation in the 1970s, which was severed from China politically and culturally, confronted with a new set of social relations, and served by a media void of local references. The mythic function of social integration was well performed by the new domestic medium of television.

The identity of the local generation was fostered in the relatively autonomous television culture of the 1970s. The television of Hong Kong, at least during the early stages, did not initially appear to be the ideological apparatus of either the colonial government or of the capitalistic economy. Although Hong Kong has been a hard-line follower of market-led capitalism, descriptions of television as a hege-monic agent of colonial capitalism cannot be applied to the Hong Kong television medium of the 1970s, at least not in a straightforward way. There are two major factors needed for the development of a relatively autonomous television culture:[28] the separation of polity from the media, and the surplus economy of the television industry.

Minimal links between polity and the media

Hong Kong was acquired by the British not for territorial gain but as a strategic midway port to relay its political and economic interests. Hong Kong is far away from Britain and close to China. As S.K. Lau notes, 'Hong Kong's geographical proximity to China and the predominant Chinese majority in the colony made China a ubiquitous factor in the mind of the colonial government' (1990:3). The colonial government suppressed any spontaneous emergence of antagonistic political forces. Pro-China and anti-China fractions were closely monitored and political threats were vigorously eliminated. On the other hand, China, for economic and diplomatic reasons, tolerated the existence of the British and 'subsidised' colonial rule by immunising the colonial government from the threat of anti-colonial assaults (Lau 1990:3). To maintain a delicate balance between these competing political forces, the colonial government suppressed dissent, restrained from high-handed colonial rule, and ran the colony by elite co-option.

The above political background was one of the major reasons for the economic *laissez-faire* and social non-interventionist policy of post-war Hong Kong. The socio-political system has been characterised as 'minimally integrated', compartmentalising the political, social, and cultural realms (Lau, 1982). There was a clear separation of polity and society. Political power had been firmly controlled in the hands of the colonial government. The government was administered under the Crown by a British governor, who was assisted by an Executive Council and Legislative Council, to which members were appointed. The councils consisted largely of entrepreneurs and established businessmen (Hook, 1983, 1993; Miners, 1991). Limited election to the legislative seats was introduced only in 1991; there was no democratic institution or mechanism for political participation. It was not until recently and in the final years of the colonial rule that the British hurriedly proposed democratic reforms which they said were deserved by the people of Hong Kong.

Nevertheless, the colonial government had sustained legitimacy through compartmentalisation of the social and political realms and as a result Hong Kong had enjoyed a high level of autonomy for some years. The British government confined its operations to the basic provisions required by a capitalist economy. In the late 1970s, there was a considerable government effort to build a better public infrastructure to cope with the increasingly complicated social conditions, but intervention was limited to basic social and urban services such as housing and transportation. The government deliberately avoided involvement in both the economy and in Chinese society. In the 1960s, the political campaigns in mainland China often emerged as a fatal combination of nationalism and a denunciation of imperialism. The Hong Kong government was extremely careful not to provoke anti-British sentiments among the leftists in the territory. The government co-opted local political forces and established its governing authority by what King (1975) calls the ruling process of 'administrative absorption of politics' – a process whereby the government recruited the elite into an administrative decision-making body. Limited administrative participation was opened to the non-British elite, with the general public largely left out of the political game. On the surface, non-interventionism was welcomed by the majority of the public. Hong Kong people were described as primarily motivated by economic aspirations, blatantly pragmatic and deliberately apolitical. These descriptions were deceptively straight-forward. In reality, there had been sporadic political demands from local groups in the post-war decades, especially among the more aggressive elite of the local generation (Cheung, 1988; So and Kwitko, 1990). This is not to suggest that the general public in the 1960s and 1970s were necessarily interested in local politics. However, the continued emphasis placed on the supposed political apathy of the Hong Kong people actually hampered the request for constitutional reform and helped to maintain the minimally integrated socio-political system. The govern-ment was consciously steering the people's interests away from politics (Young, 1994). The invisibility of colonial politics was itself a highly political choice.

The confinement of the polity was also reflected in what Kuan and Lau termed 'the minimally integrated media-political system'. They noticed that 'interactions between the mass media and the local political institutions have until recently been restricted. There is neither the transmission-belt journalism as in communist societies, nor development journalism as in the Third World nations' (Kuan and Lau, 1988:2). Hong Kong government officials and the mostly Chinese-speaking media elite were two distinct types of people. 'They do not speak the same language, do not go to the same clubs and do not mix . . . with each other' (ibid.). The media were generally left to their own devices.

This non-interventionism also applied to government broadcasting. Besides two commercial television broadcasters, Hong Kong has the government broadcasting company Radio Television Hong Kong (RTHK). RTHK has a full radio broadcasting service with seven chan-nels; but the television arm, established in the early 1970s, does not have its own television channel. The government requires the two commercial broadcasters to each set aside three prime-time hours and about ten fringe-time hours per week to carry RTHK programming. Although the official aims of the government broadcaster are to inform the public of government policy and to provide non-commercial programming,[29] RTHK enjoys a high degree of editorial autonomy in its daily operations. It has evolved less as a government mouthpiece and more as public television run by a politically neutral team of civil servants. Although a few RTHK programmes serve the aim of explaining and promoting government public policy, it is not difficult to find RTHK programmes that are critical of the establishment.[30] Thus RTHK can be seen as a quasi-public broadcaster which fulfils the dual role of public and government broadcasting (Ma, 1992).

In the wake of the riots of 1966 and 1967, the government started to perceive the need to bridge the gap between the government and the masses via the media. It stepped up the function of the Government Information Service (GIS) in 'managing information' (Chan, J. M., 1992). The GIS published *The Daily News Bulletin* and fed the press with official information. Although the relationship was indirect and non-coercive, most journalists promoted the official line (Lee, C., 1997), in part because of their need for quick and easily available government information. Despite the influence of the GIS, the media were not a government mouthpiece. The description of the minimally integrated media-political system was generally accurate. Except for a few partisan papers, which were funded by China or Taiwan, most newspapers usually did not involve themselves in politically controversial issues. Political discourse was almost totally absent from commercial television in the 1970s.

At least as perceived by local journalists, Hong Kong enjoys an autonomous media. The media have ample editorial freedom; however, there is no democratic institution to guarantee the continuation of such freedom. For instance, under the Television Ordinance, the colonial governor was able to grant, withdraw, or cancel the licences of broadcasters. He could also prescribe regulations to establish standards for programme contents, and was in a position to exercise tight control over the acting media. After a comprehensive survey of Hong Kong media laws, Shen concludes that 'if the [colonial] Governor in Council, the courts and the police are to translate zealously the letter and spirit of the ordinances and regulation into action, Hong Kong's mass media . . . would be drastically affected' (Shen 1972: 31; also see Leung, K. and Chan, M. (eds), 1995). However, largely because of the non-interventionist policy, in actuality the media enjoy, up to the present, a high degree of freedom and autonomy which is a result of the government's exercise of self-restraint (Kuan and Lau, 1988). This was true in the colonial years and remains so one year after 1997, except for the fact that networking between the polity and media owners has become more complicated since the 1990s (Lee, C.C., 1997). I shall return to this in the next chapter when I talk about the re-sinicisation before and after 1997.

Ironically, this 'minimally integrated media-political system' of the 1960s and 1970s, which can be seen as a political deficiency, provided a cultural space that was absent in many Asian countries. The colonial government of the past did not have any political, social, or cultural identity to promote. There had been very little government involvement in the creation and distribution of a domestic cultural product. Up to the present time, it is still true that Hong Kong television has been given virtually no cultural imperatives.

Without any imposed cultural imperative, the cultural products of Hong Kong manifest a distinctive secularity and non-commitment. The media provide a channel through which Hong Kong's society communes with itself (Curran, 1991a) and which helps foster a new Hong Kong identity, grounded in what Raymond Williams called 'rooted settlements', 'actual life', and 'knowable communities'. It evolves from within the society and not from imposed abstractions. Due to the lack of government intervention, popular culture industries in Hong Kong are largely left to the regulation of market economics. Critical media theorists might be quick to smell a rat in the commercialism of Hong Kong television culture and accordingly pose the question: Did Hong Kong television of the 1970s fall prey to the hegemony of unrestrained capitalism?

The surplus television economy

The highly commercialised television economy of the 1970s placed no direct commercial constraints upon the television culture. Hong Kong's strong economic growth fed the television industry with huge amounts of advertising dollars. The optimal business environment for the television industry was amplified by the swallowing up of the advertising share of other media.[31] Except for the introductory year of 1967, the balance sheets of TVB, the Hong Kong's most dominant television station, boasted a persistently high annual net profit rate of 50 to 60 per cent all through the 1970s and the early 1980s. That means TVB earned 5 to 6 dollars out of every 10.[32] With an ample profit margin, TVB quickly became the pioneer in producing in-house Cantonese programmes. The surplus economy was one of the reasons for the cultural vitality of localised programming. Administrative control was not restrictive. Ratings were reported much less frequently and the market imperatives had not yet been institutionalised. With a steady increase of advertising revenue, TVB granted a high degree of creative autonomy to producers.[33] The formation of a socially relevant television culture could be largely attributed to those young producers coming from backgrounds similar to those of their audience. They strongly identified with the locally born and were given relative autonomy in their creative works (Kung and Yueai, 1984).

Though enjoying lucrative profits, the television industry was very competitive. RTV was a long-time rival of TVB; and a third commercial television broadcaster, CTV, was launched in 1976, triggering several years of stiff competition before its sudden demise in 1978.[34] The competition was brief. It pressed for experimentation and innovation, but did not escalate into a prolonged ratings war which would have brought with it institutionalised commercial constraints.

The cultural vitality of Hong Kong television in the 1970s can also be seen in the process of rapid localisation of the television programmes. Hong Kong is free to import foreign programming. No quota is set for imported programmes. For a very short time in the early years, Chinese television was dominated by imported programmes dubbed into Cantonese. In fact the licensing conditions in the 1970s stipulated a minimum level of exposure for the colonial audience to Western, especially British, programming. There was not even a minimum requirement for the broadcast of local productions (Chan, K. C., 1990, 1991). In a small city-state with only a few million viewers, economies of scale clearly worked against the development of local productions. Against these classic conditions for media imperialism, the Hong Kong television screens were quickly filled with local prime-time programmes, saturated with a local outlook and aspirations (Chan, J. M., 1997).

Although media imperialism is not the focus of this book, it merits passing mention here. Among all its variants, two central postulates are recurrent. The economic argument claims that, due mainly to economies of scale, dominant countries, especially the United States, are in a more advantageous position in the uneven flow of media products across nations. This situation is intensified by the recent proliferation of channels and the increase of production costs. To fill up the ever-expanding air-time, it is more economical to import than to produce. As a result, the world's media markets are flooded with American entertainment programmes (Hoskins *et al.*, 1989). The cultural argument inherent to the imperialism thesis claims that imported media products can saturate the cultural sphere of the dependent countries to an extent that local cultural identity is subverted and inhibited (Hamelink, 1983). The cultural argument is strongly contested by recent research on cultural appropriation, which indicates that audiences construct very different meanings when they consume foreign television programmes (e.g. Ang, 1985; Liebes and Katz, 1990). But the economic argument remains strong. In a retrospective of his original critique of the American media empire a quarter of a century ago, Schiller points out again that the 'dollar and physical volumes of the outputs of the US cultural industries flowing into the international market are higher than they were then' (Schiller, 1992: 12).

However, the Hong Kong case seems to defy even the economic argument of the media imperialism argument. In the mid-1970s, the output of Hong Kong-made television programmes was estimated to be 6,000 hours per year. The obsolete colonial requirement for importing foreign programming was abolished in 1980. In the 1970s, imported programmes for Jade (the Cantonese channel of TVB) were reduced to 30 per cent. By 1985, TVB Jade had 80 per cent local programmes and 20 per cent imported programmes; in addition, nearly all its prime-time programmes were locally produced.

The vitality of the television culture also spilled over to other forms of popular culture. In the late 1970s, acclaimed television producers moved on to film production and revived the Hong Kong film industry which had collapsed in the late 1960s. They produced what the public called 'New Wave' films and won popularity and critical acclaim. They sharpened their skills in the television industry and developed new sensibilities when they moved into movie production. Television stations of the 1970s were described as the 'Shaolin Temple' (training ground) of the New Hong Kong cinema (Law, 1984). In seminars on the revival of Cantonese films, researchers reported a close thematic connection between television serials and the newly arrived New Wave films. Nearly all of the acclaimed movie directors came from the drama units of television stations.[35] TV subjects, screen characters, and actors and actresses with a large number of television followers became very popular in local movies. The interchange between the two media was then so ubiquitous that critics called the local film-making of the 1970s the period of television-based cinema (Leung, B. K. P., 1996).

Television also benefited the music industry. Theme songs from popular television drama serials became great hits. Pop singers got regular exposure on television shows and the sudden increase in television fans and record buyers provided a financial platform for the expansion of local record companies. Since 1978, more platinum awards have been given to local albums than to international ones (Lee, P. S. N., 1991).

The maturation of Hong Kong's indigenous cultural identity can be examined from yet another perspective. The booming popular culture has found its way to other Asian markets. Its secular and commercial outlook proved more popular than the nationalistic and moralistic cultural products of many Asian countries. In the 1980s, TVB exported 1,000 hours of its 2,000–3,000 hours of annual production (mostly drama serials) to 25 countries (Pomery, 1988). Hong Kong television programmes have become a part of the programming menu of broadcasters in Taiwan, China, and Southeast Asian countries (Chan, J. M., 1996). In the early 1980s, Hong Kong movies were exported to some 90 countries with an annual export value of more than HK$75 million (Leung and Chan, 1997), and Hong Kong has now become a regional production and export centre for both the television and film industries (Chan, J. M., 1997). Due to the exposure to Hong Kong-made films and television programmes, other Asian groups can easily recognise the cultural traits of Hong Kong people even without first-hand encounters. It is quite unusual for the localised cultural products of a place with a small domestic market and without a strong national identity to achieve popularity in nearly all Asian countries, with the noted exception of Japan. It is apparent that the economic argument of the thesis of media imperialism, at least on a quantitative level, does not hold for the Chinese television of post-war Hong Kong. Similar cases can be found in Brazil and Mexico, where media products show great economic resilience in the face of US domination (Lopez-Pumarejo, 1991; Martin-Barbero, 1988, 1993; Mazziotti, 1993). But Sreberny-Mohammadi (1991) cautions us that the localised media industries are not to be celebrated unreservedly because they are still dominated by large corporations and institutionalised commercial processes.

The cultural argument of the imperialism thesis, when applied to Hong Kong, reveals similar complexity. Hong Kong television is influenced by the West in terms of format and production norms, but there are significant differences too. The prevalence of the format of continued melodramatic serials instead of the American series, the popularity of kung fu and period dramas that can rarely be found in the West, and the massive use of traditional legends and heroes unique to the Chinese culture, all show a distinctive television culture very different from the West with respect to content, format, and aesthetics. The local television people admittedly imitate Western programmes, but they are actively seeking inspiration, not slavishly copying and imitating. There are copy-cat programmes, but the most popular local programmes all have their indigenous edge. It is hard to support without reservation the thesis that Western programmes are harmful to indigenous cultures. Using the case of Hong Kong, P. Lee (1991) argues that the thesis of media imperialism is deficient in its understanding of the complex process of absorbing and indigenising foreign culture. More attention should be focused on the recipient's side. The process of absorption is contingent upon the strength of the local culture, the purchasing power of local media consumers, and the demographics of the receiving population. Nevertheless, I question the easy dismissal of the cultural argument of imperialism, as Lee has implied in his essay. Hong Kong's localised media products are deeply infused with consumerism. As Tomlinson (1991) argues, imperialism is now displaced by the globalisation of consumerism of late capitalism. Although a full examination of the media imperialism thesis is beyond the scope of this book, suffice it to point out that global media domination is still a pressing problem and that the imperialism thesis cannot be dismissed lightly, instead it badly needs substantial revisions to accommodate recent contextualised development in the developing countries.[36]

Summary

In summary, Hong Kong television in the late 1960s and 1970s provided the local population with great cultural resources. It absorbed Western ingredients, transformed Chinese cultural particulars, articulated local experiences, and crystallised a distinct Hong Kong way of life. Similar to the early years of Brazilian television (Lopez-Pumarejo, 1991), Hong Kong television in the 1970s was more cultural than commercial. Its central role in identity formation was the result of historical contingencies, namely, the cultural severance from China, the coming of age of the local generation, the minimally integrated media-political system, and the optimal business environment of the television industry of the 1970s. These contextual particularities contributed to the formation of a strong television culture – all of which defies the thesis of media imperialism.

At the beginning of this chapter I mentioned that some media policy-makers believe that television has a powerful identity-conferring ability, notwithstanding the fact that research shows that television's role in identity formation is very limited. The case of Hong Kong shows that this issue can only be determined by considering other non-media factors in concrete social contexts. In Hong Kong television in the 1970, all the factors so far discussed combined to play a significant role in Hongkongers' identity formation and reinforcement. However, these contingent factors have been gradually eroded since the mid-1980s. In the political transition period from the mid-1980s through the 1990s, the once relatively autonomous television culture has been exposed to numerous interrelated political, social and economic constraints, which complicate the role of television in identity formation and maintenance. This forms the focus of the next chapter.

Chapter 3

Mediating Hong Kong identity (II): Re-sinicisation

The reversion of Hong Kong back to China brings into focus the dialectic and hybridised nature of cultural identity. Sovereignty reversion involves complicated processes of what I call mediated re-sinicisation of the Hong Kong identity. Re-sinicisation refers to the recollection, reinvention, and rediscovery of historical and cultural ties between Hong Kong and China. I shall elaborate in this chapter how this re-sinicisation process was mediated by the political economy of the media during the transition period. Hong Kong's television culture in the 1970s had produced, under a set of historical contingencies outlined in the previous chapter, a symbolic environment for the consolidation of an indigenous cultural identity. This identity formation process was characterised by the exclusion of the new mainland immigrants who flooded into Hong Kong in the 1970s. In the 1990s, Hong Kong television industry operates under much more competitive conditions and the media and society as a whole are undergoing rapid political and social changes. Compared with the 1970s, the situation in the 1990s sees the emergence of a more problematic relationship between television and identity maintenance.

Hostile television economy

Since the mid-1980s, the inadequacy of the unrestrained market system on broadcasting has become apparent. TVB received steady profits until the second half of the 1980s. For more than two decades, TVB has gained a large percentage of the ratings,[1] and the majority of the local audience habitually turn to TVB for news and entertainment. After a decade of popularity, ratings and profits started to slide[2] and TVB has been operating in less favourable financial conditions since then. The hostile television environment means that more commercial calculations and constraints are imposed upon television production. Commercial

Table 3.1 TVB profits from local broadcast and overseas
          programme sales (in HK$ millions)

Year	Net profit	Local broadcast operation		Overseas programme sales	
1981	100	86	(86%)	24	(24%)
1984	208	148	(71%)	60	(29%)
1987	350	262	(75%)	88	(25%)
1989	357	235	(66%)	122	(34%)
1990	327	196	(60%)	131	(40%)

Source: TVB Annual Reports

television, once a consolidating cultural resource, now acquires a hegemonic tint. Reasons for the decline are multiple, and some often cited reasons are the loss of the novelty of the television medium, the lack of competition, and the popularity of other new domestic entertainment media such as Karaoke and video players.[3] The direct consequence of audience erosion is the decline in advertising revenues. The weak station ATV has been in the red most of the time, while TVB also experienced for the first time a sustained decrease in its profitability in the early 1990s.[4]

As table 3.1 shows, there has been an expansion of overseas markets since the early 1980s. With the advent of video recorders in the late 1980s, TVB has started exporting video programmes to overseas Chinese in Southeast Asia and North America. Hong Kong television programmes are bought and broadcast by overseas television stations, which, in some cases, are TVB-owned subsidiaries (Chan, J. M., 1996). These overseas operations have significant implications for the domestic television culture. As more revenues originate from overseas programme sales, TVB may pay less attention to social relevancy and focus more on the basic entertainment value of their products. Due to this change in the market structure, the social integration effects of television have been reduced.

Since the early 1990s, the introduction of satellite[5] and cable television[6] has made the operations environment even more hostile. In contrast to the situation during the 1980s, when the majority of television viewers watched TVB Jade's prime-time programmes, Hong Kong viewers are now offered programmes from the more competitive ATV as well as various new television broadcasters, including satellite television STAR, cable television Wharf Cable, new regional television services, and the video-on-demand (VOD) operators (Ma, 1996). In this competitive scene, the Hong Kong television industry has been forced to institutionalise its operation by controlling costs and expanding its distribution networks and regional services. Competition may add to the pressure to innovate, but can also lead to more restrictive resources and creative controls. For TVB, the latter seems to be the case, since instead of making a greater effort to improve domestic programming, it is much easier for TVB to take advantage of its existing voluminous programme stock to dip into the expanding Asian satellite markets. On 17 October 1993, TVB launched its first satellite-via cable service TVBS in Taiwan.[7] It now provides programmes for Taiwan and is planning to expand to China and other parts of Asia. By 1994, TVBS had penetrated more than half of Taiwan's households, or 90 per cent of the entire cable audience (Chan, J. M., 1997). Beside TVBS, new regional broadcasters like Chinese Entertainment Television (CETV, folded in 1998), Chinese Television Network (CTN), Asian Business News, and Measat Broadcast Network Systems have launched their services and more regional broadcasters are likely to enter the race.

The most sought-after potential market is the television audience who share the Chinese language and culture. In the cultural market including mainland China, Taiwan, Hong Kong, and other Chinese communities worldwide, strong cultural affinities, growing economic integration, technological advancement, enhanced economies of scale, and the increasing similarity in terms of communication infrastructure, distribution channels, and market approaches, are all conducive to the development of a strong regional television market (Chan, J. M., 1996, 1997). Hong Kong television broadcasters have long been supplying Asian broadcasters with production expertise and television programmes. TVB now owns a library of more than 75,000 hours of Chinese programming that ranges from classic Cantonese films and soap operas, to musicals and sport.[8] With the competitive edge of a proven management approach and voluminous programme libraries, the local television broadcasters will emerge as strong media players when this potential television market becomes fully developed.

In this hostile and regionalised television economy, cost control becomes much more restrictive. To increase cost effectiveness, the production processes are further segmented and specialised along the production line.[9] Producers are also less autonomous. In an interview,[10] a TVB executive producer described to me the restrictive creative environment in this way: 'They [TVB] give you one dollar to cook them a dish of fried rice. But you have had too much fried rice and you want some modest changes – you want ten cents more to add in a little spice, and the answer is no.'

Critical media theories cannot be directly applied to the surplus television economy of the 1970s, but they have their explanatory power in understanding the hostile television economy in the 1990s. The Hong Kong television culture of the 1990s is what Gitlin (1983) called spin-offs, copies, and recombinant culture. The pressure of commercialism has a mainstreaming effect on the television industry, which opts for stereotypes, proven formulas, and dominant ideologies. How these patterns are expressed in televisual discourse will be examined in more detail in the case studies presented in chapters 5 and 6.

Social segmentation

Hong Kong's distinctive television culture of the 1970s evolved from within a large population of locally born Hongkongers – half of the population in the 1960s and early 1970s were under the age of 35. Although Hong Kong was a refugee community with a composite population, the common experiences of immigration and community building of the two post-war decades provided this Hong Kong generation with a large common stock of social memories. Under these circumstances, it was relatively easy to foster a collective identity in domestic television. However, Hong Kong society has undergone speedy segmentation along with a compressed and hasty process of industrialisation, a process in fact started before the introduction of locally broadcast television. Due to increased educational opportunities, sustained economic growth, continual full employment, and rising affluence, the population has been differentiated in terms of occupations, incomes, and lifestyles. Lifestyle surveys carried out in the early 1990s indicated a population of diversified tastes and habits.[11]

Compared with the social context of the 1960s and 1970s, one important demographic change in the past ten years has been the rising educational level and upward mobility among the local generations. With increased government spending on education, the proportion of the population with a college education has increased considerably. In 1971, only one in every 60 Hong Kong citizens had received a college education; but by the year 2000, this figure will increase to one in seven.[12] The increase in educational opportunities, combined with the structural expansion of the job market, has created a new, affluent, middle-class generation. Their aspirations, experiences, and lifestyles are portrayed in television dramas and have become a major feature of

Hong Kong's identity. In several social indicator projects, an over-whelming percentage of the respondents agree or strongly agree that Hong Kong is a place full of opportunities, and that it is individual efforts that count in one's success or failure (Lau and Kuan, 1988; quoted in Tsang, W. K., 1994:73). This liberal belief in a classless society full of abundant opportunities is common in social as well as academic discourses. As B. K. P. Leung (1994) indicates, class analysis was conspicuously absent in Hong Kong studies before the mid-1980s. Some suggest that the class factor is irrelevant on the grounds that opportunities for upward mobility have rendered it a relatively insignifi-cant structural force in social and political actions in Hong Kong (Lau, 1982; Lee, M. C., 1982).

However, behind this Hong Kong dream is a more complicated scenario:

- The expanded middle class is often cited as evidence of upward mobility; but this supposedly expanding new middle class in fact represents only around 10 per cent of the total population[13] and possesses both ambiguous class consciousness and doubtful political influence (Lui, 1997).

- Recent studies regarding class formation in Hong Kong show a much more complicated class structure: among the loosely defined new middle class, there are non-manual groups (especially clerical workers) and not just the professional-managerial-administrative groups. There is also a large population of skilled, semi-skilled, and unskilled workers (Lui, 1988b; Wong and Lui, 1993).

- Social mobility studies find that Hong Kong society is not as open as its residents perceive it to be. Members of the working class find it more difficult to move into other classes when compared with those in the upper and middle classes; there are visible structural constraints along class lines (Tsang, W. K., 1992, 1994; Wong and Lui, 1993).

- There is an increasing proportion of new Chinese immigrants who find it difficult to assimilate into the Hong Kong society. They are structurally confined to the lower-paid service industries with obvious earnings disadvantages (Lam and Liu, 1993).

- Some new immigrants, because of their connections with China, have found themselves particularly well placed to serve as economic and political brokers in the newly emerging

Chinese market. Ironically, the once despised mainlanders have become the instant-rich and die-hard believers in the Hong Kong dream in a strictly economic sense (Siu, 1996).

• Economic inequality has worsened in the 1980s; the official Gini coefficient rose from 0.44, to 0.45 to 0.48 for 1971, 1981 and 1991 respectively. These figures are much higher than those found in other Asian countries (Tsang, S. K., 1993). As B. Leung (1996) notes, Hong Kong's influential capitalist class is the one most able to stand the test of time. The increased networking between politicians and capitalists before and after 1997 is conducive to fostering the capitalists as the society's hegemonic class.

In the 1970s, television serials depicted a Hong Kong generation aspiring for a better life. Even if this dream had not yet been realised at that point in time, at least it was a commonly held dream; it fed the local baby-boomers with the courage to work miracles, and in fact, this dream did have some basis in reality. The fast-growing economy opened up many upwardly mobile opportunities and 'something of a miracle' did emerge from the Hong Kong economy. However, this Hong Kong dream faltered in the 1980s and has failed to revive itself in response to the social differentiation of the recent years. The axis of class division has been displaced and complicated by the social and cultural divisions between the Hongkongers and mainlanders. In addition, since the early 1990s, the structural expansion of the upper classes has slowed down and social and economic inequalities have widened. The Hong Kong dream has then become further detached from social reality and has acquired a stronger ideological tone. The 'Hong Kong Dream', the 'Economic Miracle of Asia' and the 'Pearl of the Orient' have become standard descriptions of the colony in the popular media as well as in political negotiations. The economic value of Hong Kong is repeatedly stressed in everyday conversation and in political discourse. Of course, this should not be outrightly dismissed as a dominant ideology. The Hong Kong miracle is an authentic experience to some social classes, and a source of identity and pride for most Hong Kong people. However, this brand of Hong Kong identity has acquired a hegemonic character and become alien to the experiences of some other groups of the segmented population. In the mobility surveys mentioned above, it is interesting to note that when specific questions are asked, those respondents who believe Hong Kong is a land of opportunities also recognise the harsh reality in their personal life. They have a subjective sense of upward mobility (Lau and Kuan, 1988) but also a realistic experience of actual personal limitations (Wong and Lui, 1993). As H.M. Chan (1994) observes, Hong Kong's culture of affluence is reminiscent of the ideology of opportunities and Hong Kong's prevalent culture of survival is also a reaction against the harsh reality of individual struggle. The media portrait of the ideal Hong Kong Man as smart, upwardly mobile, competitive, hard-working, and entrepreneurial obviously excludes a considerable number of Hong Kong people.

How these findings relate to the television ideologies is a rather complicated question. I shall come back to this in the case studies in chapter 5. The point to make here is that, in the 1990s, the main-streaming of television ideology has been less responsive to the segmented audiences of Hong Kong; it suppresses cultural diversity and is partly responsible for the restrictive television culture visible in the 1990s. Compared with other media, broadcast television is relatively insensitive to and less capable of responding to a diversified audience.

Re-sinicisation and media politics

Perhaps the most crucial socio-political factor to have influenced Hong Kong's media culture in the 1990s is the process of re-sinicisation. Since the early 1980s, when the issue of sovereignty reversion was first raised, the historical contingencies that were discussed in chapter 2 have gradually dissolved. After decades of political and cultural severance from China, Hong Kong people are now increasingly living under the influence of China. The partitions separating polity, society, and culture quickly dissipated in the heated political debates leading up to 1997.

Before the Sino-British negotiations on the territory's future, it was almost a cliché to describe Hong Kong as politically apathetic. But drastic changes have been going on in recent years and Hong Kong people are reported to have a growing political awareness.[14] They are more willing than before to fight for their political and social rights (Cheung and Louie, 1991). On the structural level, the most influential change was the formation of the Sino-British dualistic power structure in the transition period before 1997 (King, 1985). The once less visible colonial government was forced to step on to the front stage to meet the challenge of China. The gradual transfer of power from Britain to China was accompanied by political democratisation, a process that enhanced the legitimacy and the governing ability of the weakening colonial government. Shortly after the issue of the handover appeared on the political agenda, the colonial government had willy-nilly assumed a more prominent political role in a decolonisation process which involved, among other things, the setting up of district boards[15] and urban council elections in the early 1980s, and the first election of limited seats[16] on the Legislative Council in 1991. In the 1990s, these efforts encouraged the emergence of career politicians and the formation of pressure groups and political parties (Hook, 1993). The political socialisation process was speeded up by the reform proposal initiated by the last colonial governor, Chris Patten. Unlike his predecessors, Patten met the media regularly to promote his reform proposal for a more democratic Legislative Council. His proposal provoked prolonged Sino-British debates which dominated the media. These mediated debates became intensive exercises and 'televised political lessons' for the public at large and the newly formed political parties. Although decolonisation was a traditional policy of the British Empire, Hong Kong was a unique case of decolonisation without independence (Lau, 1990). In the transitional period China, the new master, was sharing power with the British in a dualistic way. This dualistic power structure was largely responsible for the cracks and cleavages in political and cultural discourse and was conspicuously visible in the early 1990s.

The political socialisation process was also accelerated by the Tiananmen Square incident in 1989. Demonstrations and memorial activities, before and after the June Fourth massacre, were participated in by a surprisingly large proportion of the population which was once described as being politically apathetic. One out of four Hong Kong citizens took to the streets in June 1989, and those who did not remained glued to their television sets for news updates and political commentary. The heavy emotional involvement and high level of participation left a permanent mark in the social memory of Hong Kong. It was the most memorable media event (Dayan and Katz, 1992) in post-war Hong Kong and it resulted in a restructuring of the dominant cultural pattern and a consolidation of a new collectivity among the local Chinese. Two effects on the identity framework were prominent. There was a feeling of deepening antagonism towards the Chinese communists in a us-vs.-them dichotomy: the 'authoritarian', 'brutal', 'barbaric' communists were contrasted with the 'democratic', 'humane', and 'modernised' Hongkongers. After the incident, there had been a widespread sentiment among Hong Kong residents that, being a Hongkonger and a British subject was, in human terms, arguably superior to being Chinese and a citizen of China (Tu, 1991; Yee, 1992). But paradoxically, the antagonism towards the Chinese government was accompanied by a rediscovery of ethnic ties with the mainland Chinese people. The people of Hong Kong, especially the younger generations, knew little about their Chinese heritage, but they strongly identified with the students and citizens in Beijing. Hong Kong people are ethnic Chinese, but there was a curious absence of the 'Chinese' label in everyday discourse in the 1980s. Using Harvey Sacks's (1992a, 1992b) terminology, daily and mediated dialogue indicated a sharp distinction between the 'membership category' of Chinese and Hongkonger. The category-bound inferences of 'Hongkonger' were clustered around those popular and romanticised characters in television dramas and films, which were radically different from the stereotypes held about mainlanders. The June Fourth incident broke this categorical distinction. The posters and banners carried by the Hong Kong demonstrators displayed conspicuous references to their ethnic ties with the mainlanders. Political identification and ethnic identification were mixed up with contradictory sentiments, and were expressed in the media in polysemic ways. The severance from China in the post-war decades was in reverse.

How did these processes affect the media? In the 1980s, party politics was a media taboo, but subsequently became a regular item in newspapers and on television. Interest groups rigorously fought for media space. In the early 1990s, press conferences, press releases, and acrid comments from both Chinese and British officials were all unloaded on to the media. Extensive political coverage legitimised party politics and institutionalised participatory norms. The media became the 'liminal passage' in what was once a minimally integrated social-political system. In the absence of a democratic political institution, the role of the media as a public forum of diversified viewpoints became increasingly important (Chan, J. M., 1992).

The influence is also an economic one. Political pressure can be exerted on the media via commercial means. The commercialisation of China's coastal cities under Deng Xioaping's open-door policy produced a huge potential market for Hong Kong entrepreneurs. In 1992, two-thirds of all foreign investments in China came from Hong Kong. Many of the booming commercial activities in the territory involve Sino-Hong Kong connections (Ash and Kueh, 1993; Sung, 1992). The proportion of advertising money connected with the Chinese market has been steadily increasing. Despite a recent recession in terrestrial television, TVB was able to increase its profits by 20 per cent in 1993, largely owing to the sudden increase in local advertisement revenue from China's property market.[17] The commercial media in Hong Kong are aggressively seeking opportunities in China. All electronic media are actively establishing their Chinese links, which range from visits, co-production projects, programme sales, and plans to set up broadcasting services in China. Media owners pay frequent friendly visits to China, and have regular formal and informal contacts with Chinese leaders and government officials. TVB boss Sir R. R. Shaw is among those who contribute considerably to Chinese government-endorsed charitable activities.

The convergence of political and economic power is more apparent in recent buyouts by businessmen with mainland interests. Rupert Murdoch delivered effective control of the influential English-language daily *South China Morning Post* to Robert Kuok, a businessman whose corporate empire includes sugar trading, shipping, and deluxe hotels in China.[18] Speculation that the Chinese government was behind the deal may not be totally unfounded. According to Xu Jiatun, China's chief emissary to Hong Kong, who fled to the US in 1990, Peking had plans to acquire the *Post* in the mid-1980s. In 1995, another elite paper *Ming Pao* (Enlightenment Daily) was also bought by a Malaysian-Chinese publisher Tiong Hiew King, who has significant business investments in China (Lee, C. C., 1997). Some other minor magazines were also acquired by pro-China businessmen.[19]

These commercial connections were influential in narrowing the range of ideological options available to the local media. News leaked out in 1992 that the Chinese government had forbidden Chinese-owned companies from placing any advertisements in newspapers critical of the Chinese government. In 1995, Murdoch's STAR satellite television dropped the BBC World Service from the northern part of its East Asia footprint. Another STAR channel, the Phoenix, provides entertainment programmes to China's state-owned cable system with news under strict official control (Lee, C. C., 1997). Despite claims that China would guarantee Hong Kong free media after 1997, there was mounting apprehension among media professionals that in the future anti-China stances might have political repercussions. In 1992 and 1993, two Hong Kong reporters were arrested when they travelled back to the mainland. The two were briefly detained and then released. Perhaps the most shocking event was, however, the arrest of Hong Kong reporter Xi Yang in 1994. He was arrested while in China and was sentenced to 12 years in prison. The official reason was the leaking to the press of some confidential state information, which in the eyes of Hong Kong journalists was simply run-of-the-mill, official information.[20] He was suddenly released on parole in 1997 because of health reasons.

These incidents sensitised local reporters to the political boundaries which could not be crossed. There is increasing evidence that the media in Hong Kong are exercising more restrictive self-censorship in their dealings with oppositional voices. According to an extensive survey on professional norms of media workers, 23 per cent of the respondents said they did employ some degree of self-censorship in their work, another 22 per cent said 'it depends' or 'no comment' (Chan *et al.*, 1992). The research team conducted another survey in 1996 and found that 50.3 per cent of the respondents, all practising journalists, agreed with the statement that most journalists in Hong Kong were hesitant about criticising the Chinese government and 21 per cent admitted they themselves had been hesitant.[21]

Up to the present, the process of self-censorship does not involve direct administrative interference on the part of the media owners in the work of their editors, reporters, and television producers. But as Bagdikian (1990) argues, the screening process is subtle, sometimes it does not even occur at the conscious level. The ambiguous boundaries of ideological options could be learnt by those occasional arrests and also by the journalists' awareness of the commercial interests of their bosses in China and the editorial boundaries implied. However, this is not to say that the Hong Kong media in the 1990s are not without ideological struggles. There are deep contradictions between political and market imperatives. As C. C. Lee (1997) observes, journalists may appeal to professionalism and public interest to deflect political pressure; the popular press may use market forces to defuse political forces; and the serious press may seek to balance political demands with economic interests by making peace with authorities and at times appearing to be fair, bold, and trustworthy, otherwise the erosion of professional reputation will damage economic interests. These intertwined and paradoxical imperatives of the 1990s have produced complex media texts with oscillating ideologies and unsettling polysemies.

Re-sinicisation as nationalisation

Political influence, which seeps through in economic terms, does not only work negatively (inhibiting ideological options), it can also encourage new discourses that are of interest to the political power. Nationalism is one example. Never on the television screen in previous decades had Hong Kong viewers seen as many charity shows as in the early 1990s. There were fund-raising variety shows for the poor, for the under-educated and for victims of floods and famine on the mainland. In mid-August 1993, TVB and the Chinese government-owned Central China Television (CCTV) co-produced a glamorous spectacular to fight poverty in rural China. The show was accorded the unique privilege of being staged at the Chinese People's Convention Hall, which is a place normally reserved for large-scale political meetings of the Communist Party. Familiar faces in show business turned up. On their TV screens the audience saw for the first time a harmonious mix of political and cultural icons.

After 1994 China stepped up its efforts in Hong Kong to promote patriotism and nationalism, efforts that were mixed with political commitment and loyalty to the ruling party. Chinese officials openly expressed their wish to 'interfere' with the design of textbooks for students and to promote patriotism among the general public. In the autumn of 1994, a variety show was organised to celebrate the 45th anniversary of the People's Republic of China. All seven electronic media accepted the invitation to relay the show to local audiences. Since then, this large-scale public ritual has become a routine annual event. In 1997, the handover ceremony and the anniversary of the People's Republic of China were accompanied by a large-scale firework display and public rituals, in which popular singers, television personalities, and celebrities all participated in the singing of the Chinese national anthem, the hoisting of the national flag and other extravaganzas. Nationalism is articulated into media discourse through popular icons. Pro-China ideologies get into the media more easily and thus find a more favourable platform for winning consent and assuming cultural leadership. These public rituals are new to Hong Kong people and will continue to forge a new sense of national collectivity in the post-1997 Hong Kong.

However, this new mediated process of nationalisation is not without complication. Although Chinese officials have been rehabilitating their image in the Hong Kong media, there is still a subtle public sentiment against the Chinese communist government, because China's military and xenophobic political culture is quite incompatible with the non-military and internationalised culture of Hong Kong (DeGolyer, 1993). Thus, we see in the popular media an ideological shift towards the North, but at the same time, the media, especially the entertainments media, are downplaying any direct political identification with the communist government. Instead, forgotten ethnic and historical ties with 'cultural China' have been revived. Cultural identification, unlike political identification, can please China and at the same time does not offend the Hong Kong public. This is why there is an upsurge of period dramas and infotainment shows that deal with the subjects of traditional Chinese culture. The stress on nationalism need not be in the form of obtrusive programming imperatives, it can also come about more subtly as the result of content options which are of interest to the public as well as to the Chinese government. Running through these media contents are nationalistic motifs such as the image of China as the motherland of Hong Kong, or seeing Hongkongers and mainlanders as members of one big Chinese family. The membership category of 'Chinese' is deployed to merge with the membership category of 'Hongkonger'. As Schlesinger (1991) suggests, national identity is continually constituted and reconstructed in collective action. The Sino-Hong Kong connection is certainly going to add new attributes and revive old ethnic ties to the membership category of 'Hongkonger'. Mediated culture will continue to tap into the cultural resource of an essentialist and timeless Chinese heritage.

In the 1990s, political and economic powers are more intrusive; greater weight is added to define media culture in the interest of the dominant powers. There are more elements of imposition as China overshadows the society of Hong Kong. The identity boundaries presented in the media are shifting unevenly along the lines of political and social domination, and do not necessarily correspond to the social experiences of the general public. Nevertheless, the commercial logic of the media asks for populism; the demands of the people, though distorted, can find their ways into the media. Thus, Hong Kong television culture of the 1990s is 'polysemic'. This polysemy is not an ahistorical given, but is related to the cracks and cleavages of the shifting power structure as well as to the negotiation between popular demands and the established powers. As C. C. Lee puts it, in post-1997 Hong Kong, 'the multiplicity of political and economic pressures may trigger media reactions in highly situational, erratic, uneven, partial, and even, contradictory patterns' (Lee, C. C., 1997:137).

Media, politics, and identity

Some preliminary generalisations concerning television's role in identity formation can be drawn from the socio-historical analysis in this and the previous chapter. First, in line with many other studies in identity formation, *the case of Hong Kong shows that cultural identity is historical and has fluid and shifting boundaries.* When post-war baby-boomers in Hong Kong participated in the modernisation process in the fast lane, the previously prevalent discourse of nationalism and patriotism was no longer persuasive to them. They constructed a new local identity which differentiated Hongkongers from the 'Ah Chians' – the 'primitive' mainlanders coming from China. They called themselves Hongkongers who were drastically different from the mainland Chinese. However, this de-sinicised Hong Kong identity was re-sinicised in the run-up to 1997 and beyond. The newly formed membership categories of Hongkonger/ mainlander are undergoing another turn. The antagonism between Hongkongers and mainlanders is deepening, but at the same time, the membership categories are opening up for restructuration. Some Hongkongers see the mainlanders as invaders, thus deepening the them/us divide; however, the identity categories are opening up by the sudden rediscovery of the ethnic ties between mainland and Hong Kong Chinese. Identity boundaries are further complicated by the invention of a timeless Chinese culture by the Chinese government to foster political and nationalistic commitment. Hong Kong is hence a dramatic case for demonstrating the historicity of identity formation and restructuration.

Second, *television can have a powerful reinforcing effect on the formation of cultural identity if it works in congruence with other socio-political factors.* In the 1970s, the local generation of Hong Kong was culturally separated from China and confronted with an urbanised and competitive society very different from that of the older generations. A need for a new identity was strongly felt and the sentiments of an emerging identity were very much 'in the air'. The historical contingencies of the times allowed for a relatively autonomous television culture, which served as a very powerful cultural force to consolidate these public sentiments into a new cultural identity. As H. M. Chan argues, 'in the absence of any hegemonic framework of high culture, national culture, and so forth, popular culture in Hong Kong plays the role – sets the agenda – of "culture" per se' (1994:449). The colonial government adopted a non-interventionist policy, and the media was to a large extent left to operate in the un-restrained market economy. But the surplus television economy rendered the television of the 1970s more cultural than commercial. All these factors worked together for television to perform its cultural/ritual role of social integration. Television became a ritual space in which the Hong Kong audience regularly entered into communion with an imagined Hong Kong community. In these televisual 'rituals', publicly circulated identity categorisations were emotionally charged and recharged, in the Durkheimian sense, with a sacredness that became a communally revered order of meaning, thus contributing to social solidarity and community building for a new generation of Hong-kongers. Under the contingent factors of the 1970s, the ritual function of social integration was well performed by the new domestic medium of television.

Third, *television, as an agent of cultural integration, always involves some form of ideological domination. The cultural and the ideological are dialectically bound together.* Indeed, Hong Kong television in the 1970s provided a cultural space for fostering and confirming local cultural identities, and this identity confirmation was a dual process of inclusion and exclusion. It involved drawing symbolic borders between Hongkongers and non-Hongkongers. Since the Hong Kong people of that time were themselves former mainland immigrants or their descendants, to enact a distinct Hong Kong identity which differed from mainland Chinese identities necessarily meant locating a negative reference point on the mainlanders. The mainland newcomers in the 1970s became the most important outsider group against which the locals constructed and defined their own identity. Televisual rituals consolidated the identity categories of Hongkongers and mainlanders and charged them with strong emotions of praise and blame, pride and disgrace, in-group charisma and out-group contempt. The popular media of the 1970s were filled with the images of the idealised Hongkonger and the derogatory images of the mainland newcomers. Thus televisual rituals had a strong reinforcing effect on the process of identity confirmation of the local generation, as well as the stigmatisation of the mainland outsiders. The ideological process also works on another more subtle level. Television depicted an open society for the Hongkongers, and described mainlanders as being restricted to the underclass just because of their cultural inferiority. Socio-cultural identities, because of their conspicuousness, can easily displace economic identities. The restriction of life chances, which is often economic, is explained in primarily cultural terms. Televisual rituals are simultaneously cultural and ideological.

Fourth, *during political transition, media and socio-political factors may contradict each other in the reconstruction of new identity and new relations, resulting in the production of polysemic media discourses. Nevertheless, the media are still playing a significant role in re-mapping the us/them border in response to the re-alignment of social power.* Hong Kong television in the 1990s is a contested ground of dominant political and economic powers. Before 1997, the dual political power centres of China and Britain were intrusive in media politics, resulting in a rapid process of re-sinicisation of television culture. Compared to the surplus television economy of the 1970s, the television economy of the 1990s is much more competitive and hostile, and the creative autonomy of television producers has been greatly reduced. Since television production is more affected by political and commercial calculations, identity categories are articulated by television culture in a much more complicated way. The identity categories of mainlander and

Hongkonger, as presented in television programming of the 1970s, were stable and distinct; but in the 1990s, they have become unstable and contradictory. The stigmatised mainlanders, in an ironical turn in the 1990s, were to become potentially dominant groups in Hong Kong. In the transitory period, the colony was reversing to the rule of China. The former 'Ah Chians' are now backed up by mainlanders with political and economic powers far greater than the Hongkongers have.

Since commercial television can be easily co-opted by political and economic powers, Hong Kong television, especially entertainment television, has conformed, with relative ease, to the wishes of the Chinese government in order to foster patriotism and nationalism. But instead of producing a coherent dominant ideology, Hong Kong television in the 1990s has produced a general ideological field which contains polysemic elements. The polysemies reflect the contradictions within the shifts of political powers and also the populist demands of the people. It complicates the ideological effects of television in a multifarious way. On the surface, attempts of the Chinese government to impose nationalism and patriotism on the Hong Kong people seem to have met with limited success. Television has a limited effect in identity formation if it is imposed from above, especially when the imposed identity is incompatible with local culture. However, mediated cultural identities conform more to the wishes of the powerful than to the aspirations of the people. Television is a very effective medium at shoring up support for the dominant powers. It can highlight desirable elements (ethnic connections with China) and downplay unpopular elements (political commitment) in polysemic ways. Television is thus an effective ideological apparatus in the 'war of positions' during periods of political transition. Here I see a strong connection between the concepts of polysemy and hegemony. The polysemic nature of televisual discourse can be seen as an articulation between dominant powers and textual discourses in the hegemonic struggles for cultural leadership. In times of political change, the polysemic nature of television can be exploited to win consent and contain conflicting emotions.

In conclusion, the contestation and maintenance of cultural identity come forth within imagined boundaries, where members feel more affinity than estrangement with one another. However within these imaginary boundaries, segmentation and cleavages, whether socio-cultural, economical, or political, exist in hierarchies and in inequalities. However, when the power hierarchies in the larger context shift their geometry, and previously persuasive discourses no longer persuade, and previous affinities no longer prevail, social and cultural boundaries enter a situation of fluidity and crisis. Competing social and political groups deploy strategic discourse and/or coercive forces in order to maintain or reshape the national and cultural boundaries and hierarchical orders (Lincoln, 1989). Television plays an important role in these processes, but as McLeod *et al.* (1991) argue, and the above socio-historical analysis has demonstrated, television has selective, variable, but important effects which take different forms and have distinctive processes in collaboration with specific contextual circumstances. In this chapter, I have delineated the shifting contextual power geometry of Hong Kong in the 1990s. Because of a number of factors – the hostile television economy, increasing social segmentation, the dual political structure before 1997, and the mediated processes of re-sinicisation and nationalisation – televisual texts harbour contextual cleavages and present themselves as polysemic, contradictory, and multi-layered discourses. In the 1990s, Hong Kong television does not perform the strong role of identity consolidation that it did in the 1970s; instead, it has become the competing ground of identity politics and power realignment.

Chapter 4

Outsiders on television

This chapter probes the reciprocal processes by which social power is translated into, and in return reinforced by, cultural representation. The case study presented here illustrates the socio-cultural differentiation process in which a sharp symbolic division is developed between an established majority and a newer group of residents in Hong Kong. These newcomers were Chinese immigrants who came from mainland China in the 1970s. They were stigmatised as people lacking the superior human virtues which the dominant group attributed to itself. In the process, the established group of Hongkongers was confirming its identity boundaries while at the same time excluding the newcomers as outsiders of lesser human worth. The established Hongkongers, who had come to the colony just two decades earlier, were themselves Chinese immigrants with transient collectivity like the new Chinese immigrants. There was no difference in 'colour' or 'race' between the two groups; in fact many of the newcomers had familial ties with the established populace, and some members of the two groups were even brothers and sisters, parents and children.[1] Yet, the established group was quick to cast a slur on their compatriots.

The differentiating process not only stigmatised the newcomers, but was also essential in the 'discovery' of the collective identity of the established populace. Stigmatising outsiders seems to go hand in hand with the identity formation process. The established group came to be called Hongkongers, leaving their Chinese identity in the shadows;[2] while the newcomers were given a collective name 'Ah Chian', a label carrying a derogatory sting. In Hong Kong 'Ah Chian' has been the most popular name for newcomers from mainland China for more than a decade. The name originated from a television melodrama in which a character, nicknamed Ah Chian, came to Hong Kong from China to rejoin his family.

The 80-episode melodramatic serial[3] *The Good, the Bad, and the Ugly* (henceforth abbreviated as GBU) was produced by TVB[4] in 1979. The serial was ranked the second most popular drama serial of the 1980s by the local audiences.[5] When the serial was first released, a new membership category (Sacks, 1992a) 'Ah Chian' was quickly delineated. 'Ah Chian' of the serial became the public face of the newcomers. What he did in the serial became the category-bound activities of the newly delineated group. Thus one encounters here, in a particular case in Hong Kong, as it were in miniature, an archetypal socio-cultural process. It is a case that reveals an insider/outsider configuration, in which a group of greater power, in terms of both material and symbolic resources, was asserting itself in human terms as superior to the other (Elias and Scotson, 1994). The serial actually constructed a group name, replete with the cultural imagery of the group, and set in motion a stigmatising process that has persisted for years. Thus the case provides a window of opportunities for investigating the complicated relation between identities, representations, and power.

While China and Asian countries are navigating a shifting set of power relations in fast-growing economies with global and local processes meeting at a crossroads, the question of cultural identity has become an increasingly significant issue to Chinese scholars. New research on cultural identity flourishes around the arenas of theorisation (e.g. Tu, 1991), historical analysis (e.g. Wang, 1994), and ethnographic studies (e.g. Lum, 1996; Siu, 1993, 1996). Similar to Western works, one of the core premises in identity research is that identity is constructed and maintained by cultural differentiation of the us/them border (e.g. Robins, 1996; Schlesinger, 1991). This chapter will provide a grounded case which shows how identity demarcation is constructed by the dual socio-cultural process of exclusion and confirmation. In other cases, the text–context relation may be less dramatic, or the influence of television discourse may be watered down in various degrees. The GBU case, however, is archetypal in the sense that it enables us to see the reach of a television serial.

The threat of the newcomers

The serial is a story of a 'typical' Hong Kong family of the 1970s. The parents are Chinese refugees who came to Hong Kong some decades before. The elder son Ching Wai,[6] a university graduate, and his younger sister Ching Fang, a factory worker, have been brought up in Hong Kong. The role of Ching Wai was played by Chow Yun Fat, who had been a prominent movie star in Hong Kong since the 1980s. The opening episode quickly introduces a conflict situation when the Chings receive a letter from China, telling them that their second son Ching Chain, nicknamed Ah Chian, is on his way to Hong Kong. Ah Chian has been living in China since the family moved to Hong Kong. Now he comes to rejoin the family after 20 years of separation. This turns out not to be not a happy reunion, but a threat to the family. The joyful mood of the family deteriorates as Fang reads the letter to her mother. The scene is unused in its abrupt change of background music, more common in thrillers and detective stories (#1:3).[7] There follows a succession of violent scenes. Ah Chian appears for the first time, chased by police on the Sino-Hong Kong border. He and two other illegal immigrants manage to escape but are later kidnapped by local gangsters (#1:4, 5). The female immigrant is raped and Ah Chian and his male friends are violently beaten. The gangsters ask for a large amount of money and vow to kill Ah Chian if the Chings fail to pay the ransom. This marks the beginning of the difficulties that Ah Chian brings to his family.

This kidnap sequence is intercut by another violent sequence (#1:6–15), in which another mainlander called Ngau, who is a relative of the Chings, threatens to kill his boss with a butcher's knife. He was smuggled into Hong Kong from China, settled in the city some months before, got a job through the father Ching, but was later fired by his boss. His history is briefly told by others in a dialogue (#1:6): When he first appears on the screen, he is already seen carrying a knife into the office of his boss. His boss yells: 'You kind of people are pigs, as stupid as pigs' (#1:9). Whether 'you kind of people' refers to mainlanders as an outsider group is unclear at that moment. However, television drama is quick in characterisation. The immediate key to a character can be suggested by his appearance, clothes, and name.[8] In Chinese, Ngau literally means an ox. Ngau wears a sweater and short trousers, in sharp contrast to the suits the other people in the office wear. Ngau looks strong but does not have the smart appearance of a stereotypical villain; he has a Mongolian face instead. These all help to conjure up an image of 'pig' that his boss has levelled at him. Ngau reacts violently and puts his knife to the boss's neck. Ngau retaliates: 'Am I as stupid as a pig?' (#1:9b). Ngau is thus challenging the label given to him by resorting to violence, but Ngau's stupidity is in fact 'acted out' in the prolonged confrontation that ensues. At the end of the sequence, Ching says in a 'matter of fact' way that Ngau had a fever when he was young and has been mentally ill since then (#1:15). Ngau is finally taken away by the police and is assumed to be locked up in an asylum. Using Sacks's analytic tools, these narrative arrangements are 'anti-modifier modifiers' (Sacks 1992a:45): Ngau modifies the label put on him, the others deny his modification and confirm that he *does* belong to the kind of people who are as stupid as pigs.

The first episode associates Ah Chian and Ngau with conflict and unrestrained violence and explicitly applies the generalised notion to the whole group of newcomers. After Ngau's arrest, the general director of the company engages Ching in conversation (#1:15):

Director: How long has Ngau been here?
Ching: About five months, I think. He couldn't adjust to the life in Hong Kong; perhaps he never will.
Director: There are now hundreds of thousands of these youngsters like him flooding into Hong Kong, I don't know how these troubles will end.
Ching (with a sigh): My younger son is coming too.
Director (surprised): Really? When?

The hundreds of thousands of youngsters referred to in this scene were new immigrants who fled to Hong Kong during the time the serial was being produced.[9] In 1980, it was estimated that one in 12 Hong Kong residents were new immigrants who had been living there for less than three years.[10] This group of newcomers aroused grave public concern and was widely seen as a threat to the colony. In a survey carried out in 1982 among the established populace, 75.7 per cent felt that the newcomers competed with locals for jobs and that this resulted in a reduction of wages; 40.4 per cent felt the newcomers were responsible for violent crimes; 24.3 per cent that they slowed down government public housing services; and 21.6 per cent that the immigrants were responsible for petty crimes. The highest percentage was related to the perceived economic threat, which was considered to be most vital to the locals.[11] Public opinion mostly blamed the newcomers for social ills and depicted them as 'destructive'.[12]

These outsiders, seen through the character of Ngau, were violent and dangerous. They were not only inferior socially, but inferior by 'nature' – Ngau is mentally retarded. It is unlikely that a mentally ill mainlander could survive the ordeal of crossing the border, yet a mad and violent man is picked up to typify the newcomers at the start of the serial. In the serial, the worst example of the outsiders is singled out as an emotive generalisation to represent the entire outsider group.

The dirty outsider

Ngau never reappears after episode one. The stage is left to Ah Chian and his family. In the story, Ah Chian is neither the protagonist nor the villain. The male lead is his brother Wai, who attracts all the praise. Though Ah Chian is not the villain, he acts as the millstone and the black sheep of the Ching family. He is the lost son returned, and is responsible for the misfortunes of the family. For a brief moment at the end of the story, he aligns with the main villain and points his gun at Wai (# 79). The change in allegiance and the difficulty in drawing a line for the role of Ah Chian reflects the social situation of the time. In fact, at that particular historical juncture, the society as a whole found it difficult to handle newcomers such as Ah Chian. There was no cultural category into which Ah Chian could be classified.

Hong Kong has long been a city of immigrants. It has absorbed uneven waves of refugees who have eventually asserted themselves as the cultural mainstream.[13] However, unlike 'Ah Chians' of the 1970s, the earlier immigrants were given a more friendly name. They were sometimes called 'Tai Heung-lei' (country-bumpkins). In the films of the 1950s and 1960s,[14] the Tai Heung-lei character was introduced to exploit the humour inherent in the inability of the newcomers to speak the Cantonese dialect properly[15] and to their difficulty in adjusting to city life. Tai Heung-lei became a social category in the popular media as well as in everyday life, however; this social label was far from discriminatory. The Tais were not deemed troublemakers but fellow-countrymen who needed sympathy and help. These films inevitably concluded with a harmonious resolution of differences with both locals and the Tais united in realisation that they were all Chinese.

This optimism and tolerance vapourised in the 1970s (Cheng Yu, 1990; Sek, 1988), since the locals viewed the new arrivals of the 1970s as totally different from the previous immigrants. The newcomers were no longer the clumsy yet friendly Tais; they were condemned as outsiders who threatened the stability of the established community. Allowed to stay and with a legitimate identity card, they had every right to be called Hong Kong Chinese, but were not considered so in the eyes of the established group. The cultural severance from China and the high-speed modernisation of Hong Kong had resulted in a vast cultural and economic chasm between the locals and the mainlanders. The mainlanders belonged to a generation which had grown up during the Cultural Revolution. In dramatic contrast to the 'modernised' Hongkongers, they were 20 years behind the times in matters of taste, behaviour, and cultural orientation. They were aliens, a different kind of Chinese. Although most of the newcomers had familial ties with the locals, public sentiments towards the immigrants were couched in unfriendly or even hostile terms.

There was no popular category into which the newcomers could be classified. They were no Tai Heung-lai – a label which afforded assimilation into the mainstream.[16] This new group was perceived as a threat and was quickly growing in size. It was deemed more of a danger because of being outside any recognised framework of social categorisation. As Mary Douglas (1966) argues, those objects or groups that fall outside the classification system or stay on the symbolic perimeter of an established culture are easily perceived as being dirty and polluted. Shoes are not dirty in themselves, but it is dirty to place them on the dining table. People condemn any object as dirty if it is likely to contradict cherished classification schemata. Similarly, in a study of a community near Leicester in England, Elias and Scotson (1994) found that the established group harboured the suspicion that the houses of the new arrivals were dirty. It is intriguing to see the Ah Chian character as the personification of the social imagination of the *dirty* outsider.

In the serial, Ah Chian is dirty in the factual sense of the word. In the beginning, he is seen wearing dirty and ragged clothes (#1:4). When he eats, he uses his fingers instead of the chopsticks, and has bits of rice sticking all over his mouth (#1:16). He always laughs and talks while eating (#2:7). He tramples around in a rubbish bin and then smells out the Chings' house when returns home (#24:6,7,8). Even down to the final confrontation, in which Ah Chian, his brother Wai, and the villain are locked in a confrontational scene, Ah Chian is depicted with a runny nose and greasy hair whereas the other two remain in good shape (#79:17). The character of Ah Chian is heavily imbued with references, both verbal and visual, to garbage, dirt, faeces, urine, vomit, sweat, and nasal discharges. His dirtiness is excessive when seen in retrospect, but seemed to be very natural to the producers and local audiences at the time the serial was launched. To the locals, the dirty immigrants badly needed to be contained and controlled via a discriminatory name.

Constructing a new membership category

In the serial, Ah Chian is the odd man out who is neither hero nor villain. He is a misfit in popular classification. However, the televising of the serial discursively constructs Ah Chian, the character, as a new social category, thus filling the gap in popular classification. Ah Chian instantly becomes a popular figure in social gossip and still remains one of the most popular characters in the television history of Hong Kong. The actor who played the role, Liu Wai-hung, is better remembered as Ah Chian than by his real name. There is no need to 'prove' whether the serial has actually constructed the social type. The people of Hong Kong knew no Ah Chian before the serial's release, after which the category of Ah Chian became firmly embedded in popular culture and everyday discourses. New immigrants from the mainland have been widely referred to as Ah Chians ever since. Ah Chian the character becomes the personification of all new immigrants, thus the serial did construct a new social category.

What are the category-bound activities (Sacks 1992a; 1992b) of Ah Chian? Does the specific category of Ah Chian bear the characteristics of the 'outsider' in general? In the serial, Ah Chian is akin to a clown, a comic figure, or a Shakespearean fool (Cheng, 1990). He is a figure one can poke fun at. Most of the mockery arises from his ignorance of the social norms and his violation of the sense of good taste among the established Hongkongers. The awkwardness of Ah Chian's behaviour marks him out as an outsider. When Ah Chian is rescued from the kidnappers and is brought home for the first time, he eats greedily, uses foul language, leaves the toilet without flushing it, and stays up all night watching television (#2:7, 8). All through the story, he seems to have an insatiable appetite, devouring any sort of food that he can get hold of (e.g. #3:2; #14:15; #21:11). In one scene (#9:5), Ah Chian takes up a bet and devours 30 hamburgers in return for HK$1,000. 'Cokes and hamburgers are my favourite. I came a long way from China, of course I deserve to have such nice American food,' says Ah Chian (#9:2). This insatiable appetite resonates with the public concerns about mainlanders consuming the material surplus of Hong Kong. Ah Chian goes to discos and is addicted to television and Kung-fu comics (#2:7; #3:3,4; #8:10; #15:22), which are considered by the Hong Kong middle class as habits of bad taste. Even in the disco, Ah Chian keeps stepping on his own trousers while the local youths are nimble of foot and 'graceful' in style (#13:4,5; #19:11,12).

A frequent accusation levelled at the outsiders is that they are ill-disciplined and lawless. Ah Chian dozes off at work (#12:13; #24:2), stays in bed until late afternoon, and wants to get rich but is reluctant to make any effort (#4:15,16; #8:11). He asks for a manager's salary while doing the menial job of a caretaker (#4:15). Ah Chian doesn't have the slightest sense of law and order, as he is caught by police for jay-walking (#9:9). He throws bottles out of the windows from a high-rise building

(#8:17), jumps the queue while waiting to apply for an identity card in the immigration office (#4:13), and steals from the jewellery shop where Wai works (#24:17). He mixes with his mainland buddies who are sinking deeper into the underworld of gangsters and prostitutes (#45). Together they rob the jewellery shop and are involved in a fatal shootout at the end of the story (#76).

Ah Chian is not case-specific. The stigmatisation of Ah Chian as a social group reveals many features common to other kinds of insider/ outsider configurations. Established (insider) groups usually have a code of conduct which demands a higher degree of self-restraint than is exercised by newly arrived groups. The former claim their superiority by being more 'civilised': their social code prescribes a more firmly regulated behaviour, demands a greater refinement of manners, and has more elaborate taboos. Outsiders are unusually 'uncivilised' in the sense that they have unrestrained desires, an unrefined manner, and are often seen breaking norms long cherished by the established population. Ah Chian, as many other imagined outsiders, is uncivilised, undisciplined, and lawless.

Competing identities

The existence of outsiders often provokes the established group to confirm and reinforce its own identity. Or to put it another way: only when the group shares a certain sense of collectivity can it differentiate itself from the outsiders. When the outsiders take shape, the existence of an established group is presupposed. Although there has been a physical border between Hong Kong and China for more than a hundred years, the imagined boundary that separates Hong Kong culture from mainland culture was only constructed during the post-war decades, when the Hongkongers developed a strong collective affinity and concomitantly a sense of estrangement from the mainlanders. The outsiders force the symbolic boundaries between the groups to become visible. The previous mainland immigrants to Hong Kong did not appear as outsiders, since in the 1950s and the 1960s, half of the Hong Kong people themselves were new arrivals. Not until the 1970s, when the economic boom gave Hongkongers a new-found pride, did a local consciousness begin to emerge. This birth of a new identity owed much to the historical contingencies outlined in the previous chapter. It was at this particular juncture that the mainland immigrants became differentiated as outsiders for the first time.

Thus the construction of Ah Chian as a social type can be seen as a double-edged sword – it served to strengthen the already existing local identity and stigmatised the new arrivals as outsiders. The serial shows the workings of this fine-grained socio-cultural process of membership identification and categorisation. It is a dual process of inclusion and exclusion; of self-confirmation and stigmatisation. I shall illustrate this process using the tools of membership categorisation analysis.

The concept of membership categorisation was first introduced by Harvey Sacks (1992a, 1992b). He observed that any person can be labelled in a large number of 'correct' ways. A person can be identified as a teacher, a mother, or a Catholic according to different contexts. How one is identified owes much to the workings of membership categorisation. Membership categorisation manages identities. To choose one collection of membership categories in a specific context excludes the application of another collection. The choice is not arbitrary, each collection has a configuration of categories carrying rich inferences of category-bound activities. For instance, a Catholic woman is not identified as such when she is seen comforting a crying baby. We put the woman and the baby in the collection of family, not religion. Take the scene in which Ah Chian is brought back to the family for the first time. We see all the family members in the living room (#2:7,8). The setting is inference-rich: Ah Chian, Fang the sister, and the mother are watching television, while father Ching and the elder son Wai are sitting on the couch reading newspapers. They are doing the category-bound activities as the members of a family. So Ah Chian can be seen as the brother of Wai and Fang, and the son of the Chings. However, Ah Chian stands out as Ah Chian-the-outsider because of his awkward behaviour (see analysis above). The other Chings, as well as the local audiences, instantly recognise that Ah Chian is different because he is seen breaking the norms of typical Hongkongers. Wai and Fang laugh at Ah Chian's ignorance and awkwardness. Father Ching shakes his head with a sigh, asking why two sons of the same parents look and behave so differently. These conspicuous inferences force the audience to set aside the collection of family (brother/sister/parent) and to take up the collection of cultural identity (Hongkonger/outsider).

When membership categorisation works under certain rules of application, it becomes, as Sacks calls it, a membership categorisation device (MCD). Generalising from empirical observations and conversation analysis, Sacks proposes two MCD rules: the *economy rule* holds that a single category from a collection is referentially adequate for defining a person, while the *consistency rule* holds that if a category from a collection has been used for one person, then the other relevant persons are usually automatically categorised by the related categories from the same chosen collection. I shall illustrate how these MCD rules differentiate Ah Chian as an outsider. In a scene in the second episode, Ah Chian is having a long conversation with his brother Wai for the first time. It is 4:00 in the morning; Wai wakes up to find Ah Chian watching the blank television screen flickering in the dark.

1   *Chian*: Why was it that a devil woman [white woman] appeared, some others sang a song, and then the television went blank?
2   *Wai*:   Because the station was closing.
3   *Chian*: What?
4   *Wai*:   That woman is the Queen of England, the television stations in Hong Kong always end the day's broadcast with 'God Save the Queen'.
5   *Chian*: I don't get it.
6   *Wai*:   You'll learn.
7   *Chian*: Of course I'll learn, you'll see how smart I am.
8   *Wai*:   That's good.
9   [pause]
10 *Chian*: Are you a manager or something?
11 *Wai*:   I just graduated from the university. I'm still waiting for a job.
12 *Chian*: You read a lot then?
13 *Wai*:   You could say so.
14 *Chian*: You're really lucky. Is that true you've got to read a lot to get rich in Hong Kong?
15 *Wai*:   Not really. It depends.
16 *Chian*: I really want to be rich. I won't go back until I get rich, I swore before I left.
17 [pause]
18 *Chian*: I told my fiancée that when I get rich, I'll go back and marry her.
19 *Wai*:   There is no easy money in Hong Kong. You really have to work hard before you can succeed in anything.
20 *Chian*: No matter what, I deserve to be rich, you bet I'll soon be a big shot. See how difficult it was to get here.
21 [very long pause]
22 *Wai*:   That's good. . . . Why don't you go to bed? It's really late now.
23 *Chian*: I'm serious. I told you only because you're my [brother].[17]

This was the first night that Ah Chian came home. The brothers haven't had time to talk to each other and now they are left alone in the dark living room. The situation is conducive to initiate a warm brotherly conversation for the long separated siblings. It seems natural to see the two as within the collection of brethren (brother/brother). However, the collection of cultural identity (Hongkonger/outsider) is much more conspicuous. Ah Chian does not have the social knowledge that the Hongkongers take for granted under colonial rule (lines 1–4). He thinks that all Hongkongers get rich quickly and he wants to be rich too (lines 10–16). Wai disapproves (by a pause, line 17) and tries to revise Ah Chian's misconception about Hong Kong (lines 18–19), but Ah Chian reasserts his unrealistic desire to become rich instantly (line 20). It is a little offensive to Wai, as well as to the local audience at large, when Ah Chian claims that he 'deserves to be rich'. This calls up the status anxieties of Hongkongers and could be interpreted as a threat to the local community. Although Wai gives a seemingly affirmative reply (line 22: 'That's good'), by an unusually long pause (line 21) he is actually expressing disapproval and does not accept Ah Chian's reassertion. Wai then terminates the conversation one-sidedly (line 22: 'it is really late now'). Throughout the conversation, Ah Chian is actively asking questions and showing affection, while Wai is answering half-heartedly, revising Ah Chian's misconceptions, and distancing himself from Ah Chian. The lines are inference-rich in revealing the cultural differences between Wai and Ah Chian, as a Hongkonger against an ignorant and arrogant new immigrant. Ah Chian has shown the visible category-bound inferences of an outsider and these inferences invoke the collection of cultural identity. Although the two can be correctly identified as brethren, the *economy rule* holds that defining Ah Chian as the outsider is referentially adequate. Wai shows the less visible, category-bound inferences of Hongkonger; however, the *consistency rule* holds that Wai, in this context, be categorised by the same collection which is applied to Ah Chian. The collection applied to Ah Chian is a collection of a 'two-set' class: Hongkonger/non-Hongkonger; insider/outsider. Hence, the categorisation of Ah Chian as the more visible outsider 'forces' the classification of 'the established Hongkonger' on to Wai. Even when Ah Chian expresses his wish to reclassify their relationship as brothers (line 23), his wish is weak under the weight of the insider/outsider collection that has been invoked in the conversation.

In the scene, there are two competing collections: the collection of the family, and the double collection of Hongkonger/Ah Chian (abbreviated as HA below). It is clear that on the textual level, the family collection is displaced by the HA collection. The identity of Ah Chian the outsider is so prominent that Wai and Ah Chian are not seen as brothers, despite Ah Chian's wish to be so identified. However, this is not to say that HA predominates in all 80 episodes. There is no clear cut them/us dichotomy; the identity of family member and of outsider compete with each other in the text. There are times when the narrative calls for the solidarity of the Ching family in the face of trouble and misfortune. In fact, the struggle of the two membership category collections in the text reflects the ambivalence towards the newcomers. After all, the newcomers had blood ties with the locals. These shifting identities are traceable on the textual level: In the first 20 episodes of the serial, Ah Chian still has a close relationship with the Ching family. He is especially affiliated to his mother,[18] and follows her to visit friends and relatives where he is introduced and greeted as a son of the Chings. In a scene when Ah Chian is staying home with Wai and their mother, Ah Chian exclaims: 'You see how difficult it was for me to come here, and I finally made it. This means that we are destined to be one nice family and we will be *united* together forever' (#17:5). Wai does not seek to revise Ah Chian's statement but shows a brotherly gesture by sitting shoulder to shoulder with him. The expression 'united together forever', in Cantonese, is awkward and can be easily recognised to be of mainland origin, but it does not have the strength to displace the collection of family in this particular scene. In a way, the struggle between the two identity collections opens up polysemic potentialities.

However, the HA collection becomes more and more predominant. Ah Chian is hanging around with other mainlanders (#45), he hates his brother for not lending him money (#55), and when Ah Chian is with his mainland buddies, they have a much closer relationship than when Ah Chian is with Wai. Together they express their hatred against the Hong Kong people for discriminating against them (#26:13). They vow to see each other more often to build stronger group support (#37:8, 9). Ah Chian's friends tell him that his brother Wai, like all other Hongkongers, sees him as a brother only when he has money. But they are not Hongkongers; they are mainlanders who are loyal to one another (#55:21). In another scene, they make use of the language of brother-hood by saying that although they were not born together in the same year and on the same date, they wish they could share their success in the near future (#56:16). There is a strong sense of solidarity between Ah Chian and his mainland friends. This change of alliance invokes the HA collection in such a noticeable way that in many scenes in the second half of the serial, even when Ah Chian is with his family, the collection of family is displaced by the collection of HA. In the final confrontation, Ah Chian even points his gun at Wai (#79:17). Whether Ah Chian would kill Wai or not depends on whether Ah Chian-the-brother could overcome Ah Chian-the-outlaw. The struggle of the membership categorisation becomes the main dramatic element of the final conflict. With the benefit of hindsight, we know that the HA collection prevails – the character of Ah Chian has been quickly enacted to represent the foolish outsider since the serial's release. Nevertheless, it should be noted that although textual discourse and social discourse have historically preferred the HA collection, the selection and fixing of membership categorisations do not occur without a struggle.[19]

The two-set collection

The binary opposition of Wai and Ah Chian is triggered by the membership category collection of a two-set class. Here I am not referring to the binary opposition in the essentialist sense of deep structural meaning (Saussure, 1959): instead the binary opposition here is only seen as the working of a symbolic process of social classification (Schlesinger, 1993) and the identity politics of difference (Morley and Robins, 1993). Ah Chian the character, as demonstrated in the above analysis, exhibits a polarising effect throughout the whole serial. This forces other characters to be seen under the collection of cultural identity. Wai is contrasted against Ah Chian; the process makes visible the binary opposition of Hongkongers and the new immigrants. I have already described the category-bound activities of Ah Chian the outsider. Now let us turn to Wai the Hongkonger. Ah Chian is the mirror that shows Wai (and all Hongkongers) as clever, hard-working, modern, and superior in cultural taste. In contrast, Ah Chian, like all other newcomers, is stupid, backward, dangerous, and a threat to the cherished values of Hong Kong.

In the serial, Wai mixes with artists, writers, journalists, and film directors. His close friends are making experimental films, publishing 'serious' magazines, translating classic Russian novels, and studying in prestigious foreign institutes like MIT and British Film Institute. They hang out in coffee shops, bars, and clubs. On the other hand, Ah Chian mixes with disco dancers, triads, gamblers, and kung-fu masters. He reads comics and watches television all day. He pays frequent visits to cheap massage parlours and finally opens one himself (many massage parlours in Hong Kong are brothels in disguise). This contrast of high and low cultural practices between Wai and Ah Chian may be too pretentious and exaggerated. However, these practices serve well as status markers, in the Ah Chian case as well as in other insider/outsider configurations. It builds up strong differentials of cultural capital between the two groups. For the Hongkongers of the 1970s who first tasted the attractions of modern life, their collective charisma was partly derived from these 'refined' cultural tastes that the newly emerged middle class had acquired.

At the beginning of the story, Wai is an aspiring university graduate from a local family, and he quickly becomes a successful manager (#15). In the second half of the serial, he falls from the top and is subjected to all the disgraces imaginable (#33–45); however Wai remains industrious and determined, seizing every opportunity to work his way up again, and he finally succeeds. Wai embodies the commonly held social discourse that all the aspiring Hongkongers are given the opportunities to succeed in the highly mobile Hong Kong society. In comparison, Ah Chian is ignorant and uneducated; his family supports his studies at an evening school, but he does not take the chance to better equip himself (#13). He fools around at work (#9; #12). When the family is in trouble, Wai is willing to work as a taxi driver, while Ah Chian is seen staying in bed late in the afternoon. Wai is often seen wearing sporty tracksuits and jogging in high spirits along the streets early in the morning; by contrast Ah Chian is depicted eating, dozing, or watching television late into the night.[20] Ah Chian lives with the fantasy of getting rich very quickly but cares little about the opportunities given to him. Ah Chian finally fails, trapping himself in an armed robbery at the end of the story. Although it is the bad guys who have led him astray, he fails because of his stupidity and laziness; and as the narrative suggests, he himself should take the blame.

In the serial, Wai proposes to his boss that he should 'modernise' the company by installing a computer network, launching a promotional campaign, and opening up more chain stores (#12; #13). For Hongkongers in the 1970s, computerisation, marketing, and business management techniques were symbols (no matter how crude or naïve) of leaping into the 'modern era'. Wai is also convinced that individual efforts and abilities should be the primary determinant of socio-economic advancement: 'I have my way of doing things. I want to move ahead on my own, I don't want any nepotism from family ties' (#15:4; also #15:2; #20:11; etc.). In direct contrast, Ah Chian metaphorically jumps queues, asks for favours, and exploits the advantages of family networks. In the backwardness of Ah Chian, a 'truth' about Hongkongers is displayed. Wai reflects the pride and confidence that the Hongkongers experienced in the 1970s. The self-satisfaction was not only a result of the prosperity brought about by rapid industrialisation, but was also fostered in contrast to the backwardness of the mainland. There was a widespread feeling of breaking away from the traditional Chinese ways to more modern methods of doing things; and to the Hongkongers, this breakaway proved to be successful, at least when compared to the mainland.

Here, the binary mode should not be essentialised in simplified dichotomy. It is an analytic strategy within a multi-layered narrative. In the serial, the achievement vs. ascription is also displayed by the antagonism between Wai and Joe, the leading villain. Joe is opposing Wai's attempt to 'modernise' the company (#57:3). He is in direct competition with Wai for the control of the company, and his method of accomplishing this is to marry the boss's daughter (#12:9,10). I don't want to complicate the analysis by introducing Joe into the comparison, since the opposition between Wai and Joe does not contradict the Wai/Ah Chian pairing. However, it is worth noting that binary opposition is working in multiple layers, especially within the multiple character relations of the melodramatic texts (see appendix 3 on methodology). A strictly structuralist conception of binary opposition is apparently inadequate. Binary opposition should be used flexibly as a tool instead of seeing it as a mysterious way of uncovering some kind of deep and stable meaning structure.

Another point of interest is that Joe is in fact another outsider, a vivacious Vietnamese. The Wai-and-Joe pairing is placed in the insider/outsider configuration similar to the Wai-and-Ah Chian pairing, but it is related to the anxieties about the influx of Vietnamese 'boat people' in the 1970s and early 1980s. The issue triggered the cultural imagination of violent Vietnamese both in television and films. An outstanding example is the movie *Boat People* produced by Ann Hui in 1982. For Hui, Vietnam was adopted as an allegory of Hong Kong to express sensitive feelings towards exile and escape (Teo, 1997). Since the 1970s onwards, Hong Kong had been troubled by Vietnamese 'boat people' who escaped communist rule and drifted into Hong Kong waters. The British agreed to take up the refugees temporarily in Hong Kong, but hundreds of thousands were stuck there for more than two decades. In GBU, a Vietnamese was conveniently deployed to serve as another hostile outsider.

The binary opposition between the categories of Ah Chian and Hongkongers is heavily invested with emotions of blame and praise. Ah Chian is depicted from the start as the black sheep of the family. In order to rescue Ah Chian, the Chings have to beg for ransom money from friends and relatives. Ah Chian is always asking for money thereafter and brings nothing but trouble to the family (#18:9; #24:10; #55:19; #72:8; #76:27).[21] He involves Wai in a serious crime because he robs the jewellery company where Wai works. The shame he brings becomes part of the category-bound emotions associated with the Ah Chian category. On the contrary, Wai always brings back a sense of pride to the family. He supports the family with all his might, and he is the one to whom the family can turn in times of trouble. This contrasting charisma and disgrace is one of the most important aspects of the binary opposition of the two-set collection; it builds strong emotional barriers between the divide.

As Elias and Scotson (1994) indicate, an established (insider) group tends to attribute to the whole of the outsider group the 'bad' characteristics of that group's 'worst'. In contrast, the self-image of the established group tends to be modelled on the minority of its 'best'. The membership categories in the two-set collection are usually polarised by blame and praise gossip. This polarising effect also worked during the production of the media text. The male lead was made to be an exceptionally good guy; he was the exemplary Hong Kong Man. Since the Hongkonger/outsider categorisation was so prominent in the serial, the scriptwriters found it too difficult to arrange a Hongkonger to do the dirty job of the leading villain. So it was decided that the villain would come from Vietnam, and the viewers were repeatedly reminded of his alien origin. This polarising process of symbolic construction breeds a logic of its own and cannot be simply reduced to the structural influences of the social contexts.

Having contrasted Hongkongers with Ah Chian, it is interesting that the image of the former is still less distinct than the latter. Up to the present day, the character Ah Chian remains alive in the social memory, but the character of Wai is less well remembered. Here we see a common feature of most forms of identity formation: Hong Kong acquires its identity almost by what it is *not*. In the post-war years, the strengthening of a Hong Kong identity was largely based on the negative reference point of communist China and the new mainland immigrants within Hong Kong. To see identity defined through negation implies that the identity boundaries are more visible than the actual image of that identity category. The 'them' is always clearer than the 'us'. As S. K. Lau (1990) notes, Hong Kong identity was unstable and comparative-reactive; it did not have a strong core component and was constructed by comparing Hong Kong people with mainland Chinese. Hong Kong people tended to exaggerate their positive features while denigrating their mainland counterparts. In fact, they tended to tap into their own inner conflicts and anxieties and project them on to the outsider. In the past, 'it was not uncommon for the Hong Kong people to shift back and forth from an exalted sense of self-esteem to a dejected sense of self-pity in no time' (Lau, 1990: 9). Hong Kong people were themselves mainland immigrants who were to some extent 'uncivilised', 'lazy', and 'lawless' like the newcomers. In common with other societies, the fear of un-desirable internal qualities is often projected on to immigrant groups or minority populations. The instability of the Hong Kong identity was stabilised by projecting the 'shadow' of the in-group to the out-group.

The dominant and the subordinate

The above discussion has shown how textual inferences give flesh and blood to the membership categories of Hongkongers and Ah Chian. Those textual inferences identified in the previous sections become the category-bound inferences of the two sets. What about the social relations between the Hongkongers and the new immigrants as inscribed in the text? The serial shows a clear power relation between Hong-kongers and the outsiders. Ah Chian is in approximately 300 scenes of the serial. In these 300 scenes, there are 180 featuring Ah Chian in a subordinate position: Ah Chian receives instructions and follows orders (e.g. #19:21; #21:10), he is beaten up (e.g. #19:14), ridiculed (e.g. #25:15), rebuked (e.g. #20:22; #24:8), taught how to behave (e.g. #44:22), made to kneel down (#24:20: #42:18), has his hands and feet bound up (#42:15), is told to stay away from his brother and sister (#27:17), is shot (#76:18), or simply shows himself incapable of directing conversation or taking his turn in dialogue (e.g. #28:16). In another 100 scenes or so, he is an equal partner in the conversation; however, these 100 scenes are mostly between Ah Chian and his wife, or Ah Chian with other mainlanders.

Ah Chian is in the dominant position in no more than ten scenes, in which Ah Chian is on the edge, drunk, or extremely nervous; and he often expresses regret after these emotional outbreaks (e.g. #41:4, 5).[22] Of course, the male lead Wai also experiences setbacks and humiliations throughout the drama. He is imprisoned and is almost killed in fights. These are in fact the basic ingredients of melodramas: however, unlike Ah Chian, Wai initiates ideas, takes action, overcomes obstacles, and fights against all odds. Even the villains are often seen in charge of things. Ah Chian, as a comic figure, is seen as inferior most of the time. This one-sided subordination of Ah Chian in the serial constructs a social relationship between the powerful Hongkongers and the subordinate Ah Chians.

The subordination of Ah Chian can also be seen in the narrative arrangement. Take Ah Chian's marriage for instance. In episode 42, Ah Chian is caught in bed with his girlfriend by the girl's parents. He is then locked up and forced to marry the girl. After the marriage, Ah Chian lives in the house of his parents-in-law and is obliged to work all day in their grocery shops. This is supposed to be very humiliating, because in a Chinese community, the wives generally live and work in the men's homes. However, Ah Chian's parents and their friends raise no objections; they even ask Ah Chian to behave and to be obedient in his new home. It is interesting that such an obvious humiliation does not come across as such in the narrative. It seems so natural, as if Ah Chian deserves this.

In the serial, Ah Chian and other mainlanders have derogatory labels heaped upon them. They are called pigs (#1:9), morons (#1:9), hungry ghosts (#3:2), country hicks (#21), rice buckets (#41:11), stink cans (#44:7), bugs (#44:8), turtle eggs (#44:11), and 'big circle'[23] (#77:10). There is a wide range of such terms at the disposal of the established Hongkongers to stigmatise the newcomers. These terms can cut deep because they are backed up by an uneven distribution of social power. See for instance the following dialogue taken from a scene in which Ah Chian is working in the grocery shop:

Customer A: Stink Chian!

Chian: What stink can! Brother Chian!

Customer B [walking in]: Hey! Stink Chian! Give me some mushrooms! Are they good?

Chian: I have a name! Ching Chian! Don't you hear?

Customer B: What's the deal, everyone calls you Stink Chian!

Chian: Who said that?

Customer C [walking in]: Stink Chian! Give me some white vinegar.

Chian: You guys call me Stink Chian again, and you'll get no mushrooms, no vinegar, nothing.

Cheung [Chian's father-in-law]: Stink Chian!

Chian: Dad.

Cheung: What have you done to my customers!

Chian: They were driving me mad calling me Stink Chian. . . .

Cheung: Will you die if somebody calls you Stink Chian? [Hitting Chian's head] Stink Chian! [Hitting again] Stink Chian! Did you die then?

Chian: I'm sorry, Dad.

Ah Chian and the customers are aware of the humiliation that goes with the stigmatising name. The customers comfortably use it as an appropriate name, but to Ah Chian, it hurts. He wants to shake it off, but it is made to stick by force. The 'force' may be too excessive and could trigger sympathy and oppositional readings. I shall discuss this kind of ideological resistance in a moment. Suffice it here to point out that, on the textual level, the stigma is firmly in place.

Not only does Ah Chian want to shake off the stigma of a low-life immigrant, he aspires to be a Hong Kong Man like all others, so he selects a Christian name, Robert (#15:22). He consciously wears a suit and a tie when taking a family photo (#4:6). In one scene, Ah Chian goes for an interview, wearing a suit and a tie, and the interviewer mistakes Ah Chian for a candidate for some high-ranking job in the company and opens the conversation in a formal and polite manner. However, the one who introduces Ah Chian to the company interrupts the conversation, telling the interviewer that Ah Chian should run errands because he is from the mainland. Ah Chian is then asked to take off his suit (#21:13) as an errand boy is not supposed to dress like a manager. Although Ah Chian aspires to be a stereotypical Hong Kong businessman, he is ridiculed for trying to do so. Like other new immigrants, Ah Chian finds himself facing an established group defensive of what it has gained.

Perceiving outsiders as born criminals is common in many other insider/outsider configurations. This frequently becomes a rationale for relegating the outsiders to a subordinate position. Ah Chian and his mainland buddies have lived up to this stereotypical image given to them. Frustrated by their failure to integrate into the mainstream, they become criminals, threatening the stability of the community. The 'fall' of Ah Chian reveals different layers of textual meanings at work. First, seen from the perspective of the Hongkongers, the mainlanders are inevitable criminals. Ah Chian and his mainland buddies are frequently seen saying that they have no choice but to become criminals in order to 'make it' in Hong Kong. They say things like: 'robbing is the only way out' (#41:10); 'If we don't plunder somebody, we'll be poor men until we lie in our graves' (#45:5); 'In Hong Kong, we mainlanders have no other choice; women end up as prostitutes, men as bandits' (#75:17); and 'If we need money, just do over the bank' (#68:8). These lines confirm the myth that mainlanders are lawless criminals. The audience is easily convinced of the determination of the mainlanders to commit crimes but doesn't care why they are so determined. This discursive perspective can be seen from another set of unusually frequent statements. All through the serial, Ah Chian is told by his family no less than five times that Hong

Kong is an open society and that everybody can make a living if one tries hard enough (#19:21; #42:18; #44:20; #54:2; #68:9). These comments reflect the widespread belief that Hong Kong is a land of opportunity; what logically follows is the conclusion that Ah Chian fails not because he is denied the chance to succeed but because he doesn't make the best of the chances given to him. The flaws deep within Ah Chian's identity are therefore responsible for his failure. Mainlanders are born criminals, thus they deserved to be discriminated against and are to be rejected from assimilating into the maistream.

However, stigmatising the outsiders as criminals can also trigger opposition and resistance from the subordinated. The text exposes contradictions and opens up possibilities of resisting the domination of the established groups. To the audience of the serial, the domination can easily be seen to be excessive and may arouse sympathetic reactions from some members of the established group and the antagonistic feelings from the subordinated group. As shown in the above analysis, it is evident that the text prefers the subordination of Ah Chian the mainlander, however this preference can easily backfire. The membership category collection of family may surface again, exposing the burning question of why Ah Chian the brother is suffering all these mockeries and ordeals. While the textual domination is competing for ideological closure, there are textual spaces for resistance and negotiation. The question of meaning negotiation should be considered in relation to the question of the ideological effectiveness of the serial, which will be discussed in the next section.

In the text, we see an insider/outsider configuration similar to what Ben-Rafael (1994) called 'usurpation'.[24] There is a salient inequality between the two groups, with the established group on the dominant side of the power balance. The outsider group aspires to integration. The dominant group, however, rejects fusion of the group. It sees the outsiders as a threat and seeks to place it in a subordinate role. The GBU case shows us how this is done symbolically; in GBU, there are some 100 speaking roles, seven of them are mainlanders. One of the mainlanders is raped and then degenerates into a prostitute, one goes crazy and is locked up in an asylum, and the remainder (including Ah Chian) commit serious crimes in the territory. By the end, two of them have been shot dead, one is unemployed and supported by a prostitute, another is in refuge, and Ah Chian is locked up in jail. In the last episode, all the major characters of the serial come together in the courtroom to hear the verdict of the robbery involving Ah Chian (#80:6). After the trial, the villain (a Vietnamese), and Ah Chian (a mainlander), are handcuffed and taken away in a police van (#80:7). Other major characters – all Hongkongers – come out of the courtroom and stand around the police van. In a subjective shot from the point of view of the bystanders, the villain and Ah Chian, both outsiders, are seen sitting behind the barred window of the van, safely separated from the crowd. When the van slowly leaves the scene, the Chings are chatting and strolling peacefully along the road in the sunset. The arrest of Ah Chian caused no grief. When Ah Chian appears for the last time, he is seen through the plastic window of the visiting room inside the prison, confined in a cell away from the outside world. Outside, everything resumes normality, and Wai lives happily with his family thereafter. Thus we see on the textual level a conspicuous ideological domination by the established group over the newcomers.

There has recently been a strong emphasis on the instability of televisual meaning. Indeed, audio-visual language produces slippery meanings. Television is by nature polysemic, full of fuzzy edges, loose ends, and secondary meanings. Nevertheless, popular cultural texts, such as the GBU case, are found to have codes and conventions competing for ideological closure. While acknowledging the contradictions within hegemonic ideology, Gitlin (1987) displays a list of competitive devices of ideological closure: prime-time television uses formats and genres for repetition; it builds in slants for legitimisation and delegitimisation; and it offers an individualised solution to difficult social problems. Thompson gives another detailed discussion of the 'strategies of symbolic construction' by which ideology operates through legitimisation, dissimulation, unification, fragmentation, and reification (Thompson, 1990:60–7). These are not essential characteristics of ideology, but together they form an overlapping network of 'family resemblances' between different styles of signification which one may find in ideological processes (Eagleton, 1991). The overall ideological effects of these textual devices for seamless ideological closure is questionable, but their ability to compete for such a closure should not be overlooked. Thus I am arguing that televisual discourses in GBU have various text devices competing for ideological closure. Yet what needs further elaboration is the question of how televisual discourse serves as an agent of *domination*.

In the GBU serial, the newcomers are excluded from the mainstream and confined to a subordinate social position, but Aronowitz (1992) cautions us that a socio-cultural form of ideological domination may conceal an economic one. In the serial, Wai the Hongkonger moves across social classes effortlessly. In the beginning, he rises from his grass-roots origin to become the head of a big company. He then falls from the top and becomes a taxi driver in the middle of the serial, but bounces back again to an even higher position as the story ends. For Wai, class barriers seem non-existent, and success is achievable if one tries hard enough. But Ah Chian is stuck in the underclass because of his cultural inferiority. As the serial discursively asserts, one's life chances are determined by the social group to which one belongs. This kind of narrative displaces class barriers by the more visible social barriers.

Displacing and explaining the economic barrier exclusively by cultural and social terms is itself ideological. For the mainlanders, their life chances were not only restricted by their status as newcomers but also by their class positions. For the Hongkongers, social mobility in the 1970s was less restrictive because of the structural expansion of upper economic classes; yet, class structure was not as fluid as was proclaimed in dominant discourses (see mobility analysis in Tsang, W. K., 1994; Wong, T. W. P., 1991). Thus, the serial GBU propagates ideological domination in a double-edged way: it discursively constructs the newcomers and Hongkongers in a dominant/subordinate configuration, while at the same time, it reaffirms the myth of the Hong Kong dream for the Hongkongers, and obliterates the economic inequalities experienced by the newcomers as well as by some working-class Hongkongers. Domination between classes and socio-cultural groups is articulated together, with economic power and socio-cultural powers exerted along each other's axis. It would be erroneous to forget the systematically asymmetrical distribution of economic power that cuts across socio-cultural groups. Economic power remains crucial in manipulating other forms of asymmetrical powers. Nevertheless, in the particular situation of Hong Kong in the 1970s, the conflicts between mainlander and Hongkonger came to the surface. These conflicts were deeply embedded in popular discourses, which were mobilised for ideological unification, identification, and rationalisation. Reducing these prominent socio-cultural forms of ideological domination exclusively to class terms would be overstating the case. Socio-cultural forms of domination have rich logistics of their own. It is essential to analyse how these forms of ideological domination work within textual discourses and as social controls.

Membership categorisation and social control

The previous analysis shows that GBU constructs a two-set membership category collection of Hongkongers and Ah Chian, with the former category inscribed in a much superior position to the latter. How far does this textual domination resonate with social discourse? Textually based discourse analysis is often criticised for assuming *social* domination just by showing textual domination. The construction of a dominant membership category collection in the serial alone does not necessarily mean that the domination is also working on the level of social relations. One cannot infer from textual domination that the same dominant/subordination configuration exists in social discourses. The discursive practice of textual consumption takes various forms and can activate diverse textual meanings. Here I combine qualitative and quantative data to gauge how far the HA collection works as a form of social control. My aim is *not* to display these various discursive forms and idiosyncratic meanings. Rather, I want to see whether the membership categories of the televisual texts have been projected into social practices via the discursive consumption of the text, and how effective these membership categories are as symbolic resources of social control. The most important test for the effectiveness of Sacks's membership categorisation device is the *recognisability* of those category-bound inferences and valorisations. If the categories of the serial are instantly recognisable, they become symbolic resources for social control and have the effect of regulating social meanings, regardless of whether the audiences are deriving polysemic interpretation from behind these public versions of identities.

Does the televisual discourse resonate with the public sentiments at the time the serial was released? The prejudices against the new immigrants were recorded in a series of research surveys carried out during 1979–1982. It was found that there was widespread discrimination against the newcomers in the late 1970s. In one of these surveys, more than half of the respondents felt that the new immigrants competed with the locals for jobs and public resources, and agreed with the hypothesis that they were the usual offenders in petty crimes; some even thought that the newcomers were responsible for the increase in violent crimes in the early 1980s.[25] Discrimination was also widely felt by the newcomers themselves. In a large-scale survey, the responses of the new arrivals revealed that most of them had not *personally* experienced discrimination. However, when they were asked whether Chinese new arrivals in general were discriminated against, the proportion of perceived discrimination soared.[26] As the researchers observed, the discrepancy is probably due to the Chinese practice of hiding disgrace. Although being discriminated against, they may be more willing to describe the situation in general than in personal terms. The discrimination had real social consequences. In a study conducted in December

1980, it was found that 80 per cent of the menial jobs in restaurants were given to new immigrants. They were also taking high-risk, short-term work on construction sites. Out of 165 work-related deaths from January 1979 to August 1980, 70 per cent of the deaths involved were new immigrants. Many work-related injuries occurred within the first six months of arrival. Not only were they getting the most undesirable jobs, they were also being paid systematically less than local workers (Siu, 1986).

It is difficult to use quantitative surveys to show the stigmatising effects in detail. I shall demonstrate this effect by an in-depth interview with one of my friends who has been given the nickname Ah Chian since the serial was released. His real name is Wong Wah Chian, and he was 36 years of age at the time of the interview.[27] Born locally, he was still a teenager when the serial was launched in 1979. The Chinese word *Chian* in Wong's name is the same as that of Ching Chian, the character in the serial. This is not a common name; Wong told me that he knew of no one else who shared this name. During the broadcasting of the serial, people started calling him Ah Chian, and he recalled a sense of embarrassment every time he was called by that name. The name seemed to tell him how he was supposed to be: stupid, clumsy, and ignorant. That uneasy feeling lasted for years. Now after 17 years, the derogatory effect of the name has diminished; the name even has a friendly connotation because it was used mostly among a circle of close friends. Nevertheless, he still felt uncomfortable when he introduced himself to new acquaintances. He always felt compelled to introduce his name 'Chian' with a joke in order to minimise the embarrassment.

Of more interest, however, is how he was called by his colleagues. He was a schoolteacher and was either called 'Wah', or 'Brother Chian' by his fellow teachers. It is unusual to be called by the middle name, but Wong's colleagues avoided the offensive word Chian and picked up his middle name Wah, or added a friendly word 'brother' to mitigate the discrimination associated with the word Chian. Brother Chian was one of us: he was not Ah Chian the outsider. This 'craftsmanship' in naming is not consciously worked out but is intuitively derived. What most surprised me was when Wong told me how he felt about the name 'Chian' before the serial's release. For most Hongkongers, the word 'Chian' is not a good name for sure, but Wong was once proud of the name. It made him think that his parents were educated and thoughtful to have given him such a rare and difficult name (the word Chian is very difficult to write in Chinese). The word didn't have any bad connotations before the launch of GBU: indeed, in literal use, Chian can mean brilliant and prosperous. The personal account of Wong shows how a television serial can drastically change the societal associations of a word. Once a positive word, Chian becomes Ah Chian, the name for a socially despised group. A sting has grown out of it and it haunts the person named after it. The power of fictional television is greater in the emotive sphere. The interview shows how a social stigma can have a powerfully emotive effect on the person involved, even if he or she does not subscribe to the ideology underlying the categorisation. In this case, discrimination works through the interface of language and social categorisation. The textual domination has transposed to social practices by constructing a membership collection of Hongkongers and Ah Chian; that is, by giving names, and by ascribing a publicly recognisable classification.

How does the membership categorisation of Ah Chian serve as a means of social control? What can be deduced from the above data? The data cited above do not 'prove' that the serial is directly responsible for the social discrimination, but evidently the serial is responsible for reinforcing the discrimination against the newcomers. Textual and social domination reinforce each other. In the GBU case, the serial does not *create* the negative sentiments against mainlanders; as the survey data show, these sentiments were already felt by the general public at that time. The serial had more effect on the construction of the category collection of HA, which objectified and consolidated the antagonism into a set of relatively stable stereotypes. The collection of HA was effective in the sense that it gave the Hongkongers an easily available classificatory device to cast a slur upon the newcomers. The membership categorisation was coloured with strong emotions and status differential. It was good for the ego of the established populace, and it hurt people classified under the inferior and despised name of Ah Chian. This publicly circulated categorisation was then internalised as part of the local culture, which blinded the Hongkongers to the obvious discrimination and deprivations which the newcomers were suffering. It also displaced class factors and economic inequalities by socio-cultural categorisations, and it put the conscience of Hongkongers at ease. Through the spectacles of the dominant category collection of HA, Hongkongers saw Ah Chians as people of lesser human worth, thus deserving to do the dangerous and low-paid jobs assigned to them. The domination was justified and legitimised by the categorisation device. Perhaps it is problematic to say that the subordinates accept this legitimisation of domination, but for established Hongkongers, the device serves the ideological purpose of maintaining domination and relieving any possible feelings of guilt.

The dominant membership categorisation is effective on the socio-cultural level, but the ability to stigmatise should not be equated with the ideological effectiveness in the sense suggested in the dominant ideology thesis. Dominant discourse is productive; it reproduces resistance. This resistance is usually weak within the dominant group, but is more prevalent among the subordinate group. There are more members of the subordinate group who do not accept the derogatory names hurled at them.

In another in-depth interview,[28] the hidden injuries and bitterness[29] of a mainlander came up when the conversation ventured into the mine-field of membership category. The interviewer Zhu was a classmate of mine at the Chinese University of Hong Kong. He was then a graduate student from mainland China. His mainland identity made it easier to initiate a conversation on the subject. The interviewee, mainlander Lau, was extremely aware of the prejudice felt against mainlanders and was quick to point out the distortions and misrepresentations involved. What is of interest is not the content of what he said; the noteworthy point is that the domination was clearly visible to main-landers like Lau and Zhu, but is masked and blurred in the eyes of the Hongkongers. Lau said that Hong Kong people are arrogant, childish, and self-centred in perceiving Hong Kong as an open and information-rich society. These bitter accusations are unheard of in the mainstream Hong Kong media or in the daily encounters of Hongkongers with mainlanders. Zhu told me that Lau's accusations are common within the circle of mainlanders, however it is true that they do not surface when mainlanders converse with Hongkongers. The mainlanders lack the social power to sustain and amplify their resistive discourse. Lau's accusations, which are not without support, cannot shame the established population because they are confined to the private sphere and, until recently, have not been expressed in dominant media discourse.

In his study of television's ideological power, Lodziak (1986), following Abercrombie et al. (1984), argues that television works best not by incorporating a dominant ideology on to the subordinated but by integrating the dominant groups. Dominant ideology is effective so far as it encompasses and influences those with the material power (the dominant groups) to put the discourse into practice (e.g. legislation, social policies, corporatist decisions). It is these practices as practices, rather than the discourses themselves, which have the impact on the majority, and it is through the material practices that domination is socially reproduced. The effects of television on uniting and mobilising the dominant groups are especially prominent in times of crisis and ideological shift.

As for the ideological effects on the subordinated, it is not ideological compulsion, but the prevention of opposition to circulate and gather support. Empirical data show that a considerable proportion of the subordinate classes do not subscribe to the values of the dominant classes, but the subordinated do seem to 'get along with' the dominant ideology. Television has a role in maintaining this tacit consent. Television may not be effective in ideological incorporation, but is more effective in marginalising and silencing opposition.

Some theoretical considerations

As argued in chapter 2, the socio-historical contexts of Hong Kong television in the 1970s contributed to the formation of a relatively autonomous television culture. The colonial government did not impose any cultural imperative on the commercial television; moreover, a large proportion of the population at that time shared the same social memories of settlement and rapid economic development. Added to these was the surplus television economy, which allowed for a creative autonomy rarely found in the hostile television economy of the 1990s. Thus, for the local generation, the newly established television medium became a homogenising cultural force. Similar to the experience of other countries when television was in the nascent stage, the viewing public was enthusiastic about the new medium. It was not uncommon to have viewing figures shooting up to 70 or even 80 per cent on weekday prime-time: this meant that a large proportion of the population participated in a daily ritual of television viewing. In the heyday of Hong Kong television, the magic of the medium elevated the ritual-like character of the routine broadcast (Chaney, 1986) to the status of media event. The feeling of co-presence and mutuality was so overpowering as temporarily to suspend the daily activities of the people of Hong Kong (see Dayan and Katz, 1992).[30] They were sharing meanings, adjusting differences, confirming common values, and fostering an indigenous cultural identity with which the majority of the community could comfortably and proudly identify. Indeed, this identity formation process is to be celebrated, especially by the transient refugee society of post-war Hong Kong.

Hong Kong television in the 1970s could be a good case for a liberal functionalist conception of television culture. It could be aptly called a cultural forum (Newcomb and Hirsch, 1984), or a ritual space of shared meaning (Carey, 1989). Yet there was also evidence of ideological domination, at least on the specific issue of cultural identity. Indeed, television provides a cultural space for confirming cultural identities; however, identity confirmation is always a dual process which confirms and discriminates at the same time. It involves demarcation of symbolic borders between cultural groups. The building up of in-group pride, which is in itself a positive feature of a community, often accompanies the process of stigmatising outsider groups (Elias and Scotson, 1994; Hagendoorn, 1993; Jenkins, 1994). When the television ritual consolidates public versions of identities and charges them with strong emotions of praise and blame, pride and disgrace, and in-group charisma and out-group contempt, the televisual ritual becomes simultaneously cultural and ideological. It at once fosters cultural solidarity and encourages suppression (Schudson, 1994). Here we see, in the case of GBU, the ideological tendencies of television and identity formation in a very simple form. The textual domination was not the direct result of the intervention of the 'state ideological apparatus'. As the Hong Kong media in the 1970s were characterised as a minimally integrated, media-political system, the colonial government was not intrusive to the media. The textual domination was also not the direct result of the distortion of the capitalistic media system. With a surplus television economy, there were relatively weaker production constraints that sprang from commercial calculation. Thus in the specific circumstances of Hong Kong television in the 1970s, the ideological domination could be seen as the working of the internal logic of television ideologies and cultural identities. The GBU case gives us some clues to how this internal logic works.

The cultural identity of Hongkongers, as illustrated in chapters 2 and 3, resides in the continuous play of history, culture, and power (Hall, 1990). It is not something already preordained. The people of Hong Kong have long been a mix of Chinese immigrants settling in the colony in different historical periods. Not until the rapid urbanisation and industrialisation of the 1960s and 1970s did an indigenous cultural identity begin to take shape. The newly formed Hong Kong identity evolved from a specific socio-historical context; it had a history. However, although cultural identity is susceptible to historical contingencies, it has a strong tendency towards closure. Simply showing the process of identity construction fails to recognise the crucial problem of why essentialist identities continue to be invoked and often deeply felt (Calhoun, 1994). As Larrain observes, the very term 'identity' may lead one to believe that there is a single received version of it, that one can somehow determine with some precision what belongs to it and what does not, irrespective of whether one conceives of it as immutable essence or as historical construct.

(Larrain, 1994:163)

Hongkongers in the 1970s were quick to forget their mainland origin and regarded their newly emerged identity as natural and ahistorical. They were quick to decide that the newcomers, who arrived just a few years later than they did, were outsiders and not entitled to the cherished identity of the 'modern' Hongkongers. Against the brief history of Hong Kong's identity, there was a strong tendency to claim an essentialist identity among the local Hongkongers. The historicity of the Hong Kong identity did not render it 'nomadic'. Mainlanders and Hong-kongers did not have nomadic identity choices; rather, they experienced different kinds of identity claims with different degrees of discursive forces originating from different social locations. Cultural identity has a tendency of fixation.

The identity circuit

The construction of cultural identity is a process that selects from a rich diversity of social practices to form a public version of a common identity. Since the formation of cultural identity includes a process of boundary drawing, it often presupposes the notions of 'others', and thus the confirmation of identity often involves the exclusion of others. This selection process may easily become ideological if it suppresses other identities and constructs social relations in a dominant and subordinate configuration. The process can be summarised in an identity circuit,[31] in which the public versions of identity and the variety of ways of life feed on each other. This is illustrated in Figure 4.1. I shall discuss these four components in turn.

I Ways of life

The ideological tendency of this identity circuit starts at the social basis. In a complex society, there is a rich diversity of groups practising a huge variety of ways of life. Some groups are 'more established' than others. The power deferential between groups can be extremely complicated. In some cases, power is articulated with race, in others with class. Yet regardless of other complications, the power deferential can

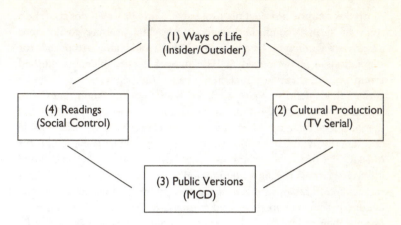

Figure 4.1 The identity circuit

be illustrated in the simplest form of insider/outsider configuration: A group of people settles in a place for some time; the seniority of the group (in terms of the length of time it has been established) is able to create the relatively higher degree of group cohesion, a commonality of norms, and a sense of group charisma. All these tend to induce the gratifying euphoria that goes with the consciousness of belonging to a group of higher value and with the complementary contempt for other groups, especially the intruding newcomers (Elias and Scotson, 1994). The seniority also implies a higher social power deferential when compared with the newcomers because the established group is supported by stronger networking and has already occupied key social positions in the community. These all imply a powerful economic base, privileging the established group. On the other hand, the outsiders, as newcomers, tend easily to violate the established norms and are therefore seen as lawless and unruly. If the incoming group aspires to assimilate into the host community, it will also trigger status anxiety on the part of the established group and is more prone to be seen as dangerous. This conflictual situation leads to a socio-psychological mechanism which urges the established group to contain the outsiders in an insider/outsider classification scheme.

2 Cultural production

The classification process is solidified by the cultural production of a public version of insider/outsider identities. Elias and Scotson (1994) show this cultural production process at work in social gossip. Their study of a small community demonstrates that praising gossips veer towards idealisation of the established identity and blame gossips towards stigmatisation of the outsiders. The status anxieties of the established group prompt them to notice immediately the behaviour of the new-comers that offends their sensibilities. Blame gossips fasten quickly on anything that could show the newcomers in a bad light. In blaming the outsiders, the established group is confirming its own sense of pride and superiority; it flatters the ego of the gossipers. The gossip mill turns quickly, because when compared with the outsiders, the established group has stronger group cohesion and more effective channels of com-munication. The antagonism of the two groups is thus enacted in the cultural practices of gossiping and so established group and the outsiders assume their public faces. However, in Elias and Scotson's study, the cultural institution of the television medium was not yet influential as the research was carried out in a small community back in the 1950s. In the case of Hong Kong, the blame and praise gossip were 'institution-alised' in the television medium. In the 1970s, Hong Kong television producers were mostly of the local generation. They held key positions in the gossip channel of television and selected from the diversity of social life some public versions of identity which they thought to be repre-sentative, while it excluded others. As members of the established group, they were more likely to classify the new immigrants in the insider/ outsider configuration. Television acted as an arena for the outpouring of public subjectivity against the new immigrants (Berger and Luckmann, 1966).

Although economic inequalities lay at the heart of the insider/ outsider domination, the cultural differences (appearance, lifestyle) between the two groups surfaced and were readily exploited in the cultural production processes. The power and status differentials of the (established) insiders and the outsiders were thus objectified in television contents. The membership categorisation of HA was constructed and became publicly circulated and recognisable. In fact, even if television producers wanted to question the mainstream sensibility, they could easily be disapproved by the viewing public. As a mass medium, tele-vision has a predisposition towards the mainstream (see chapters 5 and 6). TVB, which produced the Ah Chian category in its serial GBU, later came up with another serial entitled *Destiny* (1982). In this serial, the newcomer was conscientious, hard-working, and willing to struggle to build a happy future like all other Hongkongers – however, the serial achieved poor ratings. The public were not ready to accept a depiction of a newcomer who violated the prototype of Ah Chian (Cheng Yu, 1990).

In the cultural production process, the generic features of the melodramatic serial also contribute to the construction of the membership categorisation of Hongkonger and Ah Chian. The historicity, multiplicity, intimacy, and character-centricity of the melodramatic texts converge to confer an extraordinary power to the genre thereby engaging the audience and incorporating the socio-cultural contexts into the text, and vice versa (see appendix 3 on Methodology). The melodramatic text easily involves the discursive practices of the audience on the basis of real-life parallelism. The general public can identify with the characters, insert themselves into the gaps of the texts, and internalise the textual categorisations. I characterised the melodramatic serial as a thick textual discourse in the sense that the text and the discursive practices interpenetrate each other in an intensive and complicated manner. It is because of these particular generic particularities that the social category of Ah Chian is closely associated with the character in the serial. The character embodies the discourse. The characters of Ah Chian and Wai confer the emotions of in-group pride and the out-group disgrace that go with the membership categorisation of Hongkonger and Ah Chian.[32]

3 Public versions

Television, as an institutionalised gossip channel, constructs the two-set collection of Hongkonger and Ah Chian. The collection becomes a prominent public version of identities. This public version has its internal symbolic logic which cannot be reduced to the sociological context. It has a life of its own. The most prominent symbolic logic of the two-set collection is its polarising effect. When people start differentiating Hongkongers from mainland Chinese, they select the worst section of the outsiders and generalise the 'bad' characteristics into the category of Ah Chian; they also select the best section of the established group and generalise the 'good' characteristics into the category of Hongkonger. The two-set categorising pushes the two categories in opposite directions, focusing on the minority of the worst and the best of the respective groups, thus enabling the established group to prove their point to themselves as well as to others.

There is always evidence available to show that one group is good and the other is bad. In fact, most of the newcomers of the 1970s were poorer and less sophisticated than the established group of earlier immigrants,[33] hence the established could prove to themselves, with observable facts, that the newcomers deserved the name of Ah Chian and all that the name implied. However, the established Hongkongers did so by ignoring those newcomers who quickly assimilated into the mainstream and those mainlanders who had 'made it' in Hong Kong. They also ignored the fact that within the established group, there were Hongkongers who had retained strong mainland connections and had been separated for many years from the urbanised mainstream society.[34] There was a rich diversity in the ways of life of both the newcomers and the established, and there were similarities and differences within and outside the identity boundary of Hongkongers and mainlanders; yet, in the two-set membership category collection of Hongkongers and Ah Chian, the two groups were polarised, with one apparently superior to the other.

4 Readings

The public version of identity can become a form of social control and can consequently affect the ways of life in return. The construction of the publicly circulated category collection of HA is an objectification of subjectivity. Once the collective sentiments are objectified into a public version of membership categorisation, the categorisation influences the way in which people see themselves and the ways in which they relate to the newcomers. The influences are multifarious. First, the collection of HA is highly effective in integrating the established group. It is 'satisfying' for the established group to stigmatise the outsider since the very act of stigmatising strengthens the pride of the group and lessens their status anxieties. Prejudice against the outsiders is not only an ideological justification of domination, it is also a means of fulfilling the socio-psychological need for self-affirmation (Hagendoorn, 1993).

Second, membership categorisation arises from prevailing social sentiments. It is a process of cultural consolidation, not an outright creation. Thus categorisation and the ways of life are feeding on each other. The quantitative and qualitative data discussed above indicate that textual inferences of the television serial, the categorisations in popular memories, and the widespread social discrimination against the newcomers are all interdependent and mutually reinforcing. Television melodramatic serials, with their textual discourses, 'centripetally' draw to themselves prevalent social sentiments and consolidate them into the membership categorisation of Hongkongers and Ah Chian. The emotionally charged categorisation, in turn, 'centrifugally' projects into social practices, reinforcing the in-group pride of the locals and the out-group prejudice against the outsiders.

Third, because the newly constructed categorisation springs from widespread public sentiment, it quickly becomes the *unquestionable* classification device of the community. Although the myth that Ah Chians were human beings of lesser worth is rather ridiculous, for many years it looked natural in the eyes of the established group and has thus become ideological. It is equally ridiculous to say that Ah Chians failed in the open society of Hong Kong simply because they bore the cultural identity of Ah Chian. However this discourse of cultural identity has also been naturalised. The conspicuous socio-cultural factor has been successful in concealing the economic factors behind the domination of Hongkongers over Ah Chians.

Fourth, the category of Ah Chian becomes a stigma with a strong capacity to paralyse the people named after it. My interview with Wong demonstrates the stigmatising effect of the name. The stigma carries strong negative emotions; it hurts even if the subordinated group does not subscribe to the ideological implications of the membership categorisation. Fifth, although the category of Ah Chian carries a sting, it is quite problematic to claim that the categorisation is ideologically effective in incorporating the subordinated. Not only is the acceptance of the categorisation questionable, its excessive domination could even trigger resistive reactions. The lines of exclusion are highly visible to the outsiders and this visibility of domination can generate ideological resistance among the subordinated.

Sixth, the symbolic control does not work by making the subordinated group accept the name given to them. The symbolic control works as social control, more by marginalising and silencing alternative definitions of cultural identities. Perhaps the membership categorisation is ideologically most effective when it falls upon those with the material power (the established Hongkongers, especially those in the dominant economic class) to put the symbolic control into practice (e.g. in social policies, employment decisions, etc.). The established group has a higher power deferential and is able to discriminate against the outsiders in social practices. The dominant categorisation simply provides the dominant group with the rationale of social control. The grievances of the mainlanders seldom catch the attention of the mainstream media because the categorisation blinds the Hongkongers to their own 'barbarity' to their fellow countrymen. The categorisation reinforces their prejudice, eases their conscience, and motivates them to exclude the outsiders.

In summary, the GBU case has demonstrated that even in a seemingly autonomous television culture, the internal logic of television ideologies and cultural identities can easily produce a field of symbolic domination, and that symbolic domination and social control are interdependent and mutually reinforcing, working through the sociolinguistic interface of membership categorisation. Membership categorisation is capable of surviving the polysemic flow of televisual discourses, and its power of social control rests more on its ability to construct emotive barriers than on the fixing of cognitive meanings. As Scheff (1994) notes, the urge to belong and exclude, and the intense emotions of shame and pride associated with it, are the most powerful forces in the formation and maintenance of cultural identity.

Chapter 5

Re-imagining Hong Kong identity

In recent television studies, arguments about the polysemic nature of textual meanings and audience interpretation (e.g. Fiske, 1987) have forcefully challenged the various theoretical positions which assume the existence of a stable and unproblematic meaning system in televisual discourse. Simply stated, polysemy refers to the multiple meanings within televisual texts and the idiosyncratic readings of texts by active television audiences. However, this polysemy thesis exhibits a tendency towards cultural populism which attracts fierce criticism. Even those who have proposed the polysemic nature of televisual texts (e.g. Kellner, 1987) and audience activities (Morley, 1980) later become critics of the unrestrained celebration of idiosyncratic polysemy and audience resistance (e.g. Kellner, 1995; Morley, 1993). Scattered critiques mainly focus on the *limits* of the polysemic texts and on audience interpretative activities (e.g. Gripsrud, 1995). In response, attempts have been made to stabilise communicative meaning, mostly by emphasising the inter-pretative boundary set out by the communicative contexts (e.g. Allen, 1992).

There is a general consensus among critics that polysemies do have limits; however, little has been said about the nature and pattern of these limits. In this chapter, I shall demonstrate how the polysemic patterns of televisual discourses are overdetermined by contextual forces. In order to explore the relationship between texts and their contexts, I shall contrast televisual discourse with social discourse across time, using the issue of Hong Kong identity as a case. In the last part of this chapter, a theory of articulation will be deployed to explain how the re-imagining of Hong Kong identity is overdetermined by the historical change of the political economy in the 1990s.

Re-sinicisation as nationalisation

As I have elaborated in chapter 3, sovereignty reversion involves complicated processes of what I call mediated re-sinicisation and nationalisation of the Hong Kong identity. *Re-sinicisation* refers to the recollection, reinvention, and rediscovery of historical and cultural ties between Hong Kong and China. *Nationalisation* of the Hong Kong identity can be seen as part of this general re-sinicisation process. The Hong Kong identity emerged in the 1960s and 1970s from a cultural space with virtually no nationalistic imperatives. Political movements in China were prevented from influencing the colony, while the colonial government forfeited political commitment from its colonial subjects. Thus Hong Kong has developed an indigenous cultural identity which is affiliated with a territory, a way of life, and a general identification of a commonly accepted set of values. Furthermore the Hong Kong identity of the colonial years did not have a strong nationalistic component nor political affiliation with sovereign states. However, the sovereignty reversion has initiated a nationalisation process which changes the spaces of public culture so as to limit or expand the realm of what might constitute meaningful choice and identity positions (Chun, 1996). The previously absent nationalistic discourse and icons are being introduced to the media, crafting new spaces of identity for Hongkongers as a result. The changing power hierarchy of the larger society is being mapped on to to mediated discourse in ways very different from those of the 1970s.

From the post-war years up to the present, Hong Kong has been acquiring and revising its identity almost by 'what it is not' (Siu, 1996), and the boundaries of Hong Kong identity have been drawn largely through the negative reference point of the mainlanders in communist China and mainland immigrants within Hong Kong. This cultural differentiation involved the dual process of the stigmatisation of mainlanders and the affirmation of a local identity. As described in the previous chapter, the identity categories of Hongkonger and Ah Chian the mainlander were relatively stable in the late 1970s and the early 1980s. There was a sharp differentiation between mainlanders and Hongkongers in popular media and social discourses. In the mid-1980s, when China announced its determination to reclaim Hong Kong in 1997, mainlanders appeared in populist films as lethal invaders threatening the well-being and continuity of the colony. Mainlanders often appeared in negative, comic, or villainous roles (Yung, 1991). In films like *Bank-Buster* (1978) and *The Long Arm of Law* (1984), mainlanders appeared as outlaws threatening the law and order of Hong Kong. On the other hand, the term Hongkonger emerged as a popular and self-congratulatory term for the people of Hong Kong.

In the years before and after 1997, the contradictory Sino-Hong Kong identity boundary still persisted in social discourse, but it has started to be resolved in media discourse. No longer can one see the unrestrained stigmatisation of mainlanders in the vivid social imagination of the popular media, as commonly portrayed in the 1970s and the 1980s. Chinese immigrants have played more sympathetic roles in films such as *Mr Coconut* (1989), *All for the Winner* (1990) and *Her Fatal Ways* (1990). An interesting case is the award-winning *Comrades, Almost a Love Story* (1996), which romanticises the story of mainland immigrants of the 1980s and represents Hong Kong as a city built by mainlanders rather than a city apart from China. A film entitled *Bodyguard from Beijing* (1995) even features movie star Jet Li as a veteran Beijing bodyguard protecting wealthy people in Hong Kong. While some populist movies feature mainland heroes who are modern, sophisticated, and superior, some soap operas depict the virtuous characters of mainlanders associated with grand Chinese traditions. Television dramas feature traditional legends and stories while numerous television documentaries reconnect the Hong Kong story with contemporary Chinese history and traditional culture. The motif of Hong Kong being a member of the big Chinese family has emerged in television variety shows. There are also award-winning television advertisements featuring Hong Kong's social history rooted in Chinese culture.[1] In media discourse, the Sino-Hong Kong identity border is now being remapped and made less clear-cut by placing Hong Kong within the continuous Chinese history under the canopy of nationalism.

However, this re-sinicisation is complicated by fears and hostilities: to some, the communists are seen as invaders and the Sino-Hong Kong reunion is seen as an end to Hong Kong's way of life. Although film-makers are prevented from addressing these antagonisms directly, a few manage to do it indirectly. Films like *A Better Tomorrow III* (1989), *Song of the Exile* (1990), *Farewell China* (1990), and *Chinese Torture Chamber Story* (1994) express the suppressed fears and anxieties in esoteric and allegorical ways (Sek, 1997). Period television dramas, such as the long-running *Judge Pao* series, which builds around the story of traditional legendary figures, feature stories of how justice is achieved only after all kinds of trials and tribulations. In these film and television dramas, there are scenes of tanks mowing down dissidents; there are characters whose identity crises build up to tragedies; and as in many other popular dramas, there is torture, corruption, treason, injustice, and massacres. However, they have become political allegories for those who articulate them with the prevalent political discourse of Hong Kong in the 1990s.

By examining in detail two television programmes of the 1990s, this chapter tries to capture the changing media representations of Hong Kong identity under the contradictory processes of mediated re-sinicisation and nationalisation. By these two significant cases, I try to chart the contours of the shifting boundary of the re-imagined Chinese/Hong Kong identity. The first case is a 40-episode television serial, entitled *Great Times* (henceforth GT),[2] produced by TVB[3] in 1992. The second case is a heavily promoted non-fiction series, *Hong Kong Legend* (henceforth HKL),[4] produced by TVB in 1996–1997. The second case is a non-fiction light infotainment programme. I include this because since the early 1990s, television dramas have lost their appeal, while infotainment programmes have emerged as a dominant genre in prime-time programming. Besides, HKL, which features local history, can illustrate how television represents Hong Kong in the key moment of political transition. As the following analyses will show, these texts are polysemic and unstable, and are overdetermined by the shifting power geometry of the larger socio-political context.

TV serial: *Great Times*

Great Times is a serial of 40 episodes. GT comes to my attention because some audiences[5] saw the villain in the drama as a communist invading the colony, but in fact, not a single reference to a mainlander can be found in the narrative. Thus GT is an illuminating example of how power relations can be subtly mapped on to televisual discourse.

The stock market is the central arena of the drama. The leading character[6] Fong comes from a rich family. His father, the founder of the 'Chinese Stock Exchange Association', is bankrupted and then killed by the leading villain Ting Hian. Fong becomes a loafer in his twenties, but he suddenly realises that he is talented in stock speculation and is destined to fulfil his potential in the stock market. This enlightenment is brought to Fong by a mythical figure, Yip, a half-genius, half-lunatic mentor who proclaims himself 'God of Wall Street'. After Fong meets his mentor Yip, he changes overnight to become a hard-working office boy in the stock market. Meanwhile, Ting's family, the villain gang, deliberately or accidentally kill all of Fong's three sisters and his stepmother. Despite these tragedies, Fong manages to work his way up to become a billionaire, echoing the myth that has been retold many times in Hong Kong. Finally Fong takes revenge on Ting's family by outsmarting them in the stock market.

The Hong Kong dream

Fong, the office-boy-turned-stock-market-tycoon, embodies the identity of an 'exemplary' Hong Kong Man. Most illustrative is the sequence in episode 8, which is a turning-point of the narrative. Fong hides himself on a street corner. He tries to sleep and forget, as he always does, but then Yip appears and asks him to stand on his own two feet. Fong then follows Yip to his house in a wasteland. The discursive scene[7] is saturated with visual cues of mythical legends: there is a graveyard, a foggy night, and a narrow footbridge; the wall of Yip's house is covered over with the graffiti of stock indexes and figures. It should be remembered that GT is a drama set in concrete social context, not in the genre of legend or folklore. In the narrative, Yip is neither ghost nor god; he was once a professional stockbroker and is now retired, living alone in this deserted house. The mythic setting heightens the 'sacred' nature of the discourse. Inside his home, Yip tells Fong the secret of success:

Yip: You should find your own world. Only in your world can your potential be realised.

Fong: My father told me about stocks, I knew it when I was five. Stocks are what I want. Now I know why I had never been committed to anything; it is because I only belong to the stock market.

Yip: You deserve to be the disciple of the God of the Stock Market.

Fong: Now I've found my world. What should I do next?

Yip: Go find a place in the market!

The *mise-en-scène* and the dialogues are filled with awkward elements, especially when this scene is contrasted to the realistic setting of other scenes in the serial. Here, stock speculation is represented as God-sent and unquestionable; it is the sacred destiny of the protagonist. Similar discourses are numerous: whenever Fong's girlfriend complains about the risky business of stock speculation, she is convinced once again by Fong's ability to win by intuition, by risk-taking, and by sheer luck. He always convinces his girlfriend that speculating is much better than making a living by routine work. He pours all the money they have into speculation and gets all he wants: revenge, money, and recognition. Fong fits into the dominant membership category of a successful Hongkonger who is competitive and ambitious and finally gets rich.

In the final confrontation between Fong and the villains, Fong triumphs because three other mythical figures help him out. The mythical characters have names, appearances, and even accents of three famous Hong Kong entrepreneurs, including legendary tycoon Li Ka-shing. They are widely known as the exemplary Hong Kong Men because they have managed to get on to the shortlist of the world's richest. In the story, Fong asks them nothing; he believes he can share in their luck just by being near them and having their 'spiritual support'. The rich entrepreneurs are celebrated as Hong Kong Men at their best and are mythologised as having the power to bring luck and success. The dominant discursive construction of GT highly endorses the supreme goal of moneymaking by opportunism. Tradition, superstition, and luck are central themes of this serial. The identity constructs of 'efficient' and 'hardworking' Hongkongers are subtly undermined. This can be related to the prevalent mood over stock and real estate speculation in the 1980s and early 1990s. In this context, GT is legitimising the unique brand of opportunistic capitalism which Hong Kong considers as the most important asset of the people in the unstable social environment of the 1990s.

This discourse analysis describes how popular television promotes the prevailing view of Hong Kong as an open society, and legitimises the social values related to speculation and investment. In Hong Kong, survey data show that the myth of uninhibited upward mobility is widely held by the general public (Tsang, W. K., 1992). Besides, the ideology of *laissez-faire* is enthusiastically propagated by the government and the business sector, and has widespread support from the public. In a survey carried out in 1988, 54 per cent and 3.5 per cent of the respondents respectively agreed or strongly agreed with the *laissez-faire* policy of Hong Kong (Lau and Kuan, 1991). However, on closer examination, the responses on other more specific questions of perceived individual constraints, of the economic function of government, and of businessmen revealed intense contradictions (ibid.). The discrepancy between the general support of dominant myths and the abrupt contradictions of the specifics behind these myths, indicates that dominant ideologies successfully appear as relatively stable public and media discourses, but are contested in the everyday routines of individual practices.

Sino-Hong Kong antagonism

The television drama GT spans the period from the 1970s to the 1990s. The Chinese title *Dashidai*, which means 'Great Times', motivates the

Table 5.1 The collective value structure of the two families in *Great Times*

Fong's family	Ting's family
Heroes	Villains
Westernised	Traditional Chinese
Grassroots	Triad society
Law-abiding	Criminal
Moral	Immoral
Civilised	Fierce, violent
Defending against invasion	Invading Fong's family
Act by reason	Act by force
Upright	Corrupt
Tamed	Threatening
Typical Hongkongers	Atypical, outsider

audience to look for the sign of the times. In the run-up to 1997, political discourses were prevalent in public debates. However, GT is extremely restrained in political discourse, as there is no hint in any of the 40 episodes that Hong Kong has any problem related to politics. Hong Kong, as constructed in GT, was an apolitical society all through the 1970s, the 1980s and right up to the 1990s. In reality, the Hong Kong stock market is very much concerned by political debates, but in the drama the ups and downs of the stock market are only the push and pull between the villains and the heroes of the story.

The initial versions of the script had obvious political overtones. In one version, the story began with a stock market crash in 1997. Another version involved an accident at the Daya Bay nuclear plant.[8] A full discussion of the creative process of the drama will be reserved for chapter 7, which focuses on the production of television culture. The point to stress here is that explicit political discourse is finally suppressed. It appeared in an esoteric way. Subtle political discourse is built in the binary opposition[9] of Fong's family and Ting's family, as shown in table 5.1.

The texts do not feature one single mainland character, and thus the membership categorisation of Hongkonger and mainlander is not invoked. However, the Fongs and Tings show the strong category-bound activities of Hongkonger and mainlanders. Fong's father was educated in the West. His leisure activities are associated with bars and Western music. He plays the piano and his favourite song, *Bridge over Troubled Water* is played many times in the scenes involving the Fongs. Fong himself is good at English recitation. In contrast, Ting Hian is always quoting traditional Chinese proverbs. The names of Fong's family are very common among Hongkongers, but the Tings have atypical names with negative connotations. All their names have the Chinese character *Hian*, which means crabs, a symbol of transgression and fierceness in Chinese culture.

The Fongs have a family history recognisable to most Hong Kong people. They lived in a shanty town in the 1960s, and then moved to public housing in the 1970s. They participated in stock market speculation in the late 1970s, and shared in the colony's economic success of the 1980s and 1990s. What they experience in their daily lives on the screen rings a bell in the collective social memory of Hongkongers. In contrast, the Tings show no such references. They seem to come from nowhere and do things in mysterious ways.

The Tings are 'invading' Fong's family. They are a threat to them all throughout the story. Ting Hian wants to marry Fong's stepmother by force; his second son rapes Fong's sister; and at the end of the story, all the Fongs except the male lead die at the hands of the villain gang. The character of Ting Hian bears a resemblance to the popular image of a Chinese communist: he is violent, corrupt, yet always claims himself to be honourable, blameless, and correct – he kills and prosecutes in the name of righteousness and for the well-being of his victims. He has patriarchal control over his sons; they comply even when Ting asks them to commit suicide.[10]

This political discourse of Sino-Hong Kong antagonism is highly suppressed and esoteric. The majority of the audience sees GT as an apolitical story, but quite a number of them read the political connotations discursively. GT's executive producer said he was surprised by the letters he received from the audience. Some of the audience were commenting on the 'meaning' of the characters. The most analytical was a letter published in the letter-to-the-editor column of *Next* magazine.[11] The author of the letter noted that he took tremendous pleasure in reading the character of Ting Hian as an allusion to the Communist Party of China. Critics have long pointed out that commercial television tends to avoid controversial political issues, and GT shows a similar bias. On the surface, GT is apolitical. The political content, which is suppressed, is read by some of the audience as a political allegory.

Shifting identity boundary

I have applied membership categorisation analysis in chapter 4 to discuss the cultural identity of Hongkongers and mainlanders, but membership categorisation analysis is difficult to apply to GT at the textual level since there is no mainlander in the serial. Ting is clearly stated to have grown up in Hong Kong and is not a newly arrived Chinese immigrant. In the serial, he is seen living in Hong Kong when he is still a child. We have an 'apolitical' text, but the text seems to trigger some form of political reading. The two-set collection of Hongkonger and mainlander appears in the serial in a very complicated way. The most striking fact is that some of the audience read Ting as a mainlander and even as a communist. As the previous discussion indicates, these readings surfaced in popular magazines. To check whether these audience responses were exceptional readings, I carried out a simple survey to gain a rough idea of audience responses.[12] The results show that the reading of Ting-the-mainlander is not idiosyncratic. To my surprise, 59.6 per cent of the respondents said that Ting comes from mainland. That means that more than half of the respondents chose an answer that contradicts the factual references of the serial. When asked how Ting acts, the responses were evenly spread among four possible choices: 20 per cent said Ting acted like a Hongkonger; but many others said he acted like a mainlander (35 per cent), a Chinese (17 per cent), and even a communist (28 per cent). These polysemic readings cannot be attributed to the heterogeneity of the respondents, since most of them were college students with similar backgrounds.[13] These results call for a closer examination of the polysemic textual features of GT.

On the surface the reading of the Fongs as Hongkongers is easily recognisable through the category-bound inferences within the text (see analysis above). According to Sacks, social recognisability is the most important mechanism in the application of a specific membership categorisation. When the audiences recognise their own social memories in the family histories of the Fongs, they automatically identify the Fongs as typical Hongkongers. In the survey, an overwhelming majority (95.6 per cent) said that Fong was born in Hong Kong. Fong's identity does not display the polysemic readings found around the Tings. Fong is easily read as a locally born Hongkonger. Ting Hian, depicted in direct opposition to the Fongs (see above; the binary opposition of the Fongs and the Tings), can be identified as mainlander, or at least an outsider of the Hong Kong community. The application of the categorisation of Hongkonger/mainlander is further encouraged by the strong category-bound inferences of mainlander in Ting's characterisation. However, these category-bound inferences contradict other textual references, such as the references that Ting was brought up in Hong Kong. Therefore, the reading of Ting-the-mainlander is not unanimous. In fact, it is very difficult to say whether the Hongkonger/mainlander opposition is the preferred reading of the text. It is obviously not preferred on the surface: the Ting character is not a mainlander. Sino-Hong Kong antagonism is textually suppressed. However there are strong category-bound inferences which encourage, in an esoteric way, the application of the categorisation of Hongkonger and mainlander.

This suppressed categorisation also has a displacement effect on the identity category of the Hongkonger. GT is staged as an ambitious attempt to chart the past and the future of Hong Kong society. In the opening episode, there is even a glimpse of the future, by projecting two years ahead and looking at what Hong Kong will be like. The serial employs the device of an omnipotent narrator, announcing important historical events in the tone of a news report. However it is somewhat surprising that the much politicised Hong Kong Man of the 1990s is depicted as a one-dimensional economic man in this fictional world. In the serial, Hong Kong has been an apolitical city and will remain as such in the future. This suppression of the political aspects shifts the Hong Kong identity towards the economic aspects. GT retells the history of post-war Hong Kong and characterises the emergence of the Hong Kong Man in a strictly economical sense. What is noteworthy are the things not told. As I have discussed in chapter 3, the local generation derives a sense of collectivity not only from the economic success of the colony but also from their increasing concern over local affairs. Some members of the new middle class are found to have been influential in the democratic process of the 1980s and the 1990s.[14] However, this social consciousness cannot be found in GT. In the serial, the male lead acquires his pride primarily through his economic success.

When compared with the relatively more 'stable' case GBU of the 1970s, GT of the 1990s exhibits many more contradictory and polysemic features. Commercial dramas have multiple imperatives: they have to please a large, heterogeneous audience, to avoid offending established powers, to mainstream their ideologies, and to cling to widely shared cultural categories. These commercial imperatives shape the televisual text of GT in contradictory ways; it moulds textual meaning away from Sino-Hong Kong conflicts, but it also draws on mainstream senti-ments against the 'invading' mainlanders. Thus the text shows an esoteric/polysemic configuration: beneath the apolitical textual surface, there are deep-seated antagonisms which are grounded in the popular Hongkonger/outsider categorisation.

Hong Kong Legend

The second case, entitled *Hong Kong Legend* (HKL), is part of the recent upsurge of nostalgic materials in the popular media of Hong Kong. I selected this non-fiction programme instead of a drama programme because it vividly reflects the mediated process of re-sinicisation during 1997. The programme, which comprised 39 hour-long episodes, is a significant case because it was broadcast not on the fringes of the Hong Kong television schedule, but was produced and heavily promoted by TVB, the most powerful commercial broadcaster, which commands the dominant share of local and regional television markets. Produced by the entertainment division, the programme does not follow journalistic norms; it is more mythical than factual, more narrative than informational. The programme was launched in the summer of 1996 and ended in May 1997. It was initiated by and produced under the guidance of TVB's top executives. Thus it is an appropriate case to study how the institutional logic of TVB plays out in the construction of collective memories.

As a complex organisation, commercial television produces televisual history, heritage, and memories in organisational processes that inevitably involve commercial and political calculations. Television's capacity for local, regional, and global articulation invites various contextual retouches of the collective memories that television produces. Here, *Hong Kong Legend* is used to interrogate the roles that popular television is playing in resituating Hong Kong inhabitants as members of the Chinese nation-state.[15] Although HKL is a non-fictional programme, it exhibits capitalistic and apolitical discourse that is very similar to the fictional programme GT.

Unfailing capitalism

Hong Kong Legend celebrates the territory as a land of opportunities and attributes its success to the unique characteristics of its people. The economic miracle becomes a major component of the programme. In fact, the discourse of unfailing capitalism has a grain of truth and cannot simply be dismissed as purely ideological and illusory. Despite the ups and downs of the world economy, Hong Kong experienced a persistent economic growth all through the post-war decades. Contrary to popular prediction, political transition did not hamper economic growth and the Hong Kong economy was still going strong in the mid-1990s. Not until 1998 did Hong Kong face a major financial crisis, along with other Asian countries.

Backed up with such an economic achievement, HKL expresses a full-blown capitalistic discourse. Often repeated is the phrase 'Hong Kong has evolved from a small fishing port to a leading financial centre of the world.' This discursive statement is either made explicit or becomes the underlying logic of many episodes. In the second episode, land property agents and entrepreneurs talk about a bright future for the real estate market despite the fact that inflated real estate prices in 1996 and 1997 were widely condemned and had surpassed the affordable limit of an average middle-income family. There are many stories of successful entrepreneurs who stress their personal ability to seize the opportunities presented to them. In episode 3, a young billionaire is interviewed.[16] The selling point of his story is that 'a 39-year-old Hong Kong man is able to make 200 million dollars.' This line is consciously used by the programmers in programme teasers and promotions. There has been virtually no sad story of the social underclass or of the poor. Even members of subordinate social groups, if they appear on the programme, seem satisfied with their living conditions. The message is that those who participate and work hard can eventually make a success here. For Hongkongers, economic success is a source of pride and a constant reassurance in a time of uncertainty. Personal life stories of successful businessmen tend to decontextualise the success by highlighting personal endeavour and downplaying family background. In the programme, these stories are further situated in the ideological framework of capitalism and are grounded within a historical narrative. This positioning further essentialises capitalistic ideology as an inseparable part of Hong Kong identity. This 'excessive' capitalistic discourse is parallel to the discursive position offered to Hong Kong by the international community. It is also politically correct since Hong Kong is continuously defined by China as a commercial and apolitical city. The body social and political is masked and restricted under this unrelenting and excessive capitalistic discourse (Chiu, 1996).

Hong Kong re-imagined

HKL reconnects Hong Kong to China. The sharp Sino-Hong Kong identity border described in the GBU case of the 1970s is now re-mapped by placing Hong Kong within the tides of continuous immigration from China (episode 1). The previously invisible ethnic tie is made visible again, while the previously visible differentiation between Hongkongers and mainlanders is rendered invisible. The motif of a 'melting pot' is deployed (episode 8) to portray a harmonious mix of different ethnic groups of Chinese immigrants in Hong Kong. The history of emigration from China to the territory is rediscovered as the lifeline of Hong Kong, providing the city with hard-working immigrants and the entrepreneurial skills of mainland merchants. The inter-connectedness between Hong Kong and China is put in a 'proper' perspective. The programme also features traditional legends, festivals, and long-forgotten ritual practices (episodes 9, 10, 11), which are now replayed and highlighted to enhance the membership of Hong Kong within Chinese culture from time immemorial. Thus, HKL is remembering Hong Kong within a re-imagined community. The once de-sinicised Hong Kong is now re-sinicised televisually to become a member of the Chinese nation-state.

This 'remembering' is also accompanied by active 'forgetting'. Rather than dealing comprehensively with the major historical moments of post-war Hong Kong, the first episode of HKL elides significant moments of political turmoil. Popular street demonstrations in 1967, a watershed event in Hong Kong that is often seen as marking the emergence of a local political consciousness, is characterised in this documentary as a rebellion against colonial rule. Yet the spillover of China's Cultural Revolution into the territory, which was the underlying and widely remembered cause of the resulting violence, is conspicuously absent in the programme. On closer examination, the episode reveals how textual ideology is sensitive to changes in political power. In the 1990s, China has had a strong political influence on local Hong Kong affairs. Under the shadow of China, the politically correct facets of collective memory can easily permeate perceived ideological barriers to become the public version of the collective past. The opposite is also true. Politically sensitive aspects of history might easily be suppressed.

The riot in 1967 was a multi-faceted incident which had political, social, and industrial dimensions. It was *industrial* because it was triggered by the conflicts between Hong Kong citizens, factory workers, and industrialists; riots and industrial conflicts hampered local industries and brought about grave economic loss. The incident was *social* because it had its origins in the frustration of the population over the unjust colonial administration. From a *cultural* perspective, the riot signalled the rise of local consciousness and an emerging indigenous cultural identity. The riot also had a very obvious *political* dimension. It is widely remembered that the Cultural Revolution was the cause of the resulting violence. Local leftists seized the opportunity to activate nationalistic and anti-colonial sentiments. Widely remembered were protesters holding the 'Little Red Book' which contained the quotations of Mao Zedong. In the programme, archive film clips clearly show how the protesters held that Little Red Book and waved frantically outside the Government House. Some extremists, who were labelled 'left guys', started to plant bombs in an attempt to challenge colonial rule. However, neither the narrator nor the interviewees in the HKL mention anything about the connection between local riots and the political movement on the mainland. The audience can hear loudly and clearly the industrial, cultural, and social aspects of the riots, with the anti-colonial argument pushed to the fore. As the British handed over its power to China, the colonial government became an easy target, while for China the Cultural Revolution is still perceived as a politically problematic issue.

In the case of GT, the suppressed political discourse of the 'apolitical' text is decoded by audiences in a polysemic way. Similarly, the suppressed political discourse of HKL also triggered oppositional reading. The omission in the first episode of HKL should not lead one to the conclusion that all Hong Kong media in the 1990s are producing the politically correct History of Hong Kong. There are competing histories in public and private discourse. After the first episode was screened, the audience made itself heard in radio phone-in programmes, and offered details of what they remembered but was not retold on HKL.[17] Critical reviews appeared in the columns of elite newspapers, accusing the programme of political censorship.[18] One article even described HKL as administering ideological poison to the audience in order to make people forget about the past.[19] Suppressive discourse is productive and it activates opposition and negotiation. When there is a drastic contradiction between televised and personal memory, people speak out if the channels are available. The Hong Kong media are neither monolithic nor operating in an authoritative environment. On television screens, there were other programmes offering alternative versions of the 1967 riot. The non-commercial broadcaster RTHK, due to institutional differences, produced programmes which covered the history of the Cultural Revolution and the pro-democracy demonstration in 1989 for both Hong Kong and China. In 1996 and 1997, another documentary, *The Vicissitudes of Hong Kong*, produced by Beijing's China Central Television (CCTV), was shown in mainland China and relayed to the Hong Kong audience by the Hong Kong cable operator Wharf Cable. The documentary is an official televised history of Hong Kong which exhibits strong nationalistic and anti-colonial sentiments. Thus there were competing histories produced by TVB, RTHK, and CCTV. The differences in the political economy of these 'electronic memories' contribute to their ideological differences.

Contextual articulation

The texts of GT and HKL show polysemic and shifting identity categories. This textual complicity resonates with the prevalent social discourse of the 1990s, when a new nationalistic discourse is carving out new identity spaces for the people of Hong Kong. The adoption and/or resistance towards this new Chinese nationalistic identity depends on and is reflected by emotive and attitudinal responses towards the cultural and national icons flooding into the media. Since the 1980s, as the transfer of sovereignty of Hong Kong back to China became a *fait accompli*, various factors – cultural evolution, social metamorphosis, political changes, and the historical development of Hong Kong – have reshaped, in a multi-dimensional manner, Hong Kongers' self-perception of their cultural identity.

In 1996 I conducted a survey with Anthony Fung on identity issues of Hongkongers in political transition.[20] The results of the survey can shed light on the larger discursive context in which the two televisual texts HKL and GT were situated. When asked about their self-perception of the Sino-Hong Kong identity, 25 per cent of the respondents said that they were 'Hongkonger' while 26 per cent saw themselves as 'Chinese'. However, 33 per cent of the people felt they were 'Hongkonger but also Chinese' while 15 per cent of the people considered themselves 'Chinese but also Hongkonger'. A significant portion (48 per cent) of the respondents cognitively located themselves along the Chinese-Hong Kong identity border and identified themselves both as Chinese and as Hong Kong people: this implies the blurring of the boundary. This duality has existed for years, but the sovereignty reversion prompted it to resurface.

However, the blurring of Sino-Hong Kong identity is also accompanied by a persistent differentiation between the image of Hongkonger and Chinese. In the 1990s Hong Kong has been undergoing a re-sinicisation in which the media have been rediscovering the historical, cultural, and economic ties with China. In the survey, respondents were asked to rate the image of Hongkonger and Chinese respectively for the same 16 identity traits[21] on a 5-point scale. Results showed that respondents in general thought that the images of 'Hongkonger' and 'Chinese' were very different. Among the 16 characteristics, 14 of them are significantly different, indicating that Hong Kong people see themselves as having a distinct identity. The five most important differences are that Hong Kong people think they are more 'Westernised', 'self-disciplined', 'sympathetic', 'outspoken', and 'able to act promptly and cleverly'. Only two items are almost the same.

Respondents conceived that both 'Hongkonger' and 'Chinese' are 'enduring' but not so 'humble'. Despite a strong mediated current of re-sinicisation, which has emerged since the early 1990s, there is thus still a visible and distinctive Sino-Hong Kong identity border.

Identities are built around icons and symbols embedded in media discourse and social practices. These icons are emotional 'anchors' of identification. We selected icons about sovereignty transfer which frequently appear in the media in general and in television in particular. The results show that Hong Kong people in general harbour mixed feelings towards cultural, military, and national icons. They identify strongly with Chinese cultural and historical icons (such as the Great Wall of China) but are hesitant about national and military icons (such as the national flag, the national anthem, and the People's Liberation Army). In sum, the survey results suggest a complicated and multi-dimensional negotiation of identity changes in the 1990s: although large numbers of Hong Kong people think that they are both Chinese and Hongkongers, there remains a very distinctive image distance between the two. There is also a sense of unease towards the new Chinese national identity. These public sentiments concur with the polysemic and contradictory textual discourse of GT and HKL.

Besides contradictory and polysemic identity categories, the textual analyses above have also shown that GT and HKL suppress politically incorrect contents and produce an excessively capitalistic discourse. The apolitical and capitalistic textual ideologies are congruent with Hong Kong's socio-political situation, in which Hong Kong has increasingly been under the influence of Chinese politics and served, in economic terms, as a gateway between China and the West. Re-sinicisation involves the inhibition of politically incorrect ideologies and the installation of nationalistic identity. HKL, and the recent upsurge of nostalgic material in Hong Kong media, serve as agents to re-historicise and re-sinicise Hongkongers into a continuous Chinese history. The text-context resonance suggests a process of over-determination of textual ideology through the articulation of commercial television.

Textual representations of HKL and GT are strongly interrelated with the social contexts, not in a simple and direct way, but are instead mediated through organisational processes that involve conscious and unconscious political and commercial calculations (see chapter 7). Editorial influence is achieved through political and commercial net-working within and beyond media corporations. As Hong Kong's first commercial terrestrial television station, TVB dominated a rapidly growing broadcasting and advertising market throughout the 1970s and

1980s. In the 1990s, increasing competition from other media producers and new technologies, along with a stagnant advertising market, caused TVB's profits to fall. Pressured to develop new sources of revenue, TVB executives began aggressively to pursue expansion into mainland and overseas Chinese markets. This corporate strategy requires TVB to maintain good relations with the Chinese government, thus articulating with relative ease the ideologies of socio-political powers into televisual discourse. However, commercial television has to win popularity among audiences, which means popular televisual texts have to incorporate widespread public sentiments. As a result, the texts of HKL and especially the esoteric texts of GT harbour contradictory and polysemic elements. Here, multiple contextual imperatives, including national positioning, local politics, commercial pressure, corporate strategy, the pursuit of regional markets, perceived political pressure, and popular demands, although somewhat unconnected, are nevertheless *articulated* in the political and economic powers in the production of textual ideology in polysemic and contradictory manner.

Discussion: A theory on articulation

In this final section, I want to relocate the case studies in this chapter into the theoretical debate of ideological articulation. As noted in the beginning of this chapter, the polysemy thesis appears to be a rebellion against the linear transportation model of the positivistic perspectives and especially, the rigid instrumentalism of the Marxist perspectives, which can be illustrated most succinctly by the dominant ideology thesis. This dominant ideology thesis sees the media as carrying and constructing a relatively coherent ideology which is effective in reproducing social relations of domination in modern capitalistic societies. The polysemy thesis poses a serious challenge to this brand of critical television studies. It renders textual analysis problematic, and production research trivial. If audiences are active and able to negotiate meanings beyond the limits of media texts, textual meanings cannot rest on the assumed structures uncovered by textual analysts. If texts are open to democratic readings, researchers need not be concerned with how meanings are processed selectively by the political and economic imperatives of media organisations. Polysemy thesis challenges the economism of political economy; it also challenges the culturalists' postulate of preferred reading and sees it as too restricted.

Because of these challenges, critical media theories have undergone substantive revisions. Within critical media studies, there is a fuzzy spectrum of theoretical positions on the consistency and effectiveness of dominant ideology, with some political economists and structuralists at the one end favouring a 'strong' version of ideological incorporation, and some culturalists at the other end favouring a 'weak' version of ideological articulation. In response to the challenges of the polysemy thesis, the strong versions of media ideological effects are very much suppressed. However, the weak versions still have a strong hold in recent academic writings. In this context, the more flexible culturalists' argument of ideological articulation (see Morley and Chen, 1996) has become the major theoretical development that revitalises critical media studies. The concepts of over-determination and contradiction in ideological articulation are much more flexible than the earlier forms of the dominant ideology thesis.

In this articulation theory, contextual definers and televisual ideologies are articulated together; but the linkages are only effective at specific conjunctures, and can be disarticulated and rearticulated in shifting power hierarchies. If there is no one-to-one correspondence between social forces and ideological themes, neither is there a completely arbitrary relationship between the two. Television texts are embedded in social and ideological contexts without a simple governing law that guarantees determinacy. Polysemic structures do not have genetic origins in class structure; nevertheless, the ideological field is overdetermined by multiple contextual forces. This involves the Gramscian concept of hegemony, which is sensitive to historic contingencies and pragmatic political strategies. Assimilating national-popular demands, the dominant ideological field is shifting along with complicated social alliances to achieve hegemonic leadership in specific historical circumstances. The media occupy a space that is constantly being contested by the economic, the cultural, and the political in specific historical contexts.

The dominant ideology thesis sees capitalism as the sole rigid historical determinant of the media. This is too mechanistic and fails to account for the powerful influences of specific historical milieux. The contingent nature of the influence of political economic definers is well illustrated in the historic analysis of the media. The influences of the media on prevalent social hierarchies have been shown, in various works of research, to vary enormously from one period to another within the same nation (Curran, 1986; Gallagher, 1982; Schudson, 1991).

The polysemy thesis is equally inadequate when it comes to socio-historical definers. Pluralists often describe television polysemies as ahistorical givens. Polysemy is taken for granted as the innate nature of the modern television medium. However, historical comparisons have shown that polysemy is a relatively recent development. Media analysts have shown that television has become increasingly polysemic as it has come of age (e.g. Taylor, 1989). The growth of television literacy can produce more sophisticated demands for textual complexity; the accumulation of television programmes can also produce more inter-textual meanings in television programmes (Bondebjerg, 1992). A thesis of polysemy will be far from complete if these socio-historic influences are ignored.

The articulations between the contextual definers and televisual discourse, as indicated in the analyses in this and the previous chapters, have been shown to vary from one period to another. Comparing GBU, GT, and HKL across time, the identity category of the main-lander, as inscribed in televisual texts and circulated in social discourse, was relatively more stable in the 1970s. In the late 1970s, when political and economic interventions from the Chinese and colonial government were weak, television producers, standing in the discursive positions of the established Hongkongers,[22] drew on the prevalent public sentiments of the time and constructed identity categories that worked in the interests of the established social powers. This symbolic order was structured, predominantly, by the hierarchy of society, in which the established group of Hongkongers exerted a greater social power over the outsiders. However, in the early 1990s, the dual political power centres of China and Britain became intrusive in media politics (Chan, J. M., 1992). The identity categories of mainlander and Hongkonger, as presented in Hong Kong television of the 1990s, have become unstable and polysemic. The polysemic configurations reflect the contradictions within and between the dual political powers and also the populist demands of the population. The deep-seated categorisation of main-landers and Hongkongers is strongly activated by social and political contestation, but out of the desire for reconciliation, commercial television is suppressing the derogatory membership categorisation of the mainlanders, resulting in the apolitical, esoteric, and polysemic configuration of the televisual discourse of GT. In the drama, the problematic identity of the villain, both as a Hongkonger and a main-lander, is a dramatic example of such conflicting articulation.

In the HKL case, the differentiation between mainlanders and Hongkongers is diluted and remapped by selective processes of remem-bering and forgetting. There are contradictory signals behind the apolitical textual surface and the suppressed political subtext. The discrepancy between the images of Maoist protesters and the apolitical narration is an obvious example. These polysemic patterns would make little sense outside the wider context of historical analyses. Ignoring contextual articulation, television polysemies might easily be taken as being random and idiosyncratic. Although semiotic excess of commercial television provides a space for multiple readings, socio-political contexts confine and limit the possibility that such readings will occur. Comparing the relatively stable GBU of the 1970s with the polysemic texts of HKL and GT of the 1990s, this chapter has shown that the re-imagining of the Hong Kong identity is deeply embedded in contextual powers mediated by television.

Chapter 6

Public voices/private anxieties

The GBU case discussed in chapter 4 demonstrates a cultural process in which a Hong Kong television serial, by constructing a stigmatised identity for the mainlanders, simultaneously confirmed the identity of the established Hongkongers. However, the stigmatised outsiders gradually began to gain political power in the 1990s. As the colony reverted to the rule of China in 1997, the social affiliation and estrangement captured in the once-dominant categorisation of Hongkongers and Ah Chians underwent another dramatic turn. The insider/outsider configuration has shifted its power-geometry (Massey, 1991), which is articulated in the television culture in a much more complicated way. The complexity of the articulation demands a more refined analysis of the discursive relations between the societal and the televisual.

Institutional dispersion of television ideologies

In the theoretical discussions and empirical analyses of the previous chapters, I spent some time exploring how television ideologies can be overdetermined, in multiple articulations, by 'contextual definers' on the wider social level. The general argument, simply put, is that television ideologies converge to a considerable extent with the dominant assumptions within society. Textual producers, regardless of the kind of television organisation to which they belong, pick up meanings from a world of widely circulated commonsense values embedded in the wider social, cultural, and political contexts. These 'pick-up meanings' are not in the text itself but are the active product of the text's social articulation, of the web of connotations and also cultural codes into which the text is inserted.[1] This text/context articulation can be illustrated by the relatively stable representations of Hongkonger and mainlander of the 1970s, which were resonant with the socio-cultural differentiation of the two groups in the larger social context of the time. Also, the unstable, polysemic, and sometimes contradictory identity categories of the 1990s are related to the cleavages of the dominant social discourses. The textual representations give symbolic form to pre-existing power relations.

However, contextual articulation, if standing alone, is inadequate to account for the discursive relationship between the media and society. Apart from the general level of signification, there is another level of institutionalised encoding practices of media organisations. At the institutional level of signification, dominant contextual discourse is differentially articulated and/or dispersed into different forms and patterns of televisual ideologies and polysemies. Though not always directly, the production side of television regulates, delimits, or dramatises the kind of discourses that can be produced. Neglecting this institutional level of signification would result in a misconception which sees the media as *always* overdetermined by dominant contextual discourse to yield a convergent output, irrespective of the possible divergence between different media.

In the Hong Kong case, the differentiation and dispersion effects of television organisations were less prominent in the 1970s because of specific circumstances: The 'minimally integrated media-political system' (Kuan and Lau, 1988) and the surplus television economy of the 1970s allowed a relatively autonomous organisational environment for media workers, who were by and large left to their own devices. They drew on the public sentiments of the time and constructed identity categories in the interests of the established social powers. An insider/outsider configuration was constructed symbolically and was then widely used in social practices to confirm the superiority of the established group and to discriminate against the newcomers. This symbolic order was structured, predominantly, by the hierarchies in society, in which the established group held greater social power, especially economic power, over the outsiders.[2] Thus the contextual definers played a dominant role in the signification processes. We see a strong contextual over-determination and a convergent media output. However, in the 1990s, the media institution comes into play in more influential ways. Television ideologies are increasingly articulated by the interplay between contextual and institutional influences.

In the 1990s, Hong Kong television has become a testing ground for dominant political and economic powers (see chapter 3). The dual political power centres of China and Britain intruded in media politics, resulting in intensive discursive struggles within the politicised television culture. Contrasting the surplus television economy of the 1970s, the television economy of the 1990s is more competitive and hostile. Creative autonomy has been greatly reduced. Since television production is more affected by political and commercial calculations, power relations are increasingly relayed on to television dramas through the interface of the television institutions. Institutional dispersions of media and social discourses were less important in the 1970s, but have become much more obvious in the 1990s. The discursive dispersions take two forms. First, there is an obvious ideological discrepancy between media discourse and social discourse. Since the final years of the 1980s, there has been a conspicuous fissure between everyday discourse and the discourse in the entertainment media of Hong Kong. In everyday interactions, the imagined boundary between the locals and the mainlanders is still visible, and for some, the forced Sino-Hong Kong integration heightens the antagonism against China. Some people of Hong Kong see the mainlanders as 'invaders' and 'intruders' of their community, but on commercial television, this Sino-Hong Kong antagonism is very much suppressed. The situation is very different from that of the 1970s, when public sentiments against the mainlanders were pouring into and then objectified by the televisual texts. Due to the fact that commercial television can be easily co-opted by political and economic powers, it has become more and more sensitive to anti-Chinese sentiments and tries not to provoke the Chinese government. The suppression of public antagonism against China, especially after the Tiananmen Square massacre, seems to bear witness to the intrusion of political power, expressed in the form of self-censorship in commercial television.

Discursive dispersions also take another form. There are obvious ideological discrepancies between the television outputs of public and commercial television organisations. Contextual influences of the political economy are differentially absorbed, dispersed, and translated through different television organisations, which are entangled with the cracks and cleavages within the socio-political contexts in different ways. Of course, different television organisations in the 1970s also produced different kinds of televisual discourses, but the recent discrepancies have become much more prominent. Because of the drastic socio-political changes in the 1990s, the quasi-public broadcaster RTHK[3] has produced dramas, particularly in the early 1990s, with political overtones far more controversial than any previous Hong Kong television dramas: this is in direct contrast to the mainstream commercial television, which deliberately avoids political controversy in its entertainment programming.

These institutional dispersions provide the ideological variances for studying the influences of organisational contexts on television ideologies. In this and the next chapter, I shall pay more attention to the relationship between texts and organisational contexts, exploiting the recent institutional dispersions of television ideologies. My strategy is to find two illustrative cases which can show how power relations are mapped out in different kinds of television dramas. Simply stated, the aim of these two chapters is to compare the ideological characters of commercial and pubic television dramas.

As discussed in the previous chapters, the ideological character of television has become increasingly problematic in television studies. More emphasis is placed on the polysemic nature of televisual discourses. Nevertheless, the polysemy thesis, which rose to popularity in the 1980s, has recently been contested for its neglect of the ideological influences of socio-political contexts (Budd *et al.*, 1990), of the limits imposed by syntagmatic and textual closure (Morley, 1993) and the discursive power of the dominant cultural pattern (Carragee, 1990; Condit, 1989). There is a rough consensus among critics that polysemies do have limits (e.g. Morley, 1993; Scannell *et al.*, 1992b), but little has been said about the nature and pattern of these limits. In chapter 5, I mapped the 'polysemic patterns' articulated by socio-historical forces. That chapter is more on the dialectic between the textual and the contexual. In this chapter I pay more attention to textual configurations.

Practically, texts are often situated in the intermediate positions that fall between tight ideological closure at one extreme, and unlimited polysemy at the other. The polysemy thesis is simply deficient, or even misleading, if it doesn't differentiate between these various intermediate 'polysemic configurations'. Meanings are not within free-floating polysemy but are subjected to the dominant power structure in the larger society (also see chapter 5). For instances, using Newcomb and Alley's (1983) concept of *lyric* and *choric* television, polysemy can be described as choric (which sings in resonance with mainstream heterogeneous ideologies) or as lyric (which stands out from, and negotiates with the mainstream in a personal voice). The textual analysis in this chapter will show how public television dramas are predisposed to the lyric mode, while those produced by the commercial television are predisposed to the choric mode. In the following analysis, I shall use different concepts to describe the polysemic patterns in my cases. Polysemy can be described as open (with rounded characters, rich metaphors, and twisted narratives), or as less open, or as relatively closed (with stereotypes, formulas and ideological slants and slides of the everyday). Polysemy can be *writerly* (which resembles written literature with its self-reflexivity and experimentation) or *readerly* (with an easily accessible narrative and seamless suture) (Fiske, 1987). In a social context of overt political repression, it is also helpful to differentiate some texts as *esoteric* polysemy, in which associative devices are used to mask subtle layers of controversial meanings. To complete the binary pairing, esoteric polysemy can be compared with *negotiatory* polysemy, which explicitly builds alternative and reactionary meanings to negotiate with the dominant power.

The socio-political context of Hong Kong in the early 1990s was characterised by violent discursive struggles between the British and the Chinese governments. As this chapter will show, the Hong Kong television dramas produced in the 1990s exhibit divergent polysemic forms; some dramas have esoteric meanings, others are negotiatory in their discursive position. Hence, lumping together all types of 'polysemies' into one category of producerly text is confusing and of limited analytical value. It is not at all difficult to find examples of television programmes that fit into the categories just described. A cultural programme produced by public television is often more *writerly* than a commercial television programme; independent productions usually have greater chance to be in the *lyric* mode than network prime-time dramas. Seen in the light of these categories, the polysemy thesis is more of a positive challenge than a threat to textual analysts – polysemy does not render traditional textual analysis futile, rather, it calls for a more rigorous analysis of the polysemic patterns and their relation with different socio-political and organisational contexts. These two chapters seek to examine the predispositions of different types of television organisational contexts[4] in producing different ideological patterns, thus introducing a much neglected organisational aspect to the polysemy thesis.

Comparing public and commercial television

Besides theoretical significance, this case comparison also has policy implication concerning the public vs. commercial television debate. Right now these two television models are in a state of flux on a global level. In Europe, the public television system had dominated the broadcasting scene for decades. But in the 1990s, commercial television began to mushroom all over Europe. European public broadcasters are in deep crisis (Blumber, 1992) and their cultural strengths and weaknesses are under critical examination. In America, public television is under constant commercial pressure and financial difficulties (Hoynes, 1994). In this transitory period, there are prolonged debates between advocates of the respective models, but comparative analyses have been normative and impressionistic. This and the next chapter will present case studies to illustrate the differences between the two models.

Media pluralism is an often stated goal of media policy. Some believe that it can be achieved by technological change that allows the proliferation of television channels. Others believe that media pluralism can be achieved by opening up the television market to more commercial players. Market choice, commercial competition, and consumer sovereignty go together in an open market of television products. However, critics think that instead of enhancing diversity, more channels may only provide more of the same type of programmes. The present case study will show that public and commercial television have a tendency to produce dramas with different ideological contents. If media pluralism is a stated policy objective, public broadcasting is still an important organisational form which contributes to ideological diversity in the commercialised television economy of the 1990s.

In the following analysis, I shall attempt to identify and explain the ideological diversity of prime-time television dramas by asking two sets of questions: First, are there ideological differences between the dramas produced by public and commercial television? Do the television dramas produced in these organisational contexts in Hong Kong exhibit different ideological tendencies? How differently are the socio-political powers mapped on to different television dramas? Do television polysemies and ideologies take different forms and patterns? Second, if there are ideological differences in these two types of television drama, are the differences arbitrary? Or are they systematically shaped by the organisational contexts? Can we relate organisational influences to textual polysemies and ideological diversity? What are the dynamics between contextual overdetermination and organisational dispersion?

The question of the forms of polysemies and ideologies involves textual analysis of television dramas (this chapter), while an explanation of the differences calls for an organisational analysis of the production contexts (next chapter). I shall contrast GT, the commercial drama discussed in the previous chapter, and *Below the Lion Rock* (henceforth abbreviated as BLR) produced by the public broadcaster RTHK.[5] The comparison is based on textual analysis of the programmes and taped interviews with the production staff.

A word of caution is needed at this point: RTHK was structurally a government broadcaster with the character of a public broadcaster at the time when the drama under discussion was produced. The dualistic structure of Sino-British polity before the sovereignty change created for RTHK a political vacuum whereby producers were working in an autonomous context similar to that of a public broadcaster. Up to the present time, one year after the handover, RTHK is still enjoying a high degree of autonomy.

BLR and GT, the two selected cases, are comparable since both are politically significant. My interview with the executive producer of GT indicated that the initial draft of the serial did have explicit political overtones, but these were finally suppressed in order to avoid offending China. On the other hand, what is of interest in BLR is that the series is explicit in its criticisms of China. It attracted fierce political controversy which had rarely happened to any previous television drama. Besides, both BLR and GT were conceptualised and produced within the same period,[6] both with the intention of reflecting the changes taking place in Hong Kong. GT and BLR are fictional representations of Hong Kong society; they provide a chance for a comparative investigation of the media representations of Hong Kong. Moreover, the two selected dramas are significant productions of their respective television organisations. Both GT and BLR were designated by the executives of the respective television stations to be the most important productions of 1992. All TVB production staff interviewed said that GT was a prestigious assignment, while BLR was considered by the RTHK staff as one of the most ambitious productions of RTHK's drama unit in recent years. The production teams of GT and BLR represent the collaboration of the best staff of TVB and RTHK respectively. Out of the 20 RTHK and TVB staff interviewed, all except three had worked in their respective television stations for more than 10 years, and five of them for more than 20 years. Thus, both programmes can be regarded as exemplary productions of the respective television systems. In this chapter, I shall delineate the different forms of televisual polysemies and ideologies represented in the two selected dramas. The question of organisational differences will be discussed in the next chapter.

The opening sequences

Raymond Williams argues that television is a ceaseless flow of contents which differs from the discrete closure of film or novel (Williams, 1990). In the flow of television contents, the title and the opening sequence of a series or serial, shown repeatedly in every episode, are important devices to mark off the programmes and provide an interpretative context of the televisual discourses. How do the opening sequences of GT and BLR stage their televisual discourses? The Chinese title of GT is *Dashidai*, which means 'Great Times' or 'Great Era'. Despite minor variations, the opening sequence usually begins with this Chinese title, in bold strokes, and with a rippling special effect of the nightline of Hong Kong's Victoria Harbour, suggesting that the drama is about significant events set during a significant period in Hong Kong's history. On the other hand, *Below the Lion Rock* is the title of a long-running and much welcomed RTHK series.[7] The series appeared intermittently in the 1980s. These previous runs of BLR earned the reputation of being authentic reflections of the everyday life of ordinary Hongkongers. The public image cues the audiences to look for similar stories in this new series of BLR. This time the series reappears with a new opening sequence: it shows the image of the Lion Rock Mountain, a landmark of Hong Kong, against the background of some fast-moving clouds. It is filmed in time-lapse effect to highlight the turbulent movement of clouds heralding an imminent rainstorm. These expressive images carry rich and loaded meanings of a city experiencing great and turbulent changes.

Both the openings of BLR and GT act as discursive markers which position the drama against the background of a changing Hong Kong. They are fictional constructions of Hong Kong in the 1990s. In reality, Hong Kong in the 1990s faces drastic political, economic, and cultural changes. Within this similar discursive context, how do GT and BLR construct the discourses on the cultural identity, economics, and politics of Hong Kong? Are the two constructed versions of Hong Kong similar or drastically different? The following textual analyses of GT and BLR seek to locate and delineate the discursive differences between the two dramas. Since I have already discussed GT in chapter 7, here I shall focus on the text of BLR.

Capitalistic economy

As indicated in the previous chapter, in *Great Times* rich entrepreneurs are celebrated as Hong Kong Men at their best and are mythologised as having the power to bring luck and success. The dominant discursive construction of GT firmly endorses the supreme goal of moneymaking by opportunism. It legitimises the unique brand of capitalism which Hong Kong reveals as the most important asset of the people in the unstable social environment of the 1990s. However, this capitalist ideology is highly contested in *Below the Lion Rock*. BLR is a single-play series[8] consisting of eight episodes with the same theme – Hong Kong

Table 6.1 The value structure of characters in Masks

	Chung	Chung's father
Characterisation	Negative	Positive
Personal Style		
Dress	Business suit	Artistic, casual
Impression	Rigid	Warm
Emotion	Unhappy, tired	Happy, energetic
Interpersonal	Manipulative	Caring
Profession		
Type of Job	Entrepreneur	Artist (painter)
Motivation	Ambition	Satisfaction
Reward	Fame, profit	Satisfaction
Environment	Business	Grassroots

in the 1990s. The series generally depicts the exploitative nature of the capitalistic system of Hong Kong. This stands in sharp contrast to the popular myth which celebrates Hong Kong as a land of opportunities. The second episode, entitled *Masks*, is a story of a successful entrepreneur Chung, who participates in the 1991 Legislative Council election. Behind Chung's good public image is a man whose real motive in running for election is commercial profit and political convenience. He employs illegal mainland immigrants for their cheap labour. When one of his illegal labourers is injured on duty, he stops the worker from seeing a doctor and sends him back to China. The worker is crippled as a result of the delay in treatment. This narrative arrangement condemns Chung the entrepreneur for his exploitation of mainlanders. Similar discourse is also embedded in the binary opposing character construction of Chung and his father, as shown in table 6.1.

In table 6.1, Chung the entrepreneur-turned-politician is not depicted as an exemplary Hong Kong Man at all. In stark contrast to the manipulative and exploitative behaviour of Chung, his father is happy, content, and helpful to a group of young dramatists. The positive and negative characterisations heighten the oppositional discourse against the exploitative behaviour of Chung.

Another episode, entitled *The Heritage*, presents a more complicated discourse on the destructive but irresistible influence of capitalistic development. It is a story about an old villager, uncle Tim, who wants to preserve his home against the property developer's plan to convert it into a country motel. His grand-daughter comes back from England to help settle the dispute, only to find out that her brother, Tim's grandson, has already received a deposit from the land developer without Tim's consent. Other villagers, who openly resist the development, are vociferously protesting against the project, claiming that it would damage the traditional spirit of the village. But as the events unfold, it transpires that these protests are only tricks designed to acquire more financial compensation. This story should be seen in the light of the troublesome nature of land ownership and development in Hong Kong. After the mid-1980s, real estate prices inflated at an alarming rate of a tenfold increase, which made some people rich overnight but home ownership impossible for many others. It was not until the Asian financial crises of 1997 and 1998 that prices came down. Real estate development and speculation play a significant role in the politics, economics, and culture of Hong Kong. It is in this context that the story makes its point. The negotiatory stand of the story on unrestrained capitalistic development is made explicit in the following discursive scenes:

Land developer: Why do you object? The motel can make the village prosperous. It can also bring your grandfather a large sum of money.

Grand-daughter: My grandfather is very attached to the house.

Land developer: I just don't understand, what advantage can you get from this?

Grand-daughter: People don't just do things for an advantage!

In another confrontational scene:

Grand-daughter: You make them willing to sacrifice anything for money.

Land developer: Do you really believe that without this project, people will stop chasing after money?

These dialogues are accompanied by visual commentary of the destruction by unplanned land development: country fields are turned into junkyards, polluted rivers, and deserted ruins. Finally, the old man sets fire to the house in order to quell the dispute. Here, the profit motive is seen as an irresistible but damaging force which perverts human nature. It contests the popular myth of Hong Kong's economic success through the eyes of an old villager, who is often marginalised in the discourse of the membership category of Hongkongers. In sharp contrast, GT depicts Hong Kong's capitalistic system as a God-given opportunity for personal gain of fame and fortune.

Sino-Hong Kong antagonism

GT is extremely restrained in its political discourse, there is no hint in any of the 40 episodes that Hong Kong has any problem related to politics. Hong Kong, as constructed in GT, has remained an apolitical society all through the 1970s, the 1980s, and the 1990s. The political discourse of Sino-Hong Kong antagonism in the 1990s is strongly suppressed and hidden. In contrast to GT, the Sino-Hong Kong antagonism in BLR is much more explicit. For instance, the episode entitled *Stormy Weather*, which received the highest rating of all the eight episodes of BLR,[9] is a fable about the relationship between a country named Red Circle and a small city called Fragrant Harbour, simulating the relation between China and Hong Kong. The identity of the city is explicit since Fragrant Harbour is a widely used name for Hong Kong. The story opens with a crackdown on democracy in Red Circle and then focuses on the dilemma of a television station editor over how to handle an interview with Red Circle's senior leader. The crackdown features groups of soldiers (dressed in the uniform of the People's Liberation Army of China) firing on protesting students. Though a fable, the inference to the June Fourth incident is unmistakable. As a professional journalist, the editor (a Hongkonger) has to be critical and ask for factual details of the crackdown in the interview. However, he is constrained by his boss who insists that a critical interview will harm the station's commercial interests. After painstaking negotiation and compromise, the editor fails to put even a mildly critical version of the interview on air. The interview that is finally released is an edited version, no different from an official press release from the Red Circle government. Refusing to be a tool of political propaganda, the editor resigns at the moment when the edited version is put on air.

Table 6.2 The value structure of officials in China and journalists in Hong Kong in *Stormy Weather*

Officials / Red Circle (China)	Journalists / Fragrant Harbour (Hong Kong)
Negative	Positive
Suppressive	Autonomous
Violent	Civilised
Hypocritical	Honest
Them	Us
Control Media	Honour Free Media
Totalitarian	Democratic

The dilemma built around the character sets forth a strong discursive statement against totalitarianism. In direct contrast, the team of journalists of the 'Red Circle' is submissive to authority and manipulative in dealing with the interview. The extensive encounters of the two teams of television people and officials render the identity boundaries between them highly visible. The Hongkongers are contrasted with the outsiders of the North. As shown in table 6.2, the binary opposition constructed within the narrative conveys an explicit criticism of the political system of China.

Another episode entitled *Home from Home* is a docu-drama of singer Hou Dejian, who was deeply involved with the student protest in the June Fourth incident. Against popular belief, in part one of the story, Hou says he didn't see any students being killed in Tiananmen Square on 4 June 1989. In Part II, Hou wants to hold a press conference on some sensitive political issues, but is retained and interrogated by Chinese officials immediately before the conference. A contrast between Hou and the mainlanders is shown in table 6.3.

However, the political discourse takes a subtle twist in the second half of the story; the negative characteristics of the interrogators are later depicted in a much more positive manner: they are ruthless on duty but are as friendly as ordinary people when they are off-duty. They chat with Hou, invite him to dinner, and give him friendly advice. On the surface, opposition exists between democratic and totalitarian politics; the men behind the system, on the other hand, are all ordinary Chinese sharing the same history and culture. The political discourse is critical yet sympathetic to the communist system, which is quite different from the anti-communist discourse commonly found among the people of Hong Kong. The popular membership categorisation of Hongkongers vs. Ah Chian no longer applies in the new political situation of the 1990s.

Table 6.3 The value structure of Hou and his interrogators in *Home from Home*

Hou	Interrogators
Positive	Negative
Victim	Prosecutors
Advocate free speech	Repress free speech
Authentic	Duplicitous
Democratic	Totalitarian

Shifting identities

In GT, the suppression of the political aspect eschews the Hong Kong identity in favour of the economic aspect. GT retells the history of post-war Hong Kong and characterises the emergence of the Hong Kong Man in a strictly economic sense. A few very restricted attributes are selected from a variety of ways of life to paint the public face of the Hong Kong Man. Comparatively speaking, the stories in BLR are more explicit in dealing with the sensitive issues of mainlander identity. GT has no mainlander, but there are more mainlanders in BLR than in most previous Hong Kong television dramas. There are soldiers from the People's Liberation Army, mainland policemen, students, teachers, communists, artists, and pianists – even a political leader who is characterised after China's Premier Li Peng. The popular categories of Hongkonger and Ah Chian are no longer applicable; the diversity of mainlanders makes it difficult for them to be classified into a single category of Ah Chian or mainlander. Although in BLR there is still a visible identity boundary between Hongkongers and mainlanders, the series consciously contests the two-set division. In *Masks*, the producer condemns the exploitation of mainland workers by local employers; in *Home from Home*, the producer consciously twists the negative stereotype of a communist official and playfully turns the mainlander into a friendly character at the end of the story.

In comparison, GT is fixating on the membership categorisation of Hongkonger and Ah Chian the mainlander (HA). The serial subscribes to the dominant categorisations that have persisted in the social discourse of Hong Kong for two decades. Despite the changing identity boundaries between Hongkongers and mainlanders, they are still classified in a positive/negative opposition. However, GT dares not offend the politically powerful mainlanders by openly asserting this dominant categorisation. It has a villain with the characteristics of a stereotypical mainlander who is wearing the hat of Hongkonger in the story. On the other hand, BLR is questioning the appropriateness of the categorisation of HA, and is more assertive in exposing the conflicts between the two identity groups.

Despite these differences between GT and BLR in representing identities, there is a peculiar similarity. The mainlander, once in a sub-ordinate position of the categorisation of HA, is now seen in a dominant position in both dramas. The mainlander may be hiding back-stage, as in GT, or appear front of stage, as in BLR, but he is always in a position of command. In GT, Ting is a negative character. In BLR, there are both good and bad mainlanders, but no matter whether they are good or bad, they are all strong characters who are in control of things; they are neither fools nor victims and could no longer be named Ah Chian.

Summary: choric and lyric drama

Much has been said about the polysemic nature of televisual texts and the heterogeneity of television ideologies, but little has been said about these textual forms and ideological patterns. As those who propose the polysemy thesis have repeatedly emphasised, the polysemic nature of television is a result of the semiotic excess of the medium. However, polysemies and ideological diversities are not limitless; they have shapes and forms with different degrees of closure. This textual comparison is an attempt to trace those often neglected textual forms and patterns. The comparison, as shown in table 6.4, indicates that the differences between BLR and GT are paradigmatic.

Table 6.4 Textual comparison of televisual discourses: GT and BLR

	Great Times (GT)	Below the Lion Rock (BLR)
Economics	Endorsing HK's capitalistic economy	Negotiating with HK's capitalistic economy
Politics	Suppressed Critical towards take-over by China, expressed in esoteric terms	Explicit Diversified Critical yet negotiatory
Identities of Hongkongers/ mainlanders	Suppressed Antagonistic Still subscribing to the bipolar categorisation of Hongkonger/mainlander; Mainlander more powerful	Explicit Diversified Questions the usefulness of the categorisation of Hongkonger/ mainlander; Mainlander more powerful
Television ideologies	Monolithic Mainstream Pro-establishment	Diversified Alternative Negotiatory
Polysemic structures	Readerly polysemy	Writerly polysemy
Paradigms	**Choric drama**	**Lyric drama**

The differences between BLR and GT can be discussed on three different planes of reference:

- their ideological patterns,
- their polysemic structures, and
- their textual paradigms.

Ideological patterns

With regard to the television ideologies of these two dramas, the non-commercial drama BLR exhibits an ideological pattern that is diversified and negotiatory in nature. It expresses its negotiatory stand towards the capitalistic economy of Hong Kong and the totalitarianism of communist China. BLR is more explicit in dealing with political materials, constructing Hong Kong as a society caught in political controversies. It contests the myth of Hong Kong's economic success, exposes political and social conflicts, and rethinks long-cherished cultural categories. Concerning the issue of cultural identity, there are diversified ways of treatment which indicate a greater sensitivity to the political and cultural changes of the 1990s. BLR is quick to raise questions about the rigid two-set membership category collection of Hongkonger and mainlander. There is a wide variety of mainlanders in the stories: some are hostile, some may be friendly, but all are in a position of command. The identities of Hongkongers and mainlanders, as described in BLR, can no longer be fixed into the insider/outsider categorisation of the 1970s.

On the other hand, GT constructs Hong Kong as a capitalistic and apolitical society. Hong Kong's capitalistic system is represented affirmatively as the greatest asset of the territory. Political discourse is suppressed, but the narrative esoterically presents a widely shared political ideology, which sees China as a corrupt invading force that threatens the well-being of Hong Kong. The categorisation of Hongkonger/mainlander is hiding back stage. It only comes out via category-bound inferences which define mainlanders as hostile outsiders and Hongkongers as victims. The Hongkongers can only fight back by their God-given economic vitality. These discourses echo popular myth and mainstream ideologies, which stress Hong Kong's economic success, and see it as an apolitical city. In social discourse, this ideology of *laissez-faire* was enthusiastically propagated by the colonial government and the business sector, and has recently been endorsed by the Chinese government as an example for other mainland cities. The emphasis on the economic myth and the avoidance of political discourse are articulated into the television ideologies of GT in complex and polysemic ways.

Polysemic structures

With regard to the polysemic structures of the two dramas, GT is more polysemic than BLR. This pattern is quite extraordinary and worthy of some elaboration. Despite the fact that the commercial television drama GT exhibits less diversified television ideologies, it is more polysemic in the sense that layers of meanings are arranged on different levels of explicitness, with the more controversial meaning sinking deeper into the connotative level. The identity of the mainlanders is inscribed in a textual polysemy which 'prefers' several ways of mapping the cultural identity of the characters. Fiske (1987) is right in his contention that commercial dramas may be more predisposed to a polysemic textual arrangement. Because of the multiple imperatives of commercial television, commercial drama serials have to please a large heterogeneous audience, to avoid offending established powers, to mainstream their ideologies, and to cling on to widely shared cultural categories. These commercial imperatives shape the televisual text in contradictory ways; it moulds textual meaning of GT away from Sino-Hongkong conflicts, but it also draws on mainstream sentiments against the 'invading' mainlanders. As a result, GT shows a polysemic configuration: beneath the apolitical textual surface, there are deep-seated antagonisms which are grounded in the rigid categorisation of Hongkonger and outsider. This kind of polysemic structure may be found in other situations where political powers are intrusive and popular resistance is strong.

Despite the fact that BLR exhibits more diversified ideologies, it is less polysemic when compared with GT. BLR has negotiatory ideologies: the producers are often found questioning the mainstream. Each producer might put forward a different ideological stance, therefore BLR is ideologically diversified when *seen as a whole*. However each individual story has a clear and distinct voice. BLR is polysemic, but takes a different form of polysemy. The producers of BLR are more self-conscious and reflexive. In Barthes's term, their treatment is more 'writerly', with multiple codes that refuse closure (1975). This writerly polysemy is to be differentiated from the polysemy of commercial television. The latter masks diversity by a harmonious ideological surface, but embodies competing meaning structures within the excessive semiotics of the televisual texts. The writerly polysemy of public television is relatively more consciously crafted. It plays on stereotypes, alters cultural patterns, and creates new imagery. The polysemic subtleties are more literary and elitist. Writerly polysemy is comparable with what Feuer (1987) called the MTM style, which refers to the authorial style of the works from a US production house MTM. These productions stress self-reflexivity in form, and liberal humanism in content.

Textual paradigms

These paradigmatic differences in television ideologies and polysemies can be classified under the concepts of 'choric' and 'lyric' drama. The two concepts originated from Newcomb and Alley's book *The Producer's Medium* (1983). The term choric is taken from Greek drama: 'The chorus expresses the ideas and emotions of the group, as opposed to the individuals. Its focus is on the widely shared, the remembered, the conventional responses' (Newcomb and Alley, 1983:31). When an individual's voice becomes distinct, it stands out from the chorus as lyric. In Newcomb and Alley's words: 'The lyric is rooted in . . . the acute perceptions of the sensitive individual' (ibid.:41).

GT can be classified as a 'choric drama' which 'sings' in resonance with the mainstream capitalistic ideology, while the RTHK drama BLR can be called 'lyric drama' which stands out from, and negotiates with, the ideology of the establishment in a personal voice. There are lyric elements in GT and choric elements in BLR, but the dominant discursive thrust of GT is choric while BLR is lyric.[10] Lyric drama has negotiatory ideologies. It goes for the alternatives. In lyric drama, we hear a distinct voice with less polysemic arrangements. Yet lyric drama is the craft of sensitive dramatists; its polysemy is writerly and demands more active participation and appreciation from its audiences. On the other hand, choric drama has monolithic ideologies; it has limited ideological diversity and is pro-establishment in nature; it wants to please as many audiences as possible and does not want to offend dominant powers. However, under the harmonious resonance, there are multiple layers of polysemic voices since the chorus involves the compromise and adjustment of a variety of interests.

Against the claims of limitless and random polysemic meaning, the above case comparison indicates that we can locate and classify forms of textual polysemies and ideologies. And, against the claims of media convergence within the general ideological context, the comparative study has shown a divergence of forms of polysemies and ideologies between television dramas produced by different organisations.[11] In the next chapter, I shall go on to explore the sources of these forms and patterns and see how these patterns can be related to the production contexts of the two respective television systems.

Chapter 7

The production of television culture

The textual comparison in the last chapter has shown that the TVB drama GT and the RTHK drama BLR have paradigmatic, ideological, and textual differences. GT can be classified as a choric drama which has esoteric polysemy and mainstream ideologies. BLR can be classified as a lyric drama which has writerly polysemies and negotiatory ideologies. The chapter will examine whether these patterns are arbitrary or systematically shaped by their respective organisational contexts.

Most studies of television polysemies and ideologies ignore the influences of the production contexts on televisual texts. There are only a handful of production studies in the field. This is especially the case in the area of drama programmes, despite the fact that television serials are said to be 'one of the most popular and resilient forms of storytelling ever devised' (Allen, 1995:1). In comparison, research is skewed towards various forms of reception studies and textual analysis. Reception studies often concentrate on the polysemic readings of televisual texts, while textual studies are usually limited to the analysis of the formal properties of one or several television programmes. Besides textual and audience studies, there is also a wide variety of studies on media ideologies, and, in particular, television ideologies, which, in different ways, presume the underlining argument of the dominant ideology thesis. These studies explicitly take into account contextual definers (economical, political, cultural) in the articulation of television ideologies, and see the media as the reinforcer of the socio-political system of the larger society, and the attendant systems of domination and subordination between social classes, races, and genders. This book shares with these studies the emphasis that television ideologies are overdetermined, in multiple articulations, by 'contextual definers' of the wider society. However, the danger in looking from societal definers alone is that the workings of the production process may be seen to follow automatically from society-level constraints (Peterson, 1994); this emphasis on *contextual overdetermination* may easily result in what I have pointed out earlier, a kind of unconditional 'convergence hypothesis' (Curran, 1990a), which sees the media as *always* having a convergent output, regardless of the possible divergence between different media. Hence, besides textual description, audience reception, and contextual overdeterminations, we should take into account the *institutional dispersion* of television ideologies and poly-semies. Divergent ideological patterns of televisual texts can be better studied by analysing the interplay of contextual and organisational definers. The relative influences of the internal organisational and external contextual forces are exercised in dynamic negotiations; these negotiations are contingent, but not without pattern and tendencies.

Comparing public and commercial television

In the previous chapter I identified the ideological and textual divergence in the commercial drama GT and public drama BLR. Both dramas were produced within the same timeframe and under the same socio-political context, and both are fictional representations of Hong Kong in the 1990s. Apparently, stressing contextual overdetermination is inadequate to explain the divergence of the two dramas. Here institutional dispersion comes into play. The divergence may possibly imply that the contextual definers of the societal level have been differentially absorbed and/or dispersed by the respective organisational processes.

As I have argued in the previous chapter, the *institutional dispersion* discussed in this comparative case study also has policy implications, espe-cially at a time when public television is in a state of flux on a global level. The strong current of media commercialisation in America (Hoynes, 1994; McAllister, 1996), Europe (Blumber, 1992), and Asia (Chan and Ma, 1996) has put public broadcasting in different parts of the world under tremendous pressure. This chapter will show that public and commercial television tend to produce dramas with different ideological contents. As Hoynes (1994) argues, public television is still an important institutional form which contributes to ideological diversity in the com-mercialised television economy of the 1990s. It can play a positive role in the construction and maintenance of a democratic society. With grounded analyses of organisational processes, Hoynes advocates the setting up of mechanisms that can defuse the influences from the state and the market. Like Hoynes, I shall locate the organisational sources of ideological diversity mapped out in the previous chapter. Thus this chapter deals with the organisational mechanisms of content processing in the specific television broadcasters of TVB and RTHK. However, these specificities are not unique to Hong Kong but are relevant to the production of television culture in other countries.

The following organisational analysis is an attempt to trace the possible sources of the textual variances in the textual production of the two dramas. The analysis is based on 32 hours of taped interviews with the production and creative staff of the two dramas (see appendix 1 for a list of guiding questions for the interviews). The 21 interviewees comprised key creative and managerial staff directly related to the production of BLR and GT (see appendix 2 for a distribution list of interviewees). Two executive producers outside the GT and BLR team were also interviewed as case controls. The focus of the analysis was on the sources of content variance of the two dramas, and specific attention was paid to broad similarities and differences. Statements used repetitively by the interviewees were singled out, and concepts so identified were categorised. From these categories, possible factors that influence the selection of drama content were then formulated. In order to check the heuristic value of these factors, they were used to analyse boundary cases as reported by the interviewees.[1]

The interview data show that the creative and production staff of GT and BLR had relative autonomy in their selection and creation of content. They experienced minimal interference from management, and their proposals were approved the first time they were handed in. Most of them worked harmoniously with the management and disciplinary action was rare. Evaluation systems were ambiguous. The theory that media organisation is seriously constraining the individuals (Ettema and Whitney, 1982) seems to be unfounded here. Nevertheless, both commercial broadcaster TVB and public broadcaster RTHK are getting what they want: GT is a commercial choric drama catering for the tastes of the mass audience, while BLR is a lyric drama with a social mandate. Obviously, creative staff members were not producing these dramas by taking direct and specific orders. Creative control was unobtrusive.

Organisational schemata

Overviewing the data, there are two repetitive organisational schemata[2] permeating the two sets of interviews. For all TVB interviewees, *commercialism* is the cognitive schema which unobtrusively underlies key creative decisions. While in all RTHK interviews, *public interest* is the repetitive schema that permeates the reasoning and creative process. These organisational schemata mark off 'undesirable' creative options and act as unquestioned cognitive scripts in the decision processes within the organisation.

'Since TVB is a commercial broadcaster, inevitably, its dramas have to be popular, commercial, tamed, and safe entertainment.' This line of reasoning infiltrates the perception of TVB's organisational orientation, the evaluative criteria, and the aesthetic norms of television dramas. Most noteworthy is that whenever the interviewees complained about the lack of creativity scope in TVB, the complaints were usually followed by this schema as an excuse for the organisation: 'They [TVB management] should not be blamed, they have commercial considerations that we don't quite understand.' Both the executive producer and the head writer (the most important creators of GT), said that they had developed the programme idea by 'intuition' and 'feeling'. Behind this autonomy, however, the commercial schema acts powerfully and unobtrusively in the idea development stage. There were a few idea options at the initial stage:

- *Option 1*: An Alvin Toffler type of futuristic prediction to depict what Hong Kong would be like beyond 1997.
- *Option 2*: Centred around a big collapse of the stock market just before the takeover of Hong Kong by China in the summer of 1997.
- *Option 3*: Centred around an accident at Daya Bay Nuclear Plant[3] before or after 1997.
- *Option 4*: The drama begins and ends with a miracle day in 1994 in which the Hang Seng Index rises 4,000 points in just one day.

Option 1 is social, 'serious', and analytical; options 2 and 3 are controversial and politically sensitive; option 4 is safe, optimistic, and pleasing. Option 4 was adopted. The executive producer and the head writer gave two sets of rationale for the choice. The executive producer said that the reason for turning down the other options was that they involved too many variables and were beyond his ability and the production capacity of TVB. The head writer gave a quite different explanation:

> If we talk about what Hong Kong would be like in 1997 or beyond, we are afraid that some people might be very unhappy. The audience might find the negative descriptions disturbing too. Besides, if it is concrete (realistic), people think it is too heavy. If it is vague (imaginative), it lacks the appeal.

The decision was reached by personal choice; it was not made under any *direct* influence from the management. According to the head writer, all initial proposals of TVB drama were passed to the management meeting[4] for approval. Before the meeting, the proposal would be tailored according to the perceived criteria of the management. No one wanted a veto, because a veto meant that two months of preparatory work would be wasted, and besides, it was harmful to the creator's personal prestige. So undesirable options were screened off, and favourable options were incorporated. All TVB interviewees held similarly views on the perceived criteria of desirability: 'attractive', 'commercial', 'rating is most important', 'look good', 'intensive conflicts', 'have strong emotions', 'a proposal with a decent family fighting against a disgusting family is highly saleable [referring to GT]'. When talking about the 'selling' of proposals, at one point the head writer said, 'No pressure at all, GT has many selling points, we were very confident that they [the management] would like it.' At another point he said: 'Of course there is pressure, if they say no, it is a no, there can be no explanation at all. I think their most important consideration is whether there are enough commercial elements. The key question is, does it [the proposal] look good?'

It is quite obvious that content options are controlled in a highly unobtrusive way through cognitive barriers which are understood and accepted by the management and the creative staff. First, sophisticated and subtle treatments of social and political themes are less likely to enter the commercial schema; commercial television producers prefer dramatic, familiar, and stereotyped materials. Second, controversial materials are schematically non-compatible. According to the production manager of TVB drama section, TVB tries its best to stay away from controversial subjects, because no matter which side TVB programmes align with, parties with conflicting interests would complain. Although controversial matters may generate attention, they scare off advertisers. As the most penetrative mass medium, commercial terrestrial television needs support from the widest possible social sectors; hostile criticism drains PR resources and damages commercial interests. This is especially true in the 1990s, when Sino-Hong Kong business enterprises are one of the major sources of advertisement revenue for the local television. Another organisational factor is that TVB's producers have the export market in minds. Thus the TVB drama GT tends towards abstraction and eschews a political discourse that might be too local.

The organisational schema of commercialism found in TVB demonstrates surprising similarities with what Espinosa (1982, in Gripsrud,

1995) has identified. Through participant observation of story conferences in commercial television, he argues that there are four major rules of building televisual texts:

1   Engage the audience (i.e. create entertainment);
2   Consider the audience's knowledge about the world (i.e. don't be too sophisticated);
3   Meet the audience's expectations (an extension of the second);
4   Don't divide the audience (i.e. avoid the controversial).

The development of GT exhibits a similar organisational schema as set out by Espinosa.

RTHK has a different kind of organisational ethos. All the RTHK staff argued along different lines of reasoning: RTHK should provide a non-commercial, alternative, and diversified programming that commercial television would not provide. They all thought that RTHK was using public resources, so its programmes should have a social dimension: the content should serve the interests of the public. The majority of them wanted their programmes to address significant social issues of the day. When they were asked about what they should do as a television producer, they gave answers like: 'RTHK producers should have some kind of social mission', 'I want to give my audience an alternative perspective of looking at things', 'All my works have the message of love and care'. The making of BLR came about from their collective sense of responsibility as a public television dramatist to react to social issues at this critical point of time in Hong Kong's history. The non-commercial schema emphasises the local public interest and cultural desirability. As seen in the Hong Kong specific contents of BLR, the explicit public services mission of RTHK is to address the local concerns of Hongkongers. These premises permeate creative choices and evaluative norms; they become the rationale for producing expensive television dramas by public funding and consolidate into a strong reference frame within and outside the organisation.

The two schemata of the respective stations TVB and RTHK oppose each other. The TVB interviewees positioned the social value of their programme as peripheral. TVB's creative director noted:

> The most important thing is commercial success. Social values can only come as a bonus; never should a programme be produced for a social or educational reason.

GT's executive producer also voiced a similar viewpoint:

> With television dramas, you shouldn't be too selfish, they are different from novels; they cost a lot of money to produce. It makes no sense to mention some personal things over the public air-waves. Television should cater for the mass audience.

In direct contrast, one RTHK producer remarked:

> I think my ideas are quite different from the majority, that's why some people find my programmes difficult to understand. I hope my programmes can give an alternative point of view. If they look from my perspective, they can perhaps see something new. I would not be able to do this in TVB.

It should be noted again that RTHK is officially a government department. However, in the early 1990s, the political mandate of promoting and explaining government policies was not noticeable in the organisational schema. RTHK had the editorial independence enjoyed by most public broadcasters in other open societies. Editorial interferences from the government were rare. The informal link between RTHK and the public broadcaster BBC, the political vacuum created by the decolonisation process, the non-interventionist policy of the Hong Kong government, and the aborted plan to corporatise RTHK (Lee, P. S. N., 1992), all contributed to RTHK's dual role as both government and public broadcaster. In the 1980s and the early 1990s, it was not unusual at all to find RTHK programmes that were severely critical of the Hong Kong colonial government as well as the communist government in mainland China. BLR was one illustrative case among many others. Up to the moment of writing, the organisational schema of RTHK is still inclined towards the non-commercialism of public broadcasting and appears less as an instrumental mouthpiece of the government. This dual role may not last in post-1997 Hong Kong, but at the time when BLR was produced, the production context could still be seen as that of a public broadcaster.[5]

It is interesting that RTHK's producers, like other public producers and film-makers, usually buy into the notion of auteurism and personal expression whereas the commercial broadcasters more readily acknowledge the industrialised nature of the production process. Here auteurism is contrasted with impersonal commercialism. But there is a possibility that RTHK will turn, ironically, to the impersonal government propaganda model after 1997. So far, RTHK has maintained its autonomy, but RTHK should have an institutional barrier to insulate from the pressure of the Chinese government if it is to maintain the autonomy of personal expression.

Boundary cases

Organisational schemata represent paradigmatic control. They are unobtrusive to those who have internalised the value framework of the organisation. However, this argument is quite difficult to prove, especially by one-off ethnographic study. One effective way of 'seeing' this internalisation process is by attending to some fringe or extreme cases where the schematic boundary can be made visible. I have thus identified and interviewed those individuals in TVB and RTHK who are considered not to fit well into their respective organisational schema.

A TVB producer, who is outside the GT team and is widely recognised as innovative, made this point to me: 'I don't want my programmes to look repetitive and familiar. Of course, I won't go for extreme; extremity is not for television. I only want to do something a little bit different, but I am not allowed to do so.' Despite these complaints, he was defending the system:

> I understand they [the management] have more commercial pressures than me. Investment in television production is huge. Now I am trying to prove to them that I can produce high rating shows; with these high rating shows on my track record, I can have more bargaining power to do what I want.

When he was asked to comment on the general production environment of TVB, he said: 'I am very frustrated. Things are going worse these days.' Because he was on the edge of the commercial scheme, he felt more constrained than those who had internalised the schema of the organisation. Another RTHK producer, who was described by the executive producer as the most commercial director in RTHK, made the following critical comments:

> In the last couple of years, RTHK dramas have been too high-brow, only art fans like to watch RTHK dramas. . . . If a producer does not make programmes with that kind of seemingly artistic quality, then people think he has problems. For me, I prefer to make programmes that are close to the audience. I am quite confused whether or not my style fits their expectations.

The above analysis of organisational cognitive schemata leads to this observation: a producer whose orientation is in line with the organisational schema will experience a higher degree of creative autonomy. This is what Curran described as 'licensed autonomy': media workers 'are allowed to be independent only as long as their independence is exercised in a form that conforms to the requirements of their employing organisations' (Curran, 1990a:120). There is no need for obtrusive content control, since the contents these producers selected are the desirable options within that organisational schema. On the other hand, a producer whose orientation does not fit well with the organisational schema will feel relatively more constrained. Content control becomes obtrusive, and these producers will feel the pressure of being asked to offer what the organisation wants but not always what they personally would prefer.

The organisational schema is the primary controlling device of content selection. There are some other secondary control mechanisms such as feedback systems, track records of producers, resource allocation, and programme genre options. As the subsequent discussion will show, the influence of the organisational schema cuts deep into these secondary mechanisms.

Feedback systems

Feedback systems refer to the various mechanisms that allow evaluations and viewing information from the audience to be received by the production staff. Here audiences include the viewers, critics, colleagues, and station executives. There are three main types of feedback:

- Feedback from the watching public is basically achieved through *ratings*.
- Feedback from critics appears as *media reviews*.
- Feedback from colleagues and station executives takes the form of *informal comments* or *formal evaluations and appraisals*.

How do feedback mechanisms affect the range of ideological diversity and position of television dramas? In what ways do they affect creative decision-making and content selection?

Ratings

All TVB interviewees, including those in the supervisory position, were fully aware of the inadequacy of rating figures. They all knew that ratings were not a good indicator of programme quality. Poor shows could get high ratings; what they considered good might not look good in the ratings chart. Factors like programming of rival stations, time-slots, and habitual viewing could directly affect a programme's rating performance. However, all those in supervisory positions and those in creative control were serious about ratings. The production manager and creative director said: 'Ratings are very important feedback. It is a quick way of knowing whether or not GT is welcomed by the audience.' They were reportedly very upset by the not-so-good ratings of GT in the first few weeks.[6] As reported by other interviewees, GT's executive producer looked gloomy and easily agitated when GT was first released. Ratings, understood as a weak indicator of quality, still possess tremendous evaluative effects on the commercial producers because good and poor ratings directly affect one's track record and prestige, which are highly valued in the industry.

Though ratings are deficient feedback, they are at least clear and open. Ratings circulate openly among colleagues and attract media attention. The ups and downs of GT's rating performance had a direct emotional impact on them. The influence of ratings at the psychological level is translated into the cognitive schema and strengthens it as a result. Gitlin (1983) claims that ratings success is unpredictable. Therefore, ratings pressure will push content choice towards copying the formulas of past successes. Audience tastes and elements of success are perceived and constructed conceptually and affect the creative process. Since prime-time dramas are aimed at the largest possible heterogeneous audience, the content should be easily digestible. Unconventional ideologies are avoided. Choric contents are preferred. The cognitive script of mass appeal exerts a strong mainstreaming effect on the ange of content choice. The executive producer and head writer both pointed out that losing the 4–14 age groups would result in a drop in ratings, so 'the content should be understandable to the young audiences'. Therefore, in the drama, stock market economics were treated in the simplest possible way. Stock investment, as it appeared in GT, is no different from simple win–lose gambling. In retrospect, the producers noted that the 'rating of GT is not good enough because the treatment is still too complicated, it should be less sophisticated next time'.

For RTHK, audience feedback in the form of ratings is not so influential. All BLR producers either ignored rating figures or treated them as secondary. Some didn't even know what ratings their programmes had. The executive producer was more concerned, but ratings were still secondary; he said that 'rating figures are only "ammunition" for getting resources'. The RTHK staff thought that it wouldn't be necessary to get high ratings: 'as long as ratings are kept in a reasonable or not-too-low level, things will be fine.' When asked whether they had considered audience taste in the idea development process, none of the RTHK producers gave a concrete answer. One said things like 'the audience's taste didn't pass through my mind when I developed the script'. RTHK producers selected a particular theme because they thought it was significant, interesting, or meaningful. The producers of BLR were relatively free from ratings pressure, and this allowed a much larger range of ideological options. BLR producers made content choice and then figured out what kind of target audience the content might fit. They did not have a mass audience in mind and developed content according to the perceived audience taste. As a result, the ideological content of BLR was not as restricted to the mainstream as that of GT. The range of ideological options was more diversified.

Critical review

Television dramas have another audience group – the media critics. They are more influential than the average audience because they can make their voices heard in newspapers, magazine columns, and radio programmes. As a feedback mechanism, how do reviews affect the content options of the dramas? TVB producers were generally more sceptical about media reviews; they thought reviews were 'unfair', 'biased', 'subjective', 'written on purpose by some interested parties [TVB rivals]', 'nonsense', 'out of context', etc. Many said they didn't bother to read such comments. However, most RTHK interviewees were very much affected by media reviews. Good reviews and public attention were more highly valued than good ratings. RTHK staff were especially affected by reviews from elite newspapers. One producer was so upset by negative media reviews that she took a long vacation away from Hong Kong after the BLR production. She was unhappy despite the fact that she got fair ratings from her two episodes (episodes 1 and 8). On the contrary, another producer was very satisfied with the exceptionally favourable reviews for her work despite the fact that it got the poorest ratings of all the eight episodes of BLR (episode 3). These brief descriptions are enough to make the point: RTHK drama producers take critical reviews much more seriously than TVB. However, the most important question is: how do reviews affect content?

The producer in our boundary case of RTHK made critical and revealing comments. He had already left RTHK at the time of the interview and was able to examine the issue from a distance. He thought that RTHK stressed the reviews from elite papers a bit too much. 'One positive article in *The Economic Journal* [an elite paper], can overshadow three negative ones in a mass appeal paper such as the *Oriental News!*' This bias towards the elite point of view is ultimately reflected in content choice. When a few RTHK dramas get critical acclaims in the elite papers, that type of drama, in terms of content and style, would be highly endorsed by the RTHK management and producers. This bias towards the elite point of view is ultimately reflected in content choice. BLR is for the perceived elite audience. They are cultural products for different 'taste publics' (Gans, 1974).

Another form of critical feedback is the television awards. The RTHK drama unit has a history of procuring international awards. Awards are valued because they enhance the prestige of both the producers and the organisation. One RTHK interviewee pointed out that some RTHK producers consciously made content choice according to the perceived 'needs' of these award-giving organisations. For instance, programmes that look artistic and sophisticated and describe the special features of Chinese culture and customs could attract the attention of the international audience more easily. However, when those award-winning producers were questioned about the issue, they said they were fully aware that awards were not necessarily given to 'good' programmes. 'Of course, everybody wants to be honoured, besides, awards give me the bargaining power of getting prestigious assignments,[7] but frankly, I have never tailor-made a programme for an award.' How specific awards affect content selection remains an open question, but clearly awards reinforce the elite and artistic preferences. The heavy bias towards elitist feedback contributes partly to the negotiatory ideologies of BLR. A note of differentiation should be made here. The elitist aesthetics of RTHK refers to an intellectual elite rather than an economic-political elite; moreover these groups diverge in their values and ideologies. As the textual analysis in chapter 6 has illustrated, the particular kind of elitist aesthetics of the producers at RTHK is very critical of the political-economic elite such as land developers and capitalists.

Feedback within the organisation

Within the television organisation, evaluative feedback is rare. All TVB and RTHK interviewees said they seldom had evaluative discussions about their programmes with colleagues. Those in the supervisory positions mentioned they might talk about the programmes with their subordinates, but when their subordinates were cross-checked, they said that these occasions rarely happened. RTHK producers seem to regard the judgement of their superiors to be no better than their own; they listen, but often do not comply.

The lack of feedback within the organisations is caused by at least three factors:

1   Ratings and media reviews are openly circulated within and outside the organisations;
2   Both the management and the subordinates are aware of the deficiency of ratings and reviews as evaluative measures;
3   The aesthetic norms of television drama are highly ambiguous; there is no well-established norm that is accepted by the majority.

When asked about the criteria for a good television drama, answers were extremely diverse. Aesthetic norms ranged from concrete answers such as 'good characterisation', 'strong conflicts', to vague notions such as 'look good', 'feel good'. The interviewees are veteran television dramatists, yet they disagreed among themselves on the basic question of what constitutes a good or a bad drama. The ambiguity of creative norms furthers the greater influence of the organisational cognitive schema. When the answers on aesthetic norms are differentiated between TVB and RTHK staff, the schematic bias is noticeable. The creative norms of TVB staff are slanted towards commercially attractive elements such as emotional impact and conflict. It is surprising that the notions of innovativeness and originality were not emphasised by any of the TVB interviewees. As a supervisor of the creative staff noted, it was not necessary to have 'new stuff': 'to make the story clear and understandable is much more important'. On the other hand, RTHK answers were biased towards social significance. They placed more emphasis on sophistication and subtlety. Originality was frequently mentioned to be a basic measure of a good drama. Without shared norms that can be recognised across organisations, the two organisational schemata polarise the two sets of aesthetics.

How do all these feedback mechanisms shape the range of ideological positions and the diversity of television dramas? The analyses of the feedback mechanisms of BLR and GT have shown that television drama production contexts only provide minimal direct feedback. The indirect feedback of ratings and critical reviews influences content selection by an imaginary feedback loop in which audiences' tastes and critics' comments are constructed by past experiences (Cantor and Cantor, 1992; DiMaggio, 1977; Turow, 1984). In comparison, RTHK is biased towards elitist reviews, while TVB is inclined towards mass ratings. The differences in the assumed audience and evaluative norms are sources of content variation of BLR and GT. As Crane (1992) has argued, if the perceived audiences are heterogeneous, and evaluative norms are based more on commercial success, the content delivered needs to be understandable to the mass audience and will also be more stereotyped and ideologically conventional. If the perceived significant audience (in the case of BLR, critics and elite) possess a specific combination of demographics, the programme content will be ideologically more diversified and unconventional.

Track record and resource control

Organisational schemata and feedback systems discussed above are unobtrusive controls that work at the cognitive level. The interview data also indicate the presence of more obtrusive resource controls that work at the administrative level.

Track record

This works both ways. It serves as a control device of the organisation because managers will allocate more resources to those with 'desirable' records. On the other hand, creative staff can use their 'good' track record to fight for more resources and creative autonomy. In TVB, those with a good ratings record are allocated more important assignments.[8] Because GT's executive producer had produced numerous rating hits in the past, he was given a great cast and a longer production period. He was trusted by his superiors and was given complete autonomy in his work.

In RTHK, the drama unit only has a handful of producers who enjoy the tenure of civil servants. The factor of track record in allocating assignment is not as important. However, the drama unit has a tradition of inviting film directors to work on one or two episodes of important series. These guest directors are all critically acclaimed. They can help to reinforce the image of 'quality television' for RTHK dramas.

Resource control

In the hostile television economy of the 1990s, production resources in TVB have become more and more restrictive. Resource allocations are calculated in a more precise cost-profit ratio. One TVB interviewee said: 'This limits your options, every time your story leads to some expensive scenes, you have to stop right there and think of something else.' Although RTHK producers complained of the tight production budget, they had more resources when compared with TVB. TVB allows four to five filming days for an hour of prime-time drama; RTHK producers have eight to ten days. Commercial television has a clearer standard of cost-effectiveness. Non-commercial organisations are generally more difficult to assess for cost-effectiveness. Non-commercial television drama production is even more problematic since it provides cultural products whose utility is difficult to measure (Campbell and Campbell, 1978; McQuail, 1991). As a result, the level of resource support for BLR was to a certain extent arbitrary; this in turn allowed more flexibility in creative options.

Boundary analysis

The analyses of boundary situation of BLR and GT can explain the interplay between organisational schemata, track record, resource allocation, and the relative degree of *creative autonomy* in both RTHK and TVB.

TVB gave GT's executive producer more support because he had a successful ratings record.[9] The normal production period is six months for a 40-hour drama. GT got ten months; the creative team was free to do research and choose the themes of the serial. Of course, GT's executive producer would not contravene the commercial schema by adopting complicated or political options (see above), even though he knew that his track record gave him the privilege of a higher degree of creative autonomy. He exploited this autonomy however by attempting something difficult. He consciously built a complicated character Ting Hian, who did not fit well into the conventional stereotype. He noted: 'Ting isn't a traditional villain, he's a good guy doing bad things.' However, the resource allocated to him did not allow him to indulge too much on the non-profitable creative labour of polishing the drama. Resource support was well contained within the profit margins. He could not exceed that resource limit even if he wanted to. During the final month of the production, he spent 24 hours a day in his office to meet the deadline; no extension was allowed. In fact, the broadcast time was scheduled earlier to match with the timing of a new programme on the rival station. He argued a bit and then complied. However because of this compressed production time, producers of the second half of the serial had to work mechanically with limited creative choice.

In the RTHK case, 70 per cent of the media coverage and reviews on BLR were on one single episode entitled *Stormy Weather*. The conflict between the producer and RTHK management aroused great media attention. The case could be considered as a test case of the creative autonomy of the RTHK drama unit. The producer of *Stormy Weather* had a strong track record in terms of seniority and critical recognition. *Stormy Weather* is about a crackdown on democracy in an unnamed country and the dilemma of a television station editor over how to handle an interview with that country's senior leaders. She came up with this sensitive story of political censorship and got the go-ahead from the management. She knew the story would be difficult to get through because it carried explicit references to the June Fourth massacre in Beijing and satirised some of China's senior leaders. So she lined up an exceptional strong casting which included a retired senior government official, an acclaimed magazine editor, and a prominent political figure. She had a strong rationale because her story was well inside the non-commercial schema of public broadcasting: the subject of editorial independence is socially significant, and it is what RTHK has been fighting for.[10] She also pushed to the limit of RTHK's resources control. She was allocated one broadcast hour, 10 filming days, and a HK$200,000 budget. Without prior consent of the management, she produced two broadcast hours of content, used up 21 filming days, and HK$420,000 in production cost. She asked for two broadcast hours but was rejected. With much reluctance and enormous media attention, she edited the programme to fit it into the one-hour time slot. The media was looking for references of censorship, but the short version retained the sensitive content of the long version.

The incident was not a test-case of editorial freedom but a test-case of resource controls. The incident not only reflects the relatively un-restrained nature of resource control in RTHK's drama unit, it also reveals the fact that some RTHK producers expect a much higher degree of autonomy than the organisation can allow. To ask for doubled air-time is unthinkable in commercial television. After the incident, RTHK's drama unit tightened up its resource control. The option of firing the producer had been raised by the management but was turned down. She was later transferred to the less prestigious educational television section and finally left RTHK.

Creative locus

This refers to the position that holds the autonomy and power to make independent decisions or influential input concerning the selection and creation of the drama content. Creative control is unevenly spread across the production and creative staff of GT and BLR. In TVB, the creative locus is more centralised. The line-up of production staff of GT is similar to any other TVB serial drama: the management can veto programme ideas, but normally they will not exercise that option. They may give advice and comment, but the initiation and selection of programme ideas are centralised in two positions: the executive producer and the head writer. These two work together on a programme proposal which includes key characters, central themes, and the basic storyline of the drama. Although the head writer plays a supportive role, he has an influential creative input. However, the creative role of the on-line producers is minimal; their major contribution is visualisation of the script. TVB on-line producers are autonomous and given a relatively free hand in their production work. However, their controls are on the production scene only. They can only advise the executive producer on the problems and feasibility of production; they are not involved in the creation of the scripts. Under the head writer, numerous scriptwriters are responsible for the actual writing, which is more of an executive job rather than of gatekeeping contents. In summary, the creative loci of GT are centralised with the executive producer and the head writer.

In contrast, RTHK has more decentralised creative loci. The role of the management in RTHK is similar to that of TVB: they give advice and comments and can veto a proposal, but the actual selection comes from the executive producer. Story development is the responsibility of individual producers. In the case of BLR, the executive producer initiated a broad framework. With the approval of the management, the programme was decided to be on broad issues of Hong Kong society in the 1990s. The framework was large enough for individual producers to look for the stories they wanted. They were responsible for the development of scripts and the production of programmes. The executive producer made critical comments, but the major creative loci were held by the producers. RTHK drama producers can select and hire freelance writers to work out the script according to their discretion. The involvement of the scriptwriter varies from producer to producer, but the producer is the dominant creator of each programme. The decentralised creative loci of RTHK provide more room for content diversity and individual creativity within a single series.

Creative constraints and the ideologies of television drama

I have analysed how organisational schemata and feedback systems shape the gatekeeping process of television drama contents. I have also discussed the organisational control of resource allocation. Schemata and feedback work at the cognitive level, while the control of resources works at the administrative level. Schemata and feedback are very influential in screening off non-compatible options, while resource control limits the chosen options to be produced within the cost/profit margin in commercial television and cost/utility ratio in public television. Schemata and feedback are highly unobtrusive, but resource control is often obtrusive and responsible for many organisational conflicts in television productions. TVB is relatively more restrictive in resource allocation because its commercial context has a clearer cost/profit margin. As a non-market organisation, RTHK has an ambiguous cost/utility ratio. Resource allocation is more autonomous and unrestrained.

Television studies that describe a higher degree of individual autonomy tend to talk more of content innovation and diversity (Ettema, 1982; Feuer, 1987; Newcomb and Alley, 1983). Those studies that describe a higher degree of creative constraint usually talk about the production of media contents that are mainstream and stereotyped (Cantor and Cantor, 1992; Gitlin, 1983; Tuchman, 1974). The findings of the present study support these patterns. BLR and GT are two cases that illustrate how the relatively more restrictive context of TVB produces mainstream television dramas and how the less restrictive context of RTHK allows the production of controversial dramas. The analysis suggests that more restrictive administrative control on resource allocation limits individual autonomy and thus ideological diversity of television dramas, while less restrictive administrative control of resource allocation allows a greater degree of individual autonomy and thus ideological diversity of television dramas.

Against these general organisational predispositions, I want to make another qualification. A major argument of this book is that media dynamics should be considered in a context-sensitive way. The issue of creative autonomy is no exception. It is something that is the product of political, professional, and institutional struggle in a specific historical conjuncture. It cannot be mandated. In the 1970s it existed in the surplus economy of commercial television and then in the 1990s it existed in government television due to the policy vacuum in the run-up to the handover. Thus creative autonomy is a historically specific possibility that emerges in different organisational contexts at different moments.

Case control: context and genre

As is to be expected, GT and BLR have some loose ends that resist neat comparison. An important source of possible incomparability is derived from the difference in genre types. GT is produced in the genre of a continued serial, which has a single story across different episodes. BLR is a single-play series which features different stories and characters for every episode. Previous studies have found that the genre influences the content and ideology of television programmes (Attallah, 1984; Feuer, 1992; Swidler *et al.*, 1986; Tulloch, 1990). Is the genre difference of BLR and GT a source of their content variance? If the answer is yes, then to what extent and in what direction does genre affect ideological diversity? Is the effect of genre interfering with the comparative patterns found?

To assess the influence of programme genre, I have cross-examined my interviewees, asking whether there are differences between the content selection and production processes of serials and single plays within the same station. The control analyses show the following: First, genre affects the level of creative autonomy, and thus creative options and content selection. Single plays, even when produced in TVB, have decentralised creative processes because on-line producers can initiate their own stories for different episodes. This allows a higher degree of individual creativity than in the production of serials. On the other hand, individual producers are more restrained when producing serials, since leading roles and the narrative flow have to be maintained throughout the entire episode span.

Second, the effect of genre cannot neutralise the influences of the organisational schemata of TVB (commercialism) and RTHK (non-commercialism). Single plays produced by TVB are still more restrictive than those produced by RTHK. TVB producers are inclined to opt for 'middle-of-the-road' content for single plays, whereas RTHK's on-line producers involved in the production of a serial still work in a less centralised way when compared to TVB producers. The organisational schema has a stronger influence on content choice.

Third, and most importantly, the organisational schema has a greater effect than genre: it marginalises the significance of non-compatible genres and suppresses their occurrence in the first place. TVB produces very few single plays because such one-off stories have difficulty in hooking audiences for repeated viewing. They are also expensive to produce, because each story has its own artists, settings, and costumes. The commercial schema is biased against these less profitable, single-play series. The genre choice of RTHK also has a schematic predisposition.

The drama unit of RTHK, which is about 20 years old, has only produced one serial because the genre is less flexible than single-play series. RTHK interviewees told me: 'We can do what we want with a single-play series, which allows us to examine meaningful themes and tell expressive stories, so why bother doing the restrictive and resource-consuming serial?' The control analyses show that genre can be an intervening variable: like the organisational schema, genre can affect content selection. However, schematic effect is of a higher order; it shapes content more powerfully and at the same time suppresses non-compatible genres.

Summary: the production of television culture

Television is by nature polysemic and ideologically diversified. The medium is semiotically 'excessive'. However, textual polysemies and ideological diversity are not so excessive as to allow random and limitless televisual meanings for any given televisual text; instead, they have shapes and forms with different degrees of closure. The textual comparison in chapter 6 shows that the public drama BLR and commercial drama GT exhibit different forms of television ideologies and polysemies. The differences are paradigmatic. In this chapter, I ask whether these differences have organisational roots. Organisational analyses indicate that these forms of television ideologies and polysemies are not unconditioned givens; they are overdetermined by socio-political influences which are articulated into the texts through different production processes. Contextual influences are differentially dispersed by organisational factors, resulting in different ideological configurations and textual polysemies. In the above analysis, it is found that the organisational context of GT and BLR systematically influence the ideology of the two dramas.

Like all other case studies, particularities of the selected cases prevent unconditional generalisations. Can the organisational predisposition found in TVB and RTHK be generalised to other commercial and public broadcast television? The organisational factors found in this study are closely connected to their respective organisational contexts. They are not occasional and contingent. The profit motive, the ratings system, the clear-cut cost-profit margin, etc. are innate to the context of commercial broadcast television. Whereas the non-commercial complementary programming, the cultural and social mandate, the elite bias, the ambiguous cost/utility ratio, etc., are common to other public

Table 7.1 The organisational definers of public and commercial television

	GT	BLR
Cognitive factors		
Cognitive schema		
	Commercialism	Non-commercialism
	Ritual affirmation	Social significance
	Maximise appeal	Complementary programming
	Local/regional	Local
Feedback system		
	Ratings/critical review	Critical review/ratings
	Mass audience	Elite audience
Aesthetic norm		
	Ambiguous	Ambiguous
	Commercial	Intellectual/elitist
Administrative factors		
Resources allocation	Formalised	Flexible
	Restrictive	Ambiguous
Creative locus	Centralised	Decentralised
Genre predisposition	Continued serial	Single-play series
	Restrictive	Flexible, individualistic

television contexts. There are strong internal relationships between the lyric/choric predisposition and these organisational factors. The organisation processes summarised in table 7.1 are in a way similar to commercial and public broadcasters in other countries.

These factors can be further grouped into two clusters of generalisations. First, *cognitive factors*. The schema of commercialism, working together with the mass ratings system and popular aesthetics, creates an unobtrusive cognitive framework which predisposes creative options of television dramas towards a mainstream ideology (G1). The schema of non-commercialism, working together with feedback systems of critical review and elitist aesthetics, creates an unobtrusive cognitive framework which predisposes creative options of television dramas towards negotiatory ideology (G2).

Second, there are the *administrative factors*. Centralised creative loci and more restrictive administrative controls and genre choice limit individual autonomy and thus ideological diversity of television dramas (G3).

Less centralised creative loci and less restrictive administrative controls on resource allocations and genre choice allow a greater degree of individual autonomy and thus ideological diversity of television dramas (G4).

Summarising these effects of the organisational definers: the cognitive and administrative factors in the generalisation of G1 and G3 predispose commercial broadcast television drama towards the choric mode, while the cognitive and administrative factors of G2 and G4 predispose public broadcast television drama towards the lyric mode. Under the recent trend of media commercialisation, public broadcasting is still worth defending, since its organisational processes, as summarised above, are relatively insulated from pressures of the market and the state. A mixed system of commercial and public television will contribute to the production of a more diversified and lively television culture.

I should add a note of caution: it is the specific organisational mechanisms that contribute to the ideological tendencies of the programme output. Simply wearing the hat of public television does not guarantee ideological diversity. At different points in time, the organisational barriers within public broadcasters may not be strong enough to defuse influences from the state and the market. Similar to this study, Hoynes (1994) compares programmes produced by public and commercial television, but, contrary to the findings of this study, he finds out that *MacNeil/Lehrer*, a programme made by the public television PBS, has a wider range of narrative topics but a narrower range of viewpoints than *Nightline*, the programme produced by commercial station ABC. Hoynes then relates PBS's limited ideological perspectives to the market pressure on public broadcasting, PBS's funding-driven programming, its influential corporate sponsorship, and ambiguous aims at that period of time. Thus it is essential to uphold a more dynamic view about the production of television culture. For if public television is to remain a non-market-driven institution and avoid the tendency to slide towards state or market-driven models, it will have to stay focused on those organisational processes (see table 7.1) which contribute to the production of a 'lyric' television culture.

Discussion

The above analysis explains the discursive divergence of the selected dramas by the institutional dispersion of the respective organisations involved. However, by focusing on the materialist aspects, I am not slighting the significance of the culturalist explanation of contextual overdetermination. In fact, the polysemic and ideological forms identified in chapter 6 cannot fully account for, or be reduced to, the production processes. The organisational factors alone cannot explain why GT is esoterically polysemic, why it mythologises the economic history of Hong Kong, and why the membership categorisation of Hongkonger vs. mainlander stubbornly persists in the text and in the discursive practices of textual consumption. Likewise, institutional dispersion alone cannot explain why BLR is highlighting the political discourse in such an antagonistic way, why it so consciously rebels against the dominant discourse of *laissez-faire* economics, and why it is so concerned about the membership categorisation of the mainlanders.

Perhaps a more comprehensive explanation lies in the complicated interplay between contextual overdetermination and institutional dispersion: television institutions can be conceptualised as structuring habitual spaces within the general ideological/cultural context which is overdetermined by contextual definers. Television producers, located in different institutionalised habitats, are differentially situated to the general ideological/cultural context. Organisational analysis can only tell us the institutional predisposition of televisual discourse, it cannot tell us why dominant cultural and ideological patterns pop up in those institutionally predisposed discourses (Grossberg, 1995). We have to complement organisational explanations with the signification processes of contextual overdetermination and ideological articulation. Within the general ideological/cultural context of the 1990s, the deep-seated, two-set categorisation of mainlander and Hongkonger is strongly activated by social and political contestation. The Sino-Hong Kong antagonism is so strong that it has been mapped on to the television discourse as the most dominant point of reference of the times. Even when commercial television, out of the desire for reconciliation, opts for 'amnesia' and suppresses the dominant membership categorisation of the dirty, out-lawish, and dangerous mainlanders, the ghostly representation of the mainlander still finds its way into the polysemic discourse of GT. The sense of Hongkonger-under-threat in the wider social discourse also pushes the televisual discourse towards the reaffirmation and strength-ening of the myth of Hong Kong's economic success. To mythify past economic success has the function of justifying the present and thereby contributing to, and reflecting the desire of, social stability in the face of imminent social changes. In contrast, the ideological articulations between the general ideological/cultural context and the televisual discourse of BLR work in a very different direction. Out of the social mandate of public television, BLR amplifies the Sino-Hong Kong conflicts as a sign of the times, and questions the viability of *laissez-faire* and the category collection of Hongkonger/mainlander in the new socio-political milieu. Thus, despite institutional dispersions, both dramas draw from the general ideological/cultural context the dominant discursive agendas of the times. This dialectic interplay between contextual definers and organisational definers contributes to the divergence and convergence of the textual forms located in the textual analysis of the two selected dramas.

To conclude, production contexts of television drama are dynamic rather than static. In the language of organisation theory, the television drama production context comes about less as a rational organisation and more as a loosely coupled collectivity functioning in a 'satisficing' manner (see Perrow, 1986; Scott, 1987): decisions are made not by exploring all options but by selecting between 'handy' alternatives. It is erroneous to argue for a static position that emphasises the creative autonomy of television producers and ignores the penetrating effect of organisational controls and contextual overdetermination. It is equally erroneous to overestimate the restrictive power of the hegemonic capitalist institution on creative individuals. Different production contexts have different interrelationships of controls and creative autonomy in different historical conjunctures.

These differential positions of constraints and autonomy result in the differentiation of the 'choric' drama of the commercial station TVB and the 'lyric' drama of public broadcaster RTHK. Lyric and choric dramas are two ends of a continuum; they are not mutually exclusive. Lyric dramas may have choric elements and vice versa. Commercial television may occasionally produce innovative lyric dramas and the public television context may sometimes produce commercial choric dramas, but in general, commercial broadcast television is predisposed to the choric mode while public broadcast television is predisposed to the lyric mode. Both lyric and choric ideologies are within the reach of the general ideological/cultural context. Due to the satisficing manner of creative decisions, those dominant and presignified ideological and cultural patterns are mostly likely to get through. The organisational processes can only predispose a certain range of possible discourses, but within this predisposition, the general contextual ideologies are free to articulate dominant discourses in their own logic.

Chapter 8

Rethinking television culture

The main focus of this book is to locate and explain the uneven distribution of televisual meanings with regard to the specific issue of cultural identities. I began this project with an image of a winding road that runs through different theoretical and methodological terrain. In the previous chapters I steered an analytical course which allowed me to explore the diverse field from different directions and with different emphases. Many different arguments are sketched out in different parts of the book, focusing on a variety of theoretical and empirical issues. In common with other case studies, here too there are fuzzy edges and loose ends that cannot be neatly fitted into this conclusion, but I would like, in a schematic way, to generalise from the case of Hong Kong television a few propositions that allow us to rethink television culture in the current theoretical context. The following is thus a recapitulation of the main arguments and findings of previous chapters.

Television ideologies and polysemies

Most of the arguments in the previous chapters are about textual ideologies and polysemies, which are embedded in the theoretical debates between the dominant ideology thesis and the polysemy thesis. The various forms of the dominant ideology thesis in television studies (Lodziak, 1986) make three major assertions: first, television reflects a coherent dominant ideology; second, the dominant ideology in television is a result of direct and indirect connections between the media and the dominant groups; and third, television is ideologically effective. There is a fuzzy spectrum of theoretical positions on the consistency and effectiveness of the dominant ideology, with some political economists and structuralists at one end favouring a strong version of ideological incorporation, and some culturalists at the other end favouring a flexible and multi-dimensional version of ideological articulation. In contrast, the polysemy thesis conceptualises television as a polysemic flow which defies the assertion of a coherent dominant ideology. Far from deceiving the passive audience, television, because of its 'excessive' semiotic, offers spaces for polysemic readings by an active audience.

The dominant ideology thesis and the polysemy thesis not only deal with issues of the media but also the roles of media in social formation. Their differences not only reside in different conceptions of the media but are also rooted in contrasting social theories. The dominant ideology thesis appears to be at home with critical social theory, which sees society as an ensemble of relations of domination and subordination, and the media as an ideological apparatus of the dominant groups. The poly-semy thesis is arguably more compatible with liberal views of media and society in which different interests are able to inscribe their voices into the multivocal media. However, the dominance/polysemy antithesis is more of an analytic type than an accurate intellectual division; there are variations within and convergence between the two camps. The dominant ideology thesis has its non-Marxist parallels[1] and the polysemy thesis has close connections with critical culturalist traditions and post-modern perspectives. To complicate the scene, both antithetical positions have undergone revisions in the light of criticisms put forward by their opponents.[2] There has been a general shift from a strong to a weak version of the dominant ideology thesis and from a liberal to a critical emphasis on the part of the polysemy thesis (see table 8.1). In the following I shall take a 'third alternative' and piece together critically the strengths of these revisions to form a set of multi-dimensional propositions.

I shall begin with the proposition that *television texts are constructed in a field of dominant ideology which exhibits various degrees of ideological closure.* This proposition deals with textual features, which reflect my emphasis on a textually oriented approach to televisual discourse. The emphasis on text can be seen as a corrective to the negligence of textual analysis in recent television studies, and in particular, audience studies (see appendix 3). Of course, to avoid the fallacy of 'textualism', textually oriented analysis should be done along with the analysis of textual production and reception. Yet I maintain that in the cases presented in this book, as in many others, televisual texts continue to be among the best sets of researchable data remaining from historical encounters between the text and the audience. As Gripsrud (1995) argues, it is impossible to arrive at an understanding of historically produced interpretations without performing an interpretation of the texts in

Table 8.1 The ideological character of television

	Dominant ideology thesis		The Third Route	Polysemy thesis	
	Strong → Tight closure	**Weak** Loose closure	**Revisionist** Asymmetrical field of meanings	**Critical** ← Limited polysemy	**Liberal** Semiotic democracy
Society	Class conflicts and domination		Hegemonic competition	Competing social consensus	
Ideology	Masking class exploitation		Uneven distribution of meanings	Competing values	
Mass media	Agency of class control		Arena of contest	Cultural forum	
Development Textual ideology					
Television organisation	Agent of Class Control	Networking	Institutional dispersion	–	–
Political economy	Deterministic	Overdetermination	Multiple articulation	Contingent	Contingent
Socio-historic context	Capitalism	Capitalism	Contingent alliance Hierarchical power	Multidiscursive democracy	Liberal democracy
Human agent	Determined	Determined	In 'Habitats' of interaction	Autonomous	Autonomous
Ideological effects	Producing consents	Winning consents	Winning consents	Popular resistance	Idiosyncratic interpretation
Ideological and cultural role	All ideological	Mixed	Dialectic interplay	Mixed	All cultural

question. The fact that textual analysis often arrives at different interpretations does not necessarily invalidate textual analysis; quite the contrary, the difference between textual analysis and historically constructed interpretations, if any, may lead to fruitful questions such as: 'Why did this or that feature of the text seemingly go unnoticed?' 'Did it touch on what was "unspeakable" then?' (Gripsrud, 1995: 14).

These questions are particularly relevant to the case study of the Hong Kong melodramatic serial *The Good, the Bad, and the Ugly* – the serial which has constructed the membership category of the mainland immigrant 'Ah Chian'. My textual analysis shows a highly visible domination of the established Hongkongers over the mainlander Ah Chian. In the serial, Ah Chian is assaulted by a barrage of derogatory names. In some 300 scenes involving him, more than half depict him in a subordinate position. The categorisation of Ah Chian as an unruly, dirty, and uncivilised outsider can be discerned on the textual surface. However, the interesting point is that this obvious domination was not exactly what the historically produced interpretation was about. The character of the serial has been taken as a *suitable* and *natural* representation of the mainland newcomers. Those debasing inferences in the serial remain in the popular memory, but the public seems to be blind to the crude discrimination that has been associated with the stigma of Ah Chian (see chapter 4).

Even in academic discourse, television culture of the 1970s is celebrated as the cradle of the local cultural identity. Local researchers, who are themselves members of the local generation, seem to be slow to recognise the obvious cultural domination of the Hongkongers over the newcomers. In fact, as a member of the local group, and as an audience of the serial, I myself was quite surprised by my own textual analysis. Before the analysis, I was blind to the discriminatory features of the serial; and, like many others, I thought that the serial was realistic and had done a good job of capturing the social issues of the times. The categorisation of mainlanders as Ah Chian is ideological in the sense that it justifies the established Hongkonger's view of the outsiders as less human and their subordination as natural. The membership categorisation is also ideological in another sense: it displaces economic inequalities within and across social groups, and obliterates class barriers under the more visible socio-cultural barriers of HA. This tendency of the television serial to produce a field of ideological domination is even more remarkable when one considers the less intrusive influence of the political economy on Hong Kong television of the 1970s. At the time the serial was produced, there was no interventionist government to impose a nationalistic identity; besides, the surplus television economy, to a certain extent, insulated television culture against pressure from market forces. The ideological domination can thus be seen as the outcome of the symbolic logic of television. This is particularly the case when television is involved in the specific issue of identity formation.

Cultural identity has a strong tendency towards ideological closure. Despite the fact that identity formation is fluid and contingent, the urge for essentialist identities has been a persistent and recurrent drive all over the world in the post-Cold War years. The construction of cultural identity is a process that selects from a rich diversity of social practices to form a public version of a common identity. The process may easily become ideological if it suppresses and displaces other identities and constructs hierarchical social relations. This is exactly what the serial GBU has done. When television enters into the terrain of identity construction, it tends to consolidate and reinforce the ideological domination by objectifying the categorisations of social groups. The urge of identity confirmation, as reflected in the symbolic inclusion and exclusion of social groups, casts a reasonable doubt on the kind of soft relativism that ignores power hierarchy in identity claims, glorifies individual nomadic choice, and suggests that all identity claims have the same standing in televisual representations. The reality is quite the opposite: identity categories offered by television are often invested with the strong differential of emotional appeal and binding forces. This differential distribution of symbolic power can be easily utilised to serve the ideological function of social control.

Nevertheless, to see television ideology as a field of domination does not necessarily mean that all television outputs mechanically converge along with the power hierarchy of the wider society. I argue, in my second proposition, that *within the diffused ideological field, there are traceable forms of 'polysemies' and ideologies, which sustain and regulate a different range and pattern of asymmetrical meanings.* The strong version of the dominant textual ideology simply cannot hold in the face of empirical findings. Liberal elements are found in television in large- and small-scale content and textual analysis (e.g. Rothman *et al.*, 1992; Taylor, 1989). Even in the tradition of political economy, media texts are said to 'vary considerably in their degree of discursive openness' (Golding and Murdock, 1991:27). In their study of terrorism, Schlesinger *et al.* (1983) find that television genres such as series and serials have tighter closure than single-play dramas. Practically, texts are often situated in the intermediate positions that fall between tight ideological closure at one extreme, and unlimited polysemy at the other. Even within the obvious ideological closure of the serial GBU, there is still a struggle of two membership category collections: the category collection of 'family' (Ah Chian the brother) and the collection of 'cultural identity' (Ah Chian the mainlander). At times, the discrimination against Ah Chian the mainlander can be so excessive that it backfires to invoke the category-bound sympathy for Ah Chian the brother.

When compared with GBU, the selected dramas of the 1990s exhibit features that are far more polysemic. In the case of the commercial serial GT, the villain, who is explicitly said to have grown up locally, is still recognised by some of the audiences as a mainlander, or even a communist. On the textual surface, GT does not have any mainlander/ Hongkonger categorisation, but it esoterically incorporates strong category-bound inferences of the stereotypical mainlander. This poly-semic configuration is distinctively different from that in the GBU case. Commercial dramas have multiple imperatives: they have to please a large heterogeneous audience, to avoid offending established powers, to mainstream its ideologies, and to cling on to widely shared cultural categories. These commercial imperatives shape the televisual text of GT in contradictory ways; they mould textual meaning away from Sino-Hong Kong conflicts, but also draw on mainstream sentiments against the 'invading' mainlanders. As a result, the text shows an esoteric/polysemic configuration: beneath the apolitical textual surface, there are deep-seated antagonisms which are grounded in the rigid Hongkonger/outsider categorisation.

Besides, when GT is compared with BLR – the public television drama produced within the same period – the textual divergence is even more paradigmatic. The non-commercial drama BLR exhibits an ideo-logical pattern which is diversified and negotiatory in nature. There is a wide variety of mainlanders in the stories. The identities of Hongkongers and mainlanders, as described in BLR, can no longer be generalised into the stereotypes of Ah Chian and the economically successful Hong Kong Man. The producers of BLR were more self-conscious and reflexive. In Barthes's term, their treatment is more 'writerly', with multiple codes that play on stereotypes, alter popular cultural patterns, and create new imagery. The polysemic subtitles are more literary and elitist.

I classified these *paradigmatic differences* using the concepts of choric and lyric drama. GT can be classified as choric drama, which sings in resonance with the mainstream capitalistic ideology, while the RTHK drama BLR can be called lyric drama, which stands out from, and negotiates with the ideology of the establishment in a personal voice. In lyric drama, we hear a distinct voice with less polysemic arrangements. On the other hand, under the harmonious resonance of the choric dramas, there are multiple layers of polysemic voices which reflect the compromise and adjustment of a variety of interests.

On the textual dimension, I have located the forms of polysemies and ideologies in the television dramas produced in different periods and by different organisations. Against the claims of limitless and random poly-semic meaning, the textual analyses of the selected television programmes show significant and analysable differences in their ideological and polysemic patterns.

Contextual overdetermination and institutional dispersion

In my next proposition, I try to relate those textual forms that I have located in the previous chapters with the wider socio-historical world. I propose that *the diffuse yet patterned ideological field is overdetermined by the multiple articulation of contextual definers, which appear in the form of political, economic, and socio-historical influences.* In the dominant ideology thesis, textual ideology and social determinants have a simple and necessary correspondence. On the other hand, there is uncertain correspondence between television ideology and social contexts in the polysemy thesis. In the 'third alternative' I propose here, there is 'no necessary non-correspondence' (Hall, 1985) between television ideologies and social determinants. Social domination and televisual ideologies are articulated together by linkages which are effective only at specific conjunctures. They can be disarticulated and rearticulated in shifting and contingent power hierarchies. The contingent nature of these contextual definers is well illustrated by the historic analysis of the Hong Kong case. The articulations between the contextual definers and television ideologies, as demonstrated in the historical comparison in chapters 2 and 3, vary enormously from one period to another: In the late 1970s, the 'minimally integrated media-political system' (Kuan and Lau, 1988) and the surplus television economy produced a relatively autonomous organisational environment for the media workers. When political and economic interventions are weak, the socio-cultural aspect assumes the dominant role in ideological articulations. Television producers, standing in the discursive position of the established Hongkongers, drew on prevalent public sentiments of the times and constructed identity categories in the interests of the established social powers. This symbolic order was structured, predominantly, by the hierarchy of society, in which the established group exerted greater social power over the outsiders. Thus the contextual definers, via the socio-cultural route, were playing a dominant role in the signification processes.

However, in the 1990s, the political and economic aspects of the contextual definers became more prominent. The dual political power centres of China and Britain began to intrude in media politics, while the hostile television economy became more of a constraint. The identity categories of mainlander and Hongkonger, as presented in the television of the 1990s, have become unstable and polysemic. The polysemic configurations reflect the contradictions within and between the dual political powers and also the populist demands of the people. The deep-seated categorisation of mainlanders and Hongkongers is strongly activated by social and political contestation, but out of the desire for reconciliation, commercial television suppresses the derogatory membership categorisation of the mainlanders, resulting in the esoteric and polysemic configuration of the televisual discourse of GT and the re-sinicised and apolitical discourse of HKL. These polysemic patterns would make little sense without the historical analyses of the wider contexts. Ignoring the contextual overdetermination, the polysemies may easily be taken as random and idiosyncratic.

Nevertheless, contextual overdetermination and multiple articulation, if standing on their own, are inadequate to account for the discursive relationship between media and society. In addition to the general level of signification, there is another level that is connected with the institutionalised encoding practices of media organisations. The contextual definers overdetermine the dominant ideological field; but the organisational definers differentiate the field into different patterns of televisual discourses. Neglecting the institutional level of signification would result in at least two distorted notions of the meaning production processes. The first distortion is a 'convergence hypothesis' (Curran, 1990a) which sees the media in general as having a convergent output overdetermined by the wider ideological world, regardless of the possible divergence between outputs of different media. The second distortion is the claim of the audience's cultural autonomy over and above the influence of the television economy. The surprising absence of *production analysis* in recent audience studies presupposes these faulty assumptions. To avoid either kind of distortion, it is essential to distinguish the preferences of different television organisations in the process of textual production.

Different types of television organisations and production contexts have tendencies and predispositions to produce televisual texts with different polysemic and ideological patterns. Both the dominant ideology and polysemy theses fail to differentiate the various organisational processes from which different television texts are produced: Marxist perspective is inadequate when it mixes public and commercial television together as the ideological agent of the dominant groups. In Britain, those holding this instrumental view attack the BBC as elitist, undemocratic and pro-establishment. However, as Garnham (1993) – himself a political economist – has acknowledged: the fact that the BBC is non-commercial and protected to a significant extent from direct political control represents a real social democratic gain; while it is undoubtedly true that the BBC is controlled by the dominant fraction, nevertheless the range and relative objectivity of its programmes represent a progressive contrast with the commercial media.

In characterising modern mass communication, Thompson speaks of the 'mediazation of modern culture', which he refers to as 'the general processes by which the transmission of symbolic forms becomes increasingly mediated by technical and institutional apparatuses of the media industries' (Thompson, 1990:4). Modern cultural texts are mixed products of cultural and industrial processes (Meeham, 1986). Proponents of the polysemy thesis have always stressed the cultural and neglected the material and industrial. They persistently stand apart from the arguments of political economists and the wealth of research in media organisations. However, if the duality of the logic of culture and the logic of commodity is intrinsic to television texts, then the polysemy theorists are divorcing an innate property from television texts. Because of this blind spot, polysemy theorists miss the chance to develop a deeper understanding of the organisational source of polysemy. Hence my fourth proposition is that *contextual definers are differentially absorbed, dispersed, and translated through different organisational definers to form different polysemies and ideologies within the general ideological field.*

The differentiation and dispersion effects of television organisations were less prominent in the 1970s, because the political economy was less intrusive and the ideological articulation was mainly via the socio-cultural link. However in the 1990s, television production has become more affected by political and commercial calculations, and power relations are increasingly relayed on to television dramas through the interface of the television institutions. I selected two dramas which were produced by two different television institutions in order to study the effects of organisational contexts on textual ideologies.

In the case comparison of the commercial drama GT and public drama BLR, I identified an obvious ideological and textual divergence of the two dramas. Since both dramas were produced in the early 1990s, an emphasis on the shaping effects of the social determinants alone is insufficient to explain the divergence of the two dramas. Contextual and societal explanations should be complemented by the dispersing effects of television institutions. The comparative analysis of the production processes shows that both public and commercial television have a tendency to produce different forms of televisual discourse. In commercial television, the organisational schema of commercialism, working together with popular aesthetics and a feedback system of mass rating, creates an unobtrusive cognitive framework which favours creative options with mainstream and conventional ideology. Besides cognitive controls, commercial television allocates resources by a strict cost/profit ratio, delegates responsibilities to a centralised creative locus, and prefers the more restrictive drama genre of a continued series. These restrictive administrative controls limit individual autonomy and thus ideological diversity. The resultant effects of these cognitive and administrative factors predispose commercial television dramas to the choric mode of relatively mainstream, monolithic, but polysemic discourse.

In public television, the organisational schema of non-commercialism, working together with elitist aesthetics and a feedback system of critical review, creates an unobtrusive cognitive framework which favours creative options with elitist and negotiatory ideology. On the administrative level, public television allocates resources by questionable public utility measures, delegates responsibilities to decentralised creative loci, and prefers the more flexible drama genre of a single-play series. These less restrictive administrative controls allow a greater degree of individual autonomy and thus ideological diversity. The resultant effects of these cognitive and administrative factors predispose television dramas of public broadcasters to the lyric mode of negotiatory ideologies and writerly polysemies.

The interplay between the internal organisational and external contextual definers are exercised in dynamic negotiations; these negotiations are contingent, but not without patterns and tendencies. The contingency and determinacy can be further explained by my fifth proposition: *It is through human agents – embedded in 'habitats of interaction' – that the organisational and contextual definers exert their influences in the process of ideological articulation.* Both the dominant and polysemy theses are defective in the concept of human agents. In the former formulation, human agents are strictly determined by their position in the material and social relations. In Turner's words: 'The stronger the theory of ideology, the weaker the agent' (Turner, 1990:248). The reverse is also true; in the polysemy thesis, human agents are assumed to be autonomous, free from virtually every kind of structured constraint. The audiences are said to be capable of actively creating their own meanings (Fiske, 1987). Television producers are said to be capable of producing programmes that express their own voices (Newcomb and Alley, 1983). The third route sees human agents as occupants in what Bourdieu (1977) called 'habitats',[3] which are 'schemes of thought, perception, appreciation, and action'. A habitat of interaction may be conceptualised as a set of trajectories, determined by various kinds of resources or 'capitals,' yet which still allows room for the individuals to manoeuvre in their everyday lives. These 'capitals' include economic capital (material assets of various kinds), cultural capital (knowledge and skills), and symbolic capital (prestige and recognition). The resources and capitals available to individuals are unequally distributed, thus limiting the autonomy of the 'agent-in-habitat'.

The organisational analysis in chapter 7 indicates that televisual texts are produced by human agents who are occupants in institutionalised habitats. These habitats are determined by various kinds of contextual and organisational definers, yet they allow room for the individuals to manoeuvre within their production routine. The creative staff of the dramas make their creative choices within the organisational schema of the television institutions in which they were working. Schematic control sets a cognitive boundary within which the dramatists are free to make their own choices. They may experience constraints when they try to trespass these boundaries; but most of them have internalised the organisational schema so as to perceive themselves as autonomous creators of televisual discourses. Yet all organisational controls are not absolute: cognitive boundaries are ambiguous; feedback systems are indirect and insufficient indicators of programme quality; administrative constraints can be stretched and manipulated by those with good track records. The creative agents can exploit these ambiguities and relay to popular ideologies in idiosyncratic ways. Dominant ideological patterns are easier to relay, but the human agents are able to take new paths. Television ideology is most conservative in the parts which it takes for granted, but it can be most liberal or idiosyncratic in the parts in which producers are consciously making a point. Different production contexts have different interrelationships of organisational controls and creative autonomy: their dynamic interactions will result in different forms of textual polysemies and ideological heterogeneity. Therefore, textual forms should be conceptualised as products of these complicated articulation processes which involve the contextual overdetermination and institutional dispersions related to and managed through the intentionality of the human agents.

Audience interpretations and television influences

My sixth proposition deals with audience interpretations and television influences: *Television exerts its ideological effect upon the viewers who are also located in 'habitats of interaction'; and the ideological power of television lies in those deep-seated and emotionally loaded categorisations that refuse to change in the face of polysemy.* The ideological effects of television should be seen in the same concept of agent-in-habitat, and the consistency and contradiction that go with the concept. The concept of agent-in-habitat, when applied to audience decoding activities, can help us avoid the reductionism which takes structural factors (like class and race) to be the only determinants of decoding practices, and, on the other hand, better account for the ways in which structural factors are articulated in the discursive process of reception. Audience activities, no matter how 'producerly' (Fiske, 1987), should be seen within the constraints of the habitat in which a particular audience, or a group of audiences, resides. In the habitat, an individual's belief system is contradictory and changing, yet the uneven distribution of economic, cultural, and symbolic resources results in widespread acceptance of the values of the status quo. Television viewing is always viewing-in-contexts and, as Ang (1994) notes, contexts are indefinite. Yet contextual influences are not without patterns. Viewers situated in the habitats of interaction can produce idiosyncratic meanings, but their interpretations are limited by contextual constraints: 'One obvious situation-transcending factor is presented by the institutionally-defined constraints placed upon the structural conditions in which watching television can be practised in the first place' (Ang, 1994: 376). The discursive power of the 'centralised story telling institution' (Carragee, 1990) implies the imposition of when and what people can watch. Television may present a 'menu' of multiple textual meanings for the audience to choose whatever they like (Allen, 1985), but the very composition of that menu is determined by the television industry. Ang (1994) argues that the television institutions cannot control viewing behaviour beyond the scheduling of programmes; there are millions of viewing situations to the limited programme schedules provided by the institutions. However, this underestimates the mainstreaming effect resulting from the uneven distribution of television culture. Dominant cultural and ideological patterns remain influential in audience interpretative activities. Condit's (1989) study has convincingly shown how dominant interpretation can emerge much more easily than resistant readings. Having said all this, contextual patterns remain extremely difficult to identify. They are constantly shifting and cannot be theoretically reduced to general rules.

Obviously, dominant interpretation cannot be forced into audience reading as in the strong version of the dominant ideology thesis. Survey results of public value systems suggest that the average man tends to hold conflicted normative references (Abercrombie *et al.*, 1984). He may commit to different value systems depending on the perspective he adopts at any one time – be it front-stage pragmatics or back-stage personal life (Goffman, 1959). He may express a great deal of agreement with the dominant ideology on the abstract level, but outright dissension on the situational planes, especially for those whose subordinate class experiences are in conflict with the dominant ideology. Dominant ideology is accepted as an abstract version of reality, but real-life conditions weaken its binding force in the actual conduct of affairs (Femia, 1981). An audience's reading of a novel or a television programme can be at once resistant and compliant, neither neatly coincident with the dominant ideology nor simply a terrain of spontaneous opposition (Jhally and Lewis, 1992; Lewis, 1991; Radway, 1984). The strong version of the dominant ideology thesis has put too much faith on ideological compulsion, but on the other hand, the polysemy thesis simply fails to account for the limited cultural and symbolic capitals available to the audiences.

How the audience derives meanings out of the televisual texts within a grounded habitat has been high on the research agenda recently. In this project, instead of doing an extensive ethnographic mapping of discursive practices of the audience, which time and scope would not allow, I strategically work from an opposite direction to gauge the historically constructed readings of televisual discourses. Instead of locating the polysemic readings of the audiences, I try to locate those emotionally loaded membership categorisations that are derived from televisual discourse and remain in popular memories over time. These persistent readings bring together the concept of 'interpretation' and 'influence': interpretation can be polysemic, but it is precisely within the polysemic flow of televisual meaning that television exhibits its power by reinforcing certain dominant mythic categorisations that persist in televisual and social discourses. The power of these dominant myths is more on the emotive, associational, and categorisational levels which evade the flux of cognitive meanings. These mythic categorisations have the authoritative valorisations, prestigious icons, and 'naturalised' truth-claims all mixed up in the concretised and stable signifiers of membership categorisation devices. The audience can have a polysemic reading in the cognitive sense, but still subscribe to these emotive signifiers, and can still be strongly influenced by the emotions and valorisations attached to them. The Ah Chian category had become a persistent stigma in media discourses and in social practices. Although the myth that Ah Chians were lesser humans is rather ridiculous, it looked natural in the eyes of the established group and thus became ideological. The category of Ah Chian becomes a stigma with potency to paralyse whoever is named after it. The stigma carries strong negative emotions; it hurts even if the subordinated group does not subscribe to the ideological implications of the categorisation.

In the case of the serial GT, the survey data show a more complicated discursive pattern. The persistent categorisation of the mainlander permeates the audience's readings, despite the fact that there is not even one mainlander in the serial. The leading villain was identified to be of mainland origin by 60 per cent of the respondents, even though in the serial it is stated that he grew up in Hong Kong. Furthermore, he was seen by 35 per cent of the respondents as *acting like* a mainlander; respectively 27 per cent and 17 per cent saw him as acting like a communist and a Chinese; only 20 per cent see him as acting like a local Hongkonger. These data should not be treated as hard facts in the positivist sense; they are discursive and have to be interpreted. The interpretations of the representation of the villain clearly indicate widely open polysemic readings. This polysemy, as argued above, is not entirely the result of audience idiosyncrasy. It is a result of the contradiction in the signification processes, involving the persistent negative categorisation of the mainlander in dominant social discourse, as well as the institutional suppression of this popular discourse.

Here we can see both the power and limitation of television. On the one hand, it is quite astonishing that the serial GBU could create such a persistent categorisation of the mainlander. The stereotypical image of Ah Chian had been recurring intertextually in popular media and social discourse for nearly two decades, and it could even penetrate the interpretation of a seemingly connected serial like GT. Of course this should be judged in the convergence of the contingent social circumstances of the times, but the stability of the categorisation points to the power of television to construct and reinforce the distribution of social prestige and prejudice. Seen from another perspective, the power of television lies in its ability to suppress the range of social discourse. Commercial television in Hong Kong is strongly opposed to programmes that will offend dominant powers. In the institutionalised habitat of the production end, even when the producers of GT wanted to incorporate the sensitive issue of mainland identity, those creative options were ruled out at the very beginning of the production process, resulting in an 'apolitical' serial with not even one mainland character. This limits the range of the audience's discursive practices. In the long run, this can even mean the depoliticisation of the entertainment media. However, the polysemic readings of GT also reveal the limitation of television power. Against the institutional prohibition, the creative energy of the producers found an outlet in the text in an esoteric way. Category-bound inferences to the mainlander were inscribed into the text, which provided the cue for some of the audience to produce their own poly-semic reading of identity politics. The audience, in their habitat of interaction, were able to relay other social discourse on to the televisual discourse, and then activate those suppressed textual inferences to produce their own negotiatory and resistant meanings.

Through audience survey, interviews, and other secondary social surveys it has been shown that, in the particular case of Hong Kong identities, television is an agent in the production of a field of symbolic domination. Moreover, symbolic domination and social control are interdependent and mutually reinforcing, working through the socio-linguistic interface of membership categorisation. Membership categorisation is capable of surviving the polysemic flow of televisual discourses, and its power of social control lies more in its ability to construct emotive barriers to social meaning. Although the audience can resist the identity offered to them, the television institution holds the upper hand in setting the limit of available discourse. Scheff (1994) points out that the urge to belong, and the intense emotions of shame and pride associated with it, are the most powerful forces in the formation and maintenance of cultural identity: and in these processes, television is a powerful reinforcer and regulator.

Lastly, I would propose that *television, as a diffused ideological field, provides the space for the dialectical interplay between the cultural and the ideological*. In the dominant ideology thesis, television is basically ideological in its function. As Walsh has pointed out, 'the general problem with the whole of the Marxist perspective with regard to the role of ideology in the process of cultural reproduction is that it reduces culture to ideology and ideology to structure' (Walsh, 1993:241). Television, from the dominant ideological perspective, is an agent of control used by the dominant groups to promote ideologies that sustain their domination. Whether this argument has been made with crudity or great finesse, it has denied a large pool of televisual meanings, which has no direct relation to social domination. Opposite to this is the polysemy thesis which collapses the ideological to the cultural, by mobilising televisual meanings in an almost random fashion – meanings may be unevenly distributed in television polysemies, but that uneven distribution, as the argument goes, is in a state of flux where no consistent ideological effect is possible.

The third route that I take acknowledges that televisual meanings are distributed in favour of the powerful, but that there are also clusters of meanings serving no apparent social powers. In modern societies, social stratification systems become more complex and differentiated. There are general conflicts between the dominant and subordinated groups, as well as functional interdependency between social divisions. The Durkheimian concept of organic solidarity partially captures this need for social integration (Alexander, 1988). The homogenising effect of television culture plays a significant role in this process.

The cultural role of television has been discussed in various contexts. Media fictions provide, it is argued, 'an adequate way for society to commune with itself. This is usually defined as promoting human under-standing, mutuality and tolerance, either in classic humanist or feminist terms' (Curran, 1991a:34). Television has been conceived as a ritual space in which audiences regularly extract a few hours from their daily routine and enter into communion with the 'others' on the television screen (Hartley, 1992; Silverstone, 1988). Television is able to objectify an imagined community in a homogeneous television culture. The imagined community (Anderson, 1983) becomes 'visible', especially through its daily broadcast of news and current affairs. From television, the general public experience a sense of nationhood and collective solidarity (Scannell, 1996). Cultural boundaries are mapped and negotiated in the special occasions of civic rituals which are broadcast live as media events (Dayan and Katz, 1992), as well as in the rituals of daily television viewing. That is, television can relay localised civic rituals to the national audience; and, as a medium, it also has a ritual-like character (Chaney, 1986). Television provides a wealth of images, motifs, and categorisations for the memory banks of the audience in daily instalments for a lifetime. In these television 'rituals', publicly circulated symbols and categorisations are emotionally charged and recharged, in the Durkheimian sense, with the sacredness that becomes a communal revered order of meaning, thus contributing to social solidarity and community building. These television ritual processes are reported to have played a central role in the cultural indigenisation and nationalisation in Latin America and in some Asian countries at particular historical junctures (see Choi, 1990a, 1990b; Martin-Barbero, 1995).

The conceptualisation of the ideological field thus provides ample space for television to play the cultural role of social integration. Nevertheless, seeing television as an ideological field also suggests a dialectic relation between the ideological and the cultural roles of television. Television culture cannot be easily isolated from television ideologies. Although some cultural roles of television – like promoting indigenisation, fostering national solidarity, and confirming cultural identity – do not have apparent and immediate ideological functions, they do often have latent ideological meanings with strong political and manipulative tendencies. As Curran has argued, entertainment media 'provide a way of mapping and interpreting society. This can promote a conservative, common-sense view . . . or it can offer a potentially more radical perspective in which social processes are explained primarily in structural terms' (Curran, 1991a:34).

Rethinking television as an agent of mobilising uneven distribution of meanings suggests that those clusters of polysemic meanings which do not serve an ideological function can be easily attracted to social powers and become ideological. True, the cultural indigenisation in Latin America and Asian countries seems to disprove the direct domination of the North Atlantic culture, but these indigenous cultures are deeply infused with consumption values and are often produced by institutionalised procedures controlled by large corporations (Sreberny-Mohammadi, 1991). The fostering of national solidarity is often manipulated by aggressive nation-states and appears as a project of political hegemony. Numerous recent studies have shown that the promotion and 'invention' of social memories and national traditions often serve manipulative political aims (Brett, 1996; Drummond *et al.*, 1993; Hobsbawm and Ranger, 1983; Samuel, 1989a, 1989b).

Indeed, television is providing a cultural space for revitalising and confirming cultural identities, but identity confirmation is always a dual process of inclusion and exclusion (Schlesinger, 1991). It involves drawing symbolic borders between cultural groups. The building up of in-group pride, which is itself a positive thing for a community, often accompanies the process of stigmatising outsider groups (Elias and Scotson, 1994; Hagendoorn, 1993; Jenkins, 1994). As Cohen (1985) observes, the public face of identity necessarily masks a variety of identities. When the television rituals consolidate certain public versions of identities and charge them with strong emotions of praise and blame, pride and disgrace, and in-group charisma and out-group contempt, the televisual rituals become simultaneously cultural and ideological; they are at once fostering cultural solidarity and suppressing cultural heterogeneity.

Television rituals create 'sacred symbols' which alleviate the human craving for meaning, order, and identity. In this sense television is performing a cultural function which should be positively valorised. However, the production of sacredness can also serve the institutionalisation of power and social control. It is true that television rituals can challenge hegemony; they provide the liminal spaces for the restructuring of existing hegemonic ideologies; they make the dominant orders vulnerable; they edit and re-edit collective memories (Dayan and Katz, 1992). Thus, rituals are instrumental in creating a kind of organic solidarity which is more responsive to social diversity. However, in the war of positions of hegemonic control, dominant powers gain cultural resources and gather popular support with relative ease. The resulting solidarity can thus be even more hegemonic than before. Television can perform the cultural role of fostering solidarity; but the solidarity is usually differentially organised among social groups in a complex society (Alexander, 1988; Collins, 1988). The differential organisation of solidarity can be 'cultural' to some but 'ideological' to others. As Schudson (1994) argues, integration and suppression go together, simultaneously. Hence, the conceptualisation of television as instrumental to the production of an ideological field allows us to account better for the dialectical interplay between television culture and television ideology.

As the empirical analyses of this project have demonstrated, television, as an agent of cultural integration, always involves some forms of ideological domination. Under the contingent factors of the 1970s, the ritual function of social integration was well performed by the new domestic medium of television. Television became a ritual space in which the Hong Kong audience regularly communed with the 'others' on the television screen. Television was able to objectify feelings of sociability and co-presence within a homogeneous television culture. Thus Hong Kong television was providing a cultural space for fostering and confirming a local cultural identity. However, identity confirmation was always a dual process involving the drawing of symbolic borders between Hongkongers and non-Hongkongers. Since the Hong Kong people of that time were themselves former mainland immigrants or their descendants, to enact a distinct Hong Kong identity different from mainland Chinese necessarily meant setting a boundary to exclude the mainlanders. The mainland newcomers in the 1970s became the most important outsider group against which the locals defined their own identity. It was used by the established group to confirm their cultural identity and to stigmatise the outsider groups.

The textual analyses in this book have shown that Hong Kong television in the 1990s is more polysemic. The polysemies reflect the contradictions within the shifts of political powers and also the populist demands of the people. By producing polysemic texts, television can highlight discourses that are acceptable and desirable to dominant powers and at the same time mix them with popular sentiments which are also welcomed by the general public. The polysemic nature of television opens up cultural space but at the same time it serves the ideological function of winning consent for the powerful. Television is thus an effective ideological apparatus in the 'war of positions' during a period of political transition. There is a strong connection between the concepts of polysemy and hegemony. The polysemic nature of televisual discourse can be seen as an articulation between dominant powers and textual discourses in the hegemonic struggles for cultural leadership. The cultural and the ideological are dialectically bound together.

Summary

In summary, the above reformulations can be conceptualised in the model of an inverted U, at the crown of which are television textual ideologies and polysemies regulated by a dominant ideological field. The two legs of televisual texts are embedded in the interactive habitats of the producers and receivers. Both of them are situated in similar structured social contexts which limit, but do not determine, their creative and interpretative ranges. The ideological field is diffused with asymmetrical meanings which have ideological as well as cultural consequences. Both producers and receivers have the relative autonomy for idiosyncratic creativity, but both are also subjected to the constraints of uneven distribution of resources, and thus power, of the larger social and historical contexts. At the production end, the habitat of textual production is further complicated by different organisational definers. At the reception end, the audience may be situated in different socio-cultural contexts (e.g. transnational televisions, cross-cultural reception, subculture settings, etc.) which contribute to different idiosyncratic readings. The break between production fields and reception fields results in many of the findings of producerly audience activities, but these findings should not be generalised to all other reception settings. If the habitats of producers and receivers are within a similar social context, audience interpretations will show fewer variations. But even if texts and interpretation are polysemic, the polysemy does not necessary lessen television's ideological effects, which are especially obvious in those stable emotive categorisations that are resistant to the polysemic flow of televisual meanings. The polysemy thesis has its cutting edge in the multiplicity of meanings (which to a great extent complements the reductionism of the dominant ideology thesis), but fails to account for the regulating effect of the dominant ideological field.

The third option (see table 8.1) attempts to integrate the two perspectives by emphasising the social contextualisation of the televisual texts. I am critical of the mosaic atomism and solipsism of some extreme forms of the polysemy thesis but at the same time remain an agnostic when faced with the ontological commitment of the grand narratives of the Marxist perspective. My integration is an attempt at a mid-range theory. In the above propositions, I argue that televisual texts exhibit various degrees of ideological closure but at the same time contain polysemic elements. Within this diffused ideological field, there are traceable forms of 'polysemies' and ideologies, which sustain and regulate a different pattern and range of asymmetrical meanings. The diffused but patterned ideological field is overdetermined by various kinds of contextual definers, which appear in the form of political, economic, and socio-historical influences; however, they are differentially absorbed and dispersed by different television organisations to create different forms of polysemies and ideologies. Television ideologies and polysemies are not idiosyncratic creations, but are a discursive articulation involving the interplay of human agency, institutional dispersion, and contextual overdetermination in concrete historical circumstances.

Guiding questions for interviews

About the programme

1 What is the programme about? What is the major theme?
2 Why do you choose to tell this particular story?
3 (Free discussion of programme contents)

Creative process and creative control

1 Who originates the programme idea?
2 Please describe the creative process.
3 Who is the most influential person in the process?
4 Have you turned down other alternative ideas? Why?
5 What is your role in the creative process?
6 Do you need to submit your story for approval?
7 What are the perceived criteria for approval?
8 Do you screen the creative input of your subordinate?
9 What are your criteria?
10 Have you met resistance of any kind during the programme development stage?
11 Can you/do you revise the script? How often?
12 Do you have any conflict with your superiors or subordinates?

Feedback system I: audience/ratings

1 Do you have target audience in mind?
2 Do you have any idea about their tastes and preferences?
3 Where do you get the hints of audience preferences?
4 Do perceived audience tastes affect your programme design?
5 Do you receive feedbacks from your audience?

6   Do you read rating reports? How do ratings affect you?
7   Do you think rating is a good measurement of success and/or programme quality?

Feedback system II: critical review/award

1   Do you care about reviews? How do they affect you?
2   Have you ever thought of getting awards?
3   (For TVB): How do complaints from TELA affect you? (For RTHK): How do the criticisms from pro-China press affect you?

Feedback system III: organisation

1   Does your superior evaluate your work? (How do you evaluate your subordinate?)
2   Do your colleagues talk about your programme?
3   What is the most rewarding thing for doing a 'good' or innovative programme? What are the organisational mechanisms of reward and punishment?

Aesthetic and organisational norms

1   How do you evaluate the programmes produced by you and your colleagues? What is your standard for a 'good' TV drama?
2   Please comment on the following often heard criteria for TV drama: realism, dramatic conflicts, social message, reflect society, entertaining.
3   Do you feel any expectation from your boss or from the organisation? Any do's and don'ts? Any programming policy you should follow?

Career path and ambition

1   In what year did you start working in television?
2   What was your first job in television?
3   How did you get started? Please describe your career path in the industry.
4   Why did you not join RTHK (or TVB)?
5   How do you like working in RTHK (TVB)?
6   What is the greatest satisfaction and/or frustration?
7   What do you want to achieve? Would you consider leaving the industry for other jobs? Making a movie, for example?

Perceived differences between RTHK and TVB

1 Have you watched RTHK (TVB) dramas recently?
2 What are the differences between RTHK and TVB dramas?
3 What do you think about RTHK (TVB) dramas?

Case control

1 Is *Below the Lion Rock* (*Great Times*) a typical RTHK (TVB) drama?
2 Is it a major/important production of RTHK (TVB)?
3 Please compare this specific production with other productions in the past in terms of creative autonomy and organisation constraints; any changes from the 1970s to the 1990s?
4 (For TVB's staff): Have you ever produced dramas in the format similar to RTHK's *Below the Lion Rock* (i.e. single-play series)? Are there differences in creative autonomy and constraint? (For RTHK's staff): Did you produce *Miracle of the Orient*? (i.e. RTHK only continued serial). Were there differences in creative autonomy and constraint?

Distribution of interviewees

TVB INTERVIEWEES

Production Manager of Drama Production
(1)

GT Production/Creative Team:

Creative Director
(2)

Executive Producer   Head Writer
(1)   (1)

On-line Producer
(3)

Production Assistant
(1)

Non GT Case

Executive Producer
(1)

There were six on-line producers and six production assistants in the TVB team; since they were not involved in the creative process and were only responsible for the execution, only three producers and two assistants were interviewed.

RTHK INTERVIEWEES

Head of RTHK General Programme Section
(1)

BLR Production/Creative Team

Executive Producer
(1)
Producer
(6)
Assistant Producer
(2)

Non BLR Case

Executive Producer
(1)

In the RTHK team, producers were responsible for originating ideas and developing the scripts, all six involved in BLR were interviewed. Only two out of the six assistant producers of BLR were interviewed for the same reason mentioned above.

On methodology: analysing televisual discourse

In this book, I want to locate and explain the patterns of uneven distribution of televisual meanings. Yet how to locate televisual meanings has become a very controversial issue in television studies. Recent emphasis on the instability of televisual meanings suggests that meanings of televisual texts, melodramatic texts in particular, are too polysemic to be fixed by textual analysts, and that the audience is the most significant site of meaning-making (e.g. Ang, 1994; Liebes and Katz, 1990). I shall argue in this appendix that it is more useful to think of audiences as the co-producers of meaning, that is to say that audiences are influenced potentially by textual cues in their understanding of televisual texts. Isolating either texts or audiences as the only focus of analysis confuses rather than clarifies the complex relation between text and audience in the processes of meaning production. Against the fashionable trend of destabilising the analysis of meaning, my attempt is to stabilise meaning of television by bridging text and audience with the concept of *televisual discourse*. In the first section, I try to contextualise televisual meanings against the detextualisation[1] of television studies by developing a three-dimensional concept of televisual discourse which relates text and its discursive contexts. The second section applies the three-dimensional concept in describing the melodramatic serial as 'thick' televisual discourse, which highlights the interpenetrative nature of the textual, discursive, and social dimensions of the genre. Although this appendix talks about the melodramatic serial in particular, the concepts and methods can also be applied to televisual discourse in general.

The detextualisation of television studies

One of the major contributions of recent audience studies is that they point out the problem which lies at the heart of some textual studies of the 1970s. Those studies, mostly of a structuralist kind, worked on film and television texts alone, employed sophisticated textual methods, and aimed at digging out the true meaning of texts. Against this research context, audience studies have gathered extensive empirical evidence that audiences prefer their own idiosyncratic readings, which are at times very different from those of the textual analysts; these findings lead some researchers to a conclusion that the only authentic and legitimate moments of textual meanings are those during reception.

The recent proliferation of audience studies, which often presume the above argument, has great value in specific areas. The most valuable theoretical advance is the recognition of the inadequacy of previous textual models in explaining the complexity of televisual textuality. Also, ethnographic studies in audience reception are fruitful in enhancing our understanding of the actual use of media in everyday life (e.g. Lull, 1990; Silverstone, 1994). However, problems arise when more and more research concentrates solely on the decoding moments and refrains from carrying out any serious textual analysis. Claims that assert that 'to seek the text itself is to chase a chimera' and that 'there is no text outside reading' (e.g. Bennett and Woollacott, 1987) have an element of truth but risk dissolving the necessary analytic categories of texts and audiences. Text–audience relations are extremely complex; isolating the text for investigation is indeed like chasing a chimera. Yet the new dogmatism of isolating audience reception as the exclusive site for meaning-making is, in like manner, erroneous. The complexity of text–audience relations does not mean that collapsing the two can clean up the mess. Worse, when audience activities are said to have complete autonomy, it comes close to saying that the now institutionalised and all-encompassing television textual system of our age is of little consequence in regulating the distribution of cultural meanings.

The detextualisation of recent television studies has something to do with the problematic status of televisual texts. Robert Allen asks,

> What is the critic seeking in analysing television at all? The meaning of a particular televisual text? The preferred meanings of the texts? The possible meanings of the text? The textual structures that may be responsible for meaning production? [This constellation of questions] . . . hovers over contemporary media studies like a dense fog that refuses to evaporate.
>
> (Allen, 1993:51)

In an interview, Justin Lewis asked Stuart Hall why two people, both very skilled in textual analysis, can conclude from the same text a different interpretation and both with sophisticated justifications (Cruz and Lewis, 1994). This questions Hall's encoding/decoding model, which implicitly assumes that a preferred reading can be achieved by certain 'appropriate' methods. Hall recognises the limitations of textual analysts, saying that the analysts are always 'inside meaning', and thus incapable of achieving an absolutely objectified and consistent reading:

> [I]f you have a preferred reading, you already prestructure the decoding. [Nevertheless] if you don't have a preferred reading . . . you're in a commitment that text can meaning anything. . . . So you have to risk trying to read as much as you can, as neutrally as you can . . .
>
> (Hall quoted in Cruz and Lewis, 1994:266–67)

It seems that Hall is just saying that the 'anything goes' position is much more difficult to hold than the position that texts have preferred readings. However, difficult questions remain unanswered: How can an analyst approach the preferred reading? Where are the preferring moments? Are the preferred meanings already inscribed in the text or are they situated within the reading contexts? Do the 'indicators' within the texts prefer one set of meanings over the others? How can those indicators be found? By some 'correct' textual methods or can they be fixed at all? Do different analysts have different preferences? Do audience and the analysts prefer similar readings? Is the preferring of the decoding side similar to the preferring of the encoding side?

These questions all revolve around the problematic status of the text and the speculative status of textual methods. This book is on television culture and ideologies. Cases of textual analysis, using different kinds of textual methods, are cited as evidence by scholars arguing both for and against the existence of dominant television ideologies. Obviously, a study of television ideologies and culture cannot bypass the problems of texts and methods.

Contextualising televisual meanings

One way of solving the problem is by shifting the discussion away from textual analysis towards audience reception studies. But as argued above, if used as an escape route, audience studies will only detextualise the complex textual systems of modern television and fail to provide an understanding of the relation between text and audience. By doing audience research alone, there would be little advance in dealing with the problematic status of the texts other than asserting, time and again, the indeterminacy of the decoding process. Audience readings are notoriously difficult to classify along the lines of social classes or other sociological categories (Morley, 1980). If the discursive practice of the audience is to be understood in any meaningful pattern, it should be analysed in reference to the texts and to the wider context of social practices (see Fairclough, 1992:62–100, 1995; Thompson, 1990: 272–73).

Against the detextualisation of recent television studies, this book is deliberately textual in its orientation. I contend that texts remain one of the most researchable and significant empirical data sources for television studies, especially in the present conjuncture where television studies has lost its anchorage in televisual textuality. Textual analysis plays a central role in my analysis, not as a substitute for the analysis of audience activity, but as a way of alerting us to its multi-dimensionality. Indeed, audience responses cannot be read off directly from the texts, but equally, as Murdock argues, 'an analysis that operates with an underdeveloped view of texts is bound to over-simplify the complexity of potential reactions' (Murdock, 1989b:237). The textually oriented analysis of this book is grounded in all the other three levels of analysis, namely the audience, the textual production processes, and the wider socio-cultural contexts, but I strategically centred on the text as a reference point from which the other three levels of analysis are drawn as wider contextual circles. Instead of arguing for a polysemy thesis by giving yet another account of audience idiosyncratic activities, I am going to spend more time finding those relatively stable meaning patterns that persist in the polysemic texts and within the audience communities. Instead of claiming the autonomy of audience inter-pretation freed from the constraints of television institutions, I am trying to re-establish the link(s) between the text and its production contexts. I have argued previously that the ideological power of television lies precisely in its ability to promote, in specific areas, certain stable categories, myths, and narratives in the polysemic flow of televisual meanings. The more stable these categories are, the more powerful the ideological influences are. It is revealing to study the various features of the texts, especially those interpretative frameworks and emotionally loaded categories, to see how stable they are for the udience, and how they are circulated in the wider socio-cultural world. The stability and change of textual, cultural, and ideological patterns can also be studied by comparing the text produced by different television organisations in different historical periods. The search for these stable and publicly recognisable patterns is in itself significant, no matter how polysemic the meanings that derived from them are.

Different approaches of textual analysis presuppose different concepts of texts (Rosengren, 1981). Different theories of television textuality make different kinds of textual features visible and analysable.[2] In this book, I draw mostly from discourse theory[3] in my analyses. My research questions concern the relation of cultural identities and television in Hong Kong. These research questions require a textual theory which is context-sensitive. The shifting boundaries of the Hong Kong identity intertwine with the socio-historical contexts in a complicated way. As discussed below, discourse theory has the strength to foreground the socially constructive properties of the melodramatic texts and is thus an appropriate theoretical tool for the present project.

Televisual discourse

Discourse is a widely used term in recent academic writings. There are definitions which are formulated from a wide range of theoretical perspectives.[4] I shall not go into the differentiation of different kinds of discourse theories and will only highlight the context-sensitive aspects in some of the recent discussions in the field. Among the variety of arguments, there is a general tendency to see discourse as bringing together text and its immediate contexts (e.g. Graddol and Boyd-Barrett, 1994; van Dijk, 1977). Against the structuralist's emphasis on abstract textual system, discourse relocates the process of signification into particular historical, social, and political conditions (Fiske, 1994). Discourse originates from social institutions, and is directed to other social agents. It regulates meanings that are sensitive to the power structure in the society. As a mode of address, it shapes, defines, circumscribes, and constitutes what can be, or is allowed to be said and understood about a certain area of social life (Foucault, 1972, 1981). It closes off alternative representations. In short, it interpellates (Althusser, 1971). In this sense, discourse is ideological. It can be perceived as a unified and structured 'address' equivalent to a micro unit of ideology.

Conceptualising televisual text as discourse can thus save textual studies from the crippling disabilities of previous Saussurian/structuralist models which isolate text as a self-sufficient site of textual analysis. In order better to account for the social and interactive aspects of televisual text, I have developed a three-dimensional conception of televisual discourse which is adapted from Fairclough's social theory of discourse (Fairclough, 1992:62–100).[5] As shown in figure A3.1 in this conception,

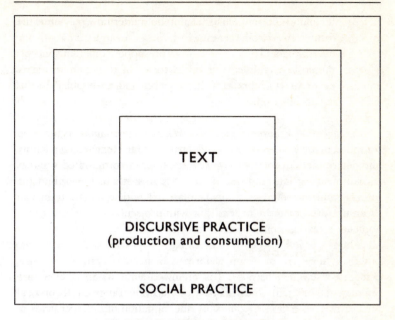

SOCIO-CULTURAL CONTEXT

Figure A3.1 Three-dimensional conception of televisual discourse

television is not seen as 'text', but as *discursive formation*, which is simulta-neously a piece of text, instances of discursive practice (including production and consumption), and instances of social practice.

The 'text' dimension of televisual discourse attends to the material features, or the materiality of discourse (Graddol, 1994). Discourse finds its expression and realisation in text by regulating a certain range of textual features. Despite all the irregularities, televisual texts rely on shared semiotic resources, and speak of common social experiences; they have recognisable forms, formats, and generic features that are *shared and anticipated* by the audiences. To say that these textual cues do not have any suggestive effects is as ridiculous as saying that text can determine interpretation. In this book, I am looking for four main elements within the texts:[6]

1 classificatory systems and identity categories which define affinities and antagonisms;
2 labels, images, stigmas, and stereotypes, which concretise and anchor key identity divisions;

3   textual structures such as relation between characters, narrative forms, emotional scenes which propose argumentation and reasoning; and

4   the positive and negative valorisations[7] of all the above textual elements which praise or denounce, cherish or despise the social agents involved.

The dimension of discursive practices stresses the production and consumption of texts. Discursive practices permeate the text as a constitutive and determinative part; they regulate and mobilise textual features; they invoke meaning into and out of the texts. For instance, words, signs, images, and stereotypes in the text are all socially motivated: their meanings are not only 'in text' but within discursive practices of the audience's textual consumption. Also, the meanings activated by the audiences are influenced by past discursive practices. As Fairclough observes, 'texts are made up of forms which past discursive practice, condensed into conventions, has endowed with meaning potential' (Fairclough, 1992:75). The discursive practices of televisual discourse are further mediated and modified by the organisational imperatives of television institutions. The different ways in which texts are produced affect the availability of certain types of discourse (Barker, D., 1994). The stress on discursive practices of production and consumption as constitutive parts of television discourse point to the fact that television is not just text, it 'converses' with the audience (Allen, 1993) in an 'institutionalised manner' (Thompson, 1990).

The social practice dimension attends more to the socio-structural circumstances of the discursive event. The social practice dimension is also constitutive and constructive to televisual discourse. In Hodge and Kress's (1988) words, 'context is meaning'. It provides the social conditions from which discursive practices and the textual dimension of discourse are grounded. Thus discourses always emerge at particular points in time and have traceable histories (Murdock, 1989a, 1989b). The tricky bit is that, analytically, the social practice dimension has a fuzzy edge which messes with the wider socio-cultural environment. The two are closely connected but should not be reduced to each other.[8] Television discourse can draw into its text the social practices of its socio-historical location; it can also project into the social practices its textual categories, images, reasoning, and valorisations. It can be an instrument of social construction (Lincoln, 1989), regulating knowledge, enacting social relations, and establishing identities (Fairclough, 1992, 1995). It is structured and structuring, for it is defined by its social practices and affects them in turn. Televisual discourse and its socio-historical location contaminate each other. This is what Hartley (1992) calls the 'dirtiness', and also the power, of television.

In this book, I am asking how television plays the role of identity construction and maintenance. The three-dimensional conception of television discourse maximises the sensitivity of the analysis to the possible interaction between text and context. The social practice dimension highlights those socio-historical definers which are constantly infiltrating into the text and the discursive practices of production and consumption. The conception also opens up the analytical possibility of exploring how television discourse can consolidate social practices.

However, this text–context interaction does not mean that the texts are totally absorbed into the context. This kind of reduction of the textual into the social is evident in Foucault's archaeological (1972) and genealogical works (1979, 1981). Foucault's main contribution to discourse analysis resides in his emphasis on the constitutive nature of discourse in social reality (in his archaeological work)[9] and the emphasis of power struggle in and over discourse (in his genealogical work).[10] Nevertheless, Foucault's discourse analyses do not involve the actual analysis of texts (e.g. conversations or written documents within and around the social institutions that he is analysing). In my textually oriented approach, text is the material expression of discourse. It is considered as holding the central position in discourse analysis.

The above is a conceptualisation of the general nature of televisual discourse. Now I shall move on to the more specific generic feature of the kind of text I am going to analyse – the melodramatic serial.

The melodramatic serial in Hong Kong

I use the term 'melodramatic serial' for the Hong Kong prime-time serial drama to distinguish it from soap operas[11] in Western countries. The genre shares many characteristics with Anglo-American *prime-time serials* in general and is especially similar to Latin American *telenovelas*.[12] Since the launch of television in 1967, the television melodramatic serial has been the most popular genre in Hong Kong.[13] In the 1970s, most melodramatic serials consisted of 40 to 100 episodes and were broadcast on prime-time television every weekday. Since the mid-1980s, the number of episodes per serial went down to 40, sometimes 20, but serials still occupied a large proportion of the prime-time hours.[14] These prime-time melodramatic serials were also rerun during the daytime in Hong Kong and were exported to Chinese and Asian communities all over the world. They attracted more local audiences than imported Western drama series and serials (Chan and Lee, 1992). It is interesting to note that a similar situation occurs in Mexico and Brazil where *telenovelas* are successful domestically and overseas (Rogers and Antola, 1985).[15]

Apart from the prominence of melodramatic serials in the Hong Kong television culture, another justification for choosing the genre lies in the fact that local opinions attribute the formation of a Hong Kong identity partly to the cultivation of these melodramatic serials (e.g. Chan, K. C., 1990, 1991; Choi, 1990b). Some Latin American researchers suggest a similar relation between the popularity of *telenovelas* and the construction of indigenous identities. *Telenovelas* are structured by and structure the modernisation and 'nationalisation' processes of various Latin American cultures (Lopes, 1995; Martin-Barbero, 1995). There is large-scale research on this subject in Latin America, but none in Hong Kong so far. The compressed process of modernisation (compared to the West) and the fast-paced social change in Latin American and Asian countries may be a reason why television serial dramas in these areas seem to be closely connected to the solidifying and fostering of new indigenous identities.

As Kress argues, 'at any given point in history and in any given social group, certain genres are available for expression of specific discourse' (1985:28). In the post-war decades, the melodramatic serials in Hong Kong played an important role in the formation and maintenance of the local cultural identities. In the following, I shall paint the most prominent textual feature preferred by the genre of melodramatic serials, with special attention given to the particularities in the case of Hong Kong.

Soap opera research

Whether called soap operas, *telenovelas*, or melodramatic serials, television serials together constitute 'one of the most popular and resilient forms of storytelling ever devised' (Allen, 1995:1). The genre has undergone a global reach in recent years.[16] Thorburn has now been proven correct when he noted, 20 years ago, that 'television melodrama has been our culture's most characteristic aesthetic form, and one of its most complex and serious forms as well, for at least the past decade and probably longer' (Thorburn, 1976:78). In 1947, James Thurber described 'soapland' as 'a country too vast and complicated that the lone explorer could not possibly hope to do it full justice.' A few decades later, the soap terrain is more vast than Thurber could have imagined (in Allen,

1985:3). The quantity of the programmes, the variety of the sub-genre (see Self, 1984), the cultural prejudices against the genre (Derry, 1985), and the unavailability of tapes for analysis, all make soap opera a difficult subject for critics and researchers. Nevertheless, more attempts have been made to understand soaps in recent years. Related studies are numerous. Here I shall only briefly highlight the major trends (see Frey-Vor, 1990a, 1990b: Mazziotti, 1993 for more comprehensive surveys). Early research on soaps was conducted within the empirical sociological traditions which stress content analysis of the soap opera world in comparison with the real world (e.g. Cassata and Skill, 1983). These studies are said to have shared the view that soap operas are somewhat alienating and manipulatory (Allen, 1985). Yet some of these studies attend to the sociology of soap opera production (e.g. Cantor, 1971; Cantor and Pingree, 1983) and do not show an explicit or implicit 'ideology of mass society' (Swingewood, 1977). The sociological tradition has continued until the present day in production studies (Buxton, 1994; Tulloch and Moran, 1986) and content studies (e.g. Rothmen *et al.*, 1992). In the 1980s, Allen (1985) provided one of the first comprehensive accounts of soap opera's textual system, combining historical, structuralist, and semiotic analysis. Allen's study was followed by more historical studies that trace soap operas back to the serial melodramas in newspapers and magazines, to the radio soaps, and the generic connection with the folklore and mythic narratives (e.g. Hagedorn,1995; Liebes and Katz, 1988; Sheehan, 1987; Tulloch, 1990; Williams, 1992). Soaps, being considered as a feminine genre, attract some researchers to analyse the relation between this genre and feminism (e.g. Brown, 1994; Brunsdon, 1995). Also, the recent proliferation of ethnographic audience studies has not left soap operas aside (e.g. Gillespie, 1995; Seiter *et al.*, 1989). Among all these trends and emphases, perhaps the most relevant to this project is the research on Latin America *telenovelas*; these studies, only recently known to researchers outside Latin American, stress the national variations of *telenovelas* and their connection with national culture and development (Martin-Barbero, 1993). The generic character of the *telenovela* and its socio-cultural content shows great similarity to the melodramatic serials in Hong Kong.

This very brief account is enough to demonstrate the vast and complicated field of television drama programmes. I shall sketch below their most significant generic characteristics through the lens of the three-fold conception of television discourse outlined in the beginning of this appendix.

Generic features

There are some arguments about the generic differences within the genre of soap. For instance, there are some researchers (e.g. Cantor and Pingree, 1983) who differentiate daytime soap from prime-time serial in terms of gender orientation (matriarchal daytime soap vs. patriarchal prime-time serial) and spatial structure (indoor vs. outdoor). There is also differentiation between mainstream dramas, 'quality television' (like the famous MTM style as described in Feuer, 1987), and 'serious' dramas (such as those selected as Britain's 'best' in Brandt, 1991; 1993). Despite all these internal variations, there is a rough consensus on the general textual features of the programmes grouped under the category of the melodramatic serial. The genre is said to exhibit the features of historicity, multiplicity, intimacy, and character centricity. I shall briefly discuss these in turn.

Historicity

The term 'serial' draws our attention to the textual feature of 'seriality', which is described by Allen (1995) as an important defining feature of the serial genre. Allen characterises serialisation as 'the organisation of narrative and narration around the enforced and regular suspension of both textual display and reading activity'; it 'produces a very different mode of reader engagement and reader pleasure than we experience with non-serials' (ibid.: 17). Serial has a unique narrative structure of movement and stasis (Geraghty, 1981). This makes the melodramatic serial resistant to many types of narrative textual analysis which presume narrative closure (Allen, 1983). Narrative textual analysis assumes that one basic narrative operation is the disruption of an initial equilibrium by posing the enigma/s in the beginning, solving the enigma/s in the middle, bringing the text to resolution, and restoring a new equilibrium at the end. The serial format, however, creates large and small enigmas not only in the beginning; new problems, new characters, new stories are initiated in the extended middle; resolution is delayed to an extent that the narrative is no longer propelled by the expectation of the ending.

Due to its extended middle, punctuated by narrative movement and stasis, a serial acquires a historical sense of time (Geraghty, 1981, 1991). It does not construct the present in terms of a future story resolution. The present is structured as a chronicle, or a diary within the narrative and between the episodes. The audience senses the passage of time within the serial stories and also the historical time outside the fictional world.

Hence, the serial format opens up the possibilities of blending two histories – one within the fictional world, one within the audience's everyday world. It provides an ongoing narrative in which time lapses between episodes and is woven into the narratives. As Ang argues, these spaces allow 'unchronicled growth' which 'construct the feeling that lives of characters go on during our absence' (Ang, 1985:52). Melodramatic serials follow the unfolding life of a community in a way that parallels the lives of the audience (Livingstone, 1990; Lozano and Sanghal, 1993).

The effect of seriality is even more intensive in the case of the Hong Kong melodramatic serials since they are broadcast daily, and like the Latin American *telenovelas*, they emphasise the romanticised upward mobility very much in line with the impulsive process of modernisation in real life. However, it should be noted that unlike the open serial, Hong Kong melodramatic serials are designed to end; though there is also an extended middle, the narrative carries teleological thrust. This particularity does not lessen the serial's ability to blend the fictional and the everyday. In fact, it heightens the emotional engagement of the audiences, especially towards the heavily promoted ending episodes.

Multiplicity

The seriality of a melodramatic serial creates many gaps and interruptions. As a result, multiple plots and multiple characters have to be deployed to propel the movement of the narrative. As early as 1976, Thorburn already pointed out the multiplicity principle of television melodrama: it is 'a principle of plotting or organisation whereby a particular drama will draw not once or twice but many times upon the immense store of stories and situations created by the genre's brief but crowded history' (Thorburn, 1976: 85). Serials have the ability to draw on the plots and stories of other television dramas to form a complicated narrative; 'two or three stories are woven together and presented to the audience over a number of episodes' (Geraghty, 1981:11). Classic narratives follow a linear cause-and-effect sequence, while the serial narrative complicates the linearity by displaying a parallel, multiple, and messy flow (Oltean, 1993). This disordered multiplicity allows the audience to identify with a number of characters and engage in different storylines.

The multiplicity principle can also operate in an intertextual mix of generic conventions. A melodramatic serial combines various generic traditions to form an excessive and overcoded textual system (Allen, 1983; Feuer, 1987). It draws on the genre of *light entertainment* which works on the 'aesthetics of escape' (Dyer, 1973). It also draws on the genre of *melodrama* which is marked by excessive and explosive emotional and moral issues (Brooks, 1976). It also draws on the genre of *realism* which provides easy reading and hides discourses (Fiske, 1987). The multiplicity of the melodramatic serial involves a range of aesthetic elements and offers a mix of generic conventions (Jordon, 1981). 'With a single episode, soaps can move from one set of conventions to another and back again and within an evening's viewing the soaps offer a surprisingly wide range of aesthetic experiences within a common narrative organisation' (Geraghty, 1991:35–36). Against this multiplicity, Gripsrud (1995) cautions us not to overrate the polysemic possibilities. The multiple storylines, unexpected twists, and hybridised conventions are largely contained within paradigmatic stability and predictable affective/emotional rides of harmony and conflict, all working together to regulate the show's receptions and its social meanings.

Intimacy

Despite its diffused and multiple narrative structure, the melodramatic serial has an extraordinary ability to involve the audience in an intimate and personal way. This powerful sense of intimacy derives from at least two textual sources. First, from the affective features of the melodramatic text. The melodramatic serial draws heavily on the conventions of the melodramatic novel. Unlike the episodic series and the situation comedy, the melodramatic serial shares with the melodrama genre the 'indulgence of strong emotionalism; moral polarisation and schismatisation; extreme states of being, situation, action; overt villainy, persecution of the good, the final reward of virtue; inflated and extravagant expression; dark plotting, suspense, breathtaking periphery' (Brooks, 1976:11–12). The convention of emotionalism becomes an 'instrument of seeing'; it 'enables' the encounter of deeply disturbing materials within the familiar and well-contained world of the melodramatic serial. The serial acts as 'a forum or arena in which traditional ways of feeling and thinking are brought into continuous, strained relation with powerful intuitions of changes and contingency' (Thorburn, 1976:80). I shall argue that the Hong Kong melodramatic serial provides a 'safe' place for the intimate and deeply troubling sentiments in the discrimination of Chinese immigrants in Hong Kong, and later, the forced integration between the mainland and Hong Kong Chinese.

Second, a sense of intimacy is also reinforced by the diminishing space and increasing scale of television's visual characteristic. The economics of serial production in Hong Kong are characterised by a limited budget and a high daily consumption rate. This limits the space represented. Although the prime-time serial in Hong Kong is not as confined to the world of interiors as in the American daytime soap, there is still a financial barrier imposed on the studio/field production ratio. Despite occasional exotic attractions, the interior/domestic is the dominant mode. Together with the factor of the restricted television screen, the world of melodramatic serials is primary represented 'spatially through the close-up and the two shot, a strategy that has the effect of focusing viewer attention almost exclusively on facial expression and figure relationship, respectively' (Allen, 1985:66). The limited space and increasing visual scale tend to simplify the genre's visual language, making it allegorical, intimate, and familiar. These generic restrictions also create an 'ideological problematic' (Brunsdon, 1983): the melodramatic serial 'emphasise[s] dialogue, continuous interpersonal conflicts, family struggles and a domestic stage that is the centre of all battles' (Lozano and Singhal, 1993:117), thus displacing the public sphere with the private and personal sphere. Anything that cannot be seen as personally motivated is omitted. Even if external powers and socio-structural problems are not omitted, they are usually expressed and solved in intimate, personal, and domestic terms (Jhally and Lewis, 1992). In the cultural context of Hong Kong, this ideological problematic is further complicated by Confucian ethics, which are constituted almost entirely as a code of regulating hierarchical social and political relations within and beyond the family (Browne, 1994). The familial institution represented within the melodramatic text is relatively easy to transpose to the realm of social practices via the discursive practice of textual consumption. Compared with Western viewers, Chinese viewers are more inclined to read into the domestics of the social hierarchy.

Character centricity

The multiplicity and historicity of the melodramatic serial defuse the ability of its plot devices (such as cliff-hangers) to attract the viewers. Instead, a melodramatic serial attracts audiences through its characters. The genre is character-driven (Williams, 1992). It captures the identification of its viewers through a large community of interrelated characters. The viewer's pleasure comes more from knowing the characters than from expecting the resolutions. As Thorburn observes, 'far more decisively than the movie-actor, the television-actor creates and controls the meaning of what is seen on the screen' (Thorburn, 1976:80). The reduced space and enlarged visual of the television mean that the actor's performance, especially facial expression, is essential to bring out the meanings of the drama. A serial often uses more characters than are 'necessary' in order to give variety, fill up gaps, and perform a multiplicity of narrative functions. Given the number of characters and the need for a quick recognition for casual viewers, characterisation has to be swift and sharp: 'an immediate sense of what a character is and what role he or she is likely to play has to be given quickly, using such elements as clothes and voice' (Geraghty, 1981:19), or even by characters' names (Sumser, 1992).

Owing to this requirement for 'recognisability' and because of the intimacy of television, characters often fuse with actors. Each actor, when playing the role through the serial's chronological time, cannot help but bring to the performance some of his or her own actual personality (Derry, 1985). The actors, characters, and viewers are also fused in a complicated way through gossip, interviews, and promotional activities. In opposition to the prejudice that soap operas are artistically inferior, the characters in soap operas are surprisingly three-dimensional: they 'embody (literally) discourse' (Fiske, 1987). As a result, character types can be a form of identity classification and social control. Hence, comparing characters, their interrelations, and their real-life parallels is one of the keys to understanding the televisual discourse of the melodramatic serial.

These generic particularities of historicity, multiplicity, intimacy, and character centricity converge to confer an extraordinary strength to the genre of melodramatic serials in engaging the audience and incorporating the socio-cultural contexts. The melodramatic serial easily involves the discursive practices of the audience on the basis of real-life parallelism. The reader can identify with multiple characters, insert himself or herself into the gaps of the text, filling them up – but only in part – according to his or her own frame of reference. 'The structuring gaps of the text, then, mark the point of the intersection between the horizon represented within the text and the horizon brought to the text by the reader' (Allen, 1985:79).

Seen through the lens of the three-dimensional conception of discourse outlined above, the melodramatic discourse is 'thick' in the sense that the text, the discursive practices, and social practices interpenetrate each other in a much more intensive and complicated manner than in other forms of televisual and cinematic discourses. It is this 'thickness' that blends together the melodramatic serial and its socio-cultural contexts in the formation and maintenance of the cultural identity of Hong Kong.

The methodological implication is the need for a multi-dimensional and contextual approach to the analysis of televisual meanings. The melodramatic serial is deeply embedded in the social and discursive contexts in which the text is produced and consumed. The three dimensions of televisual discourse each have their distinct logic which cannot be determined by, or dissolved into one another, yet they are tied together in such a complicated dynamic that concentrating on each of the individual instances risks distorting the whole meaning-making process. A contextual approach to the study of the thick televisual discourse of melodramatic serial requires the analyst to combine textual, reception, organisational, and social analysis. This kind of context-sensitive analysis can modulate the pendulum swing between extreme forms of textual determinism and unrestrained relativism which have been common in media research for the past few decades. Contextualising televisual meanings within the specificity of textual, discursive, and social dimensions implies the relativisation of the determinacy in grand media theories, and, at the same time, fixing the complex yet patterned meanings in their immediate contexts and saving reception analysis from the solipsism of audience idiosyncrasy.

Notes

1 Identity, culture, and the media

1 Researchers interested in television have long been investigating the behavioural and attitudinal effects of television content such as sex, violence, and persuasive messages. But it was not until the 1980s that more researchers started to study television as cultural and discursive texts (see Barker and Timberg, 1992, for a review). This departure from effects research, to a critical and interpretative perspective, is loosely categorised as television studies, which is still a field without well-agreed boundaries (Allen, 1992; Burns and Thompson, 1989; Hartley, 1992).

2 Detextualisation refers to the reduction of the complex textual system of television to the audience's interpretative activities alone (Allen, 1993).

3 See, for example, the emotionally charged exchange between those affiliated with cultural studies and political economy, involving N. Garnham, L. Grossberg, J. Carey, and G. Murdock (in *Critical Studies in Mass Communication*, 1995, vol. 12: 60–100). Also see Ferguson and Golding, 1997.

4 Crowley and Mitchell's words (1994).

5 Some contest this division as too simplistic (see Carey, 1995; Garnham, 1995).

6 Within the tradition which has commonly been called political economy, Murdock and Garnham differ significantly, in that the latter rejects the theory of articulation for the reason of indeterminacy, while the former is willing to explore the uncertainties of cultural articulations. Murdock (1995, 1997) thinks that research in political economy does not constitute a school or a paradigm. On the other hand, the tradition of cultural studies is entertaining even more diverse positions and arguments. Grossberg (1995) claims that cultural studies is 'both narrower and broader' than political economists assume. Reducing political economy and cultural studies into two distinct paradigms is doomed to be controversial.

7 See Schlesinger, 1990; Lodziak, 1986, for a review.

8 In Comstock's (1989) description, the penetration graph of television resembles a strike of lightning.

9 For example the case of Brazil, as described in Martin-Barbero, 1993.

10 For example the case of Canada, as described in Collins, 1990.

11 Larrain (1994) accurately points out that historicist theories that claim total contingency are ideological and are grand theories in themselves.

2 Mediating Hong Kong identity (I): De-sinicisation

1 Scholars generally agree that nations and nationalism are formed under the historical contingencies of industrialisation, the institutionalisation of education, the imperative of capitalism for collective operation on a national level, and the sense of nationhood reinforced during the imperialistic expansion and the encounter with alien culture.

2 The non-interventionist and *laissez-faire* policy in the colonial years contributed to the 'minimal integrated media-polity system' in Hong Kong. See Kuan and Lau, 1988.

3 For example Brazil, as described in Martin-Barbero, 1993.

4 For example Canada, as described in Collins, 1990.

5 In 1898, about 90 per cent of the colony was leased to Britain for a 99-year term. Then Britain had to return a large part of the colony to China on the expiration date of 30 June 1997. Also see note 6.

6 In 1842, the island of Hong Kong was ceded to Britain by China under the Treaty of Nanking. Other parts of the territory were either ceded or leased to Britain in subsequent treaties: In 1860, Kowloon peninsula was ceded to Britain by the First Convention of Peking. The New Territory (the country land north of Kowloon) was acquired by the British under a 99-year lease in 1898. The lease ran out on 1 July 1997. Now Hong Kong is a city state of just over 1,000 square kilometres on the southern coast of China. It has a population of 6 million, 98 per cent of whom are ethnic Chinese.

7 According to the 1931 Census there was then a population of 849,751.

8 In the first six months of 1950, more than 700,000 refugees poured into Hong Kong from the mainland.

9 The population had risen from 1,550,000 in 1946 to 2,614,600 in 1956, and then to 3,708,920 in 1966. Sources: Hong Kong Census and Statistics Department. Also see Luk, 1995.

10 The Anglicised Hong Kong culture can be illustratively seen in its commercial design (see Turner, 1988) and even in the naming of streets and places (see Liang Tao, 1992).

11 In October 1994, a large-scale conference was organised in Peking to celebrate the 2,545th birthday of Confucius. The celebration received unprecedented support from the communist government which had denounced Confucianism for many years after seizing power.

12 See Chai, S. 'Patriotism and civilisation', *The Hong Kong Economic Journal*, 3 Oct. 1994 (in Chinese).

13 China has been providing water and agricultural products for the colony where natural resources are very limited.

14 See the collection of essays of that period in Lo, 1983.

15 Most people in Hong Kong speak Cantonese, a southern dialect very different from the official Mandarin language.

16 Public discussion of television's identity-conferring ability rarely touches on the material basis for cultural identity.

17 See Sweeting (1992) for a review of Hong Kong education and its

relationship with the historical processes of colonisation, industrialisation, bureaucratisation, localisation, and democratisation.

18 In 1977, 31,000 arrived in Hong Kong legally or illegally; in 1978, the figure had risen to 95,000; in 1979, to 178,000. See Siu, 1986; Lingnan Colllege, 1985.

19 See CUHK Student Union, 1982; HKU Student Union, 1980.

20 TVB and ATV both have two channels, one Cantonese and one English.

21 Television households increased from 12.3 per cent of the population in 1967 to 90 per cent in 1977. The penetration reached 98 per cent in the 1980s.

22 Annual production dropped from 104 films in 1967 to one in 1971, then none in 1972 (Choi, 1990b).

23 Television Advisory Board (1974), *The Third Report on the Progress of Television in Hong Kong*, January 1973.

24 Chaney (1986) discerns that television can transform occasional civic rituals to powerful media events; and that television, as a medium, itself has the ritual-like character of a media event in its daily broadcast. To these observations, I would add that, in the heyday of Hong Kong television, the magic of the medium was in elevating the ritual-like character of the routine broadcast to the status of media event. The feeling of co-presence and mutuality was so overpowering as temporarily to suspend the daily activities of the people of Hong Kong (see Dayan and Katz, 1992). The ritual characteristics of the medium are lessened as the medium loses its novelty.

25 See Gripsrud (1995) for an interesting high culture vs. low culture debate in the reception of *Dynasty* in Norway. This high vs. low debate of television culture is not prominent in Hong Kong.

26 Membership categorisation device is an analytical tool for conversational analysis originated by Harvey Sacks (1992a, 1992b) and later adopted by David Silverman (1993a).

27 I shall come back to this dual process in chapter 4.

28 Hong Kong television in the 1970s didn't have strong political and economic constraints imposed on television producers, owing to reason discussed below. But I shall demonstrate, by a case study in chapter 4, that the 'autonomous' television culture could still serve ideological functions.

29 See the previous annual *Departmental Reports of Broadcasting*, published by the Hong Kong Government. The last report was published in 1976.

30 The role of RTHK will be discussed in more detail in chapter 7.

31 Television's percentage share of all media advertising revenue:

	1972	1974	1976	1978
Share (%)	34	41	54	59

Source: Chan, J. M., and Lee, P. S. N., 1991

32 Lee, S. L., 'TVB 25th Anniversary,' *Hong Kong Economic Journal*, 19 Nov. 1991 (in Chinese).

33 Described to the author in an interview by television veteran Ng Ho, who was formerly a programme planner and is now a programming consultant for TVB (see Ma, 1992).

34 The shutdown was due to overspending and internal management problems. After the incident, most believe that advertising revenue, generated from the small population size of Hong Kong, was incapable of sustaining three commercial broadcast television stations.

35 Seminar on 'The Impact of the Television Industry in Cantonese Films', organised by the RTHK in 1983.

36 See Chan, J. M., 1997; 1996; Chan and Ma, 1996, for the discussion on internationalisation and globalisation of Asian television.

3 Mediating Hong Kong identity (II): Re-sinicisation

1 TVB's only rival ATV had not been able to impose any real threat to TVB all through the 1980s. (ATV, formerly RTV, was renamed ATV in 1982 when the ownership of the station changed hands.)

2 Within the 10-year-period 1982–1991, TVB annual prime-time weekday ratings dropped from 45 points to 31 points (each point equals 1 per cent of all potential viewers). The combined ratings of TVB and ATV dropped 25 per cent. Sources: Media Index, SRG; Chan, K. C., 1990.

3 See Ma (1992) for a comprehensive review.

4 See *TVB Annual Reports*, HK:TVB.

5 Satellite television service was launched in 1991 by STAR. The Hong Kong-based station was acquired by Rupert Murdoch. STAR provides pro-grammes for a pan-Asian audience and receives impressive ratings in India, Taiwan, and China. STAR achieved quick penetration in Hong Kong in terms of the number of households installed for satellite reception, but actual audience share is below 5 per cent (as of 1994). The low viewership is largely due to the licence restriction on STAR to air Cantonese programmes. STAR programmes are now in English and Chinese (Mandarin).

6 Cable operator WHARF started to provide its multi-channel programmes to subscribers in October 1993. Besides movies and acquired programmes, WHARF promises to provide original programming to the domestic audience. News programmes are produced in-house, while many entertainment programmes are contracted out.

7 'TVB New Moves,' *South China Morning Post*, 17 Oct. 1993.

8 To, Y. M. and Lau, T. Y. (1994) 'The sky is not the limit: Hong Kong as a global media exporter'. Paper presented to the International Communication Association Convention, July 11-15, Sydney, Australia.

9 See the parallel situation in the US as reported in Williams, B., 1994. Newcomb observes that the 'economic conditions in the network television production context were more and more constrained, forcing both networks and studios to rethink their offering to one another and to the public' (Newcomb, 1994:135).

10 Personal interview, 1993.

11 In 1991, Survey Research Hong Kong conducted a Lifestyle Survey which was modelled after the Values and Lifestyles Project (VALS) by the Stanford Research Institute. Based on interview responses, 1,500 respondents are clustered into nine types of lifestyles of different aspirations, values, needs, and habits. What is extraordinary is the percentage shares of each lifestyle spread across the sample within the range of 5 to 15 per cent. That is, the

results show a variety of lifestyles without there being a mainstream one. See *Lifestyle Survey*, Hong Kong, 1991, SRH.

12 Proportion of college-educated population in Hong Kong:

	1961	*1971*	*1981*	*1991*
College graduates	1.4	1.7	4.3	11

Source: HK Census and Statistics Department

13 *Hong Kong Census Reports*, 1981, 1986, 1991. The professional-managerial-administrative categories.

14 Lau *et al.* (1991) of the Chinese University have conducted several massive surveys on the political culture of the Hong Kong community. Early surveys were carried out in 1982 and repeated in 1984, 1986, and 1988. They found a growing political awareness and concluded that the overall direction was the institutionalisation of a set of participatory norms. Actual participant behaviour, nevertheless, lags behind normative orientation, and the conspicuous coexistence of participatory and non-participatory norms testify to an early 'modern', and hence 'immature', form of participatory political culture.

15 Advisory bodies on district affairs.

16 Thirty per cent of the whole Council.

17 Increasing numbers of Hong Kong investors are interested in the booming China property market. Many of the property development companies in China are pouring money in to television and other media in Hong Kong for advertising and other promotional activities.

18 'Pressing Concern', *Far East Economic Review*, 23 Sept. 1993; 'Politics and profits run colony's press,' *Guardian*, 21 Oct. 1993.

19 For example, *Pai-Sing Magazine* and *Window Magazine*. Both were closed down in the mid-1990s.

20 See the special issue of *Ming Pao Monthly*, May 1994. Some interpret the arrests as a political signal of media control from China.

21 See the report in *Ming Pao*, 9 May 1997.

4 Outsiders on television

1 In a 1979 survey of 13,594 newcomers, more than 90 per cent had relatives in Hong Kong. Zhou Yongxin, 'Hong Kong faces population explosion', *The Nineties* (Nov.) 1980: 23-26 (in Chinese).

2 In a survey in 1985, about 60 per cent of locals chose 'Hongkongers' over 'Chinese' as their identity (Lau and Kuan, 1988). However, it should be noted that there is a rich diversity in the ways Hongkongers identify themselves. In the last section of this chapter, I shall discuss the process of how diversified ways of life are reduced to a few public versions of identity.

3 I use the term 'melodramatic serial' for the Hong Kong prime-time serial drama to distinguish it from soap operas in Western countries. The genre shares many characteristics with Anglo-American *prime-time serials* in general and is especially similar to Latin American *telenovelas*. Since the launch of broadcasting television in 1967, the televisual melodramatic serial has been the most popular genre in Hong Kong. In the 1970s, most melodramatic

serials consisted of 40 to 100 episodes and were broadcast on prime-time television every weekday (see appendix 3, 'On methodology').

4   TVB is the most popular terrestrial television station in Hong Kong. Its drama serials dominate the prime hours and attract the widest public attention.

5   The survey was done in 1990 by TVB. GBU got 3,823 votes and rated second in the top ten list of the favourite serial of the 1980s. (See Ma, 1992:15.)

6   Ching is the surname, which goes first in Chinese naming.

7   #1:3 stands for episode one, scene three. The scene number follows the number of the shooting script.

8   See for instance how the name 'Alexis' is 'invented' for *Dynasty* to give the character a sexually ambiguous, but motherly connotation (Gripsrud, 1995:40).

9   The influx was triggered by the liberalisation policies in China after the Cultural Revolution. It is estimated that in 1977, 31,000 arrived, legally and illegally. In 1978, another 95,000 came. The serial was produced in 1979, when immigration reached its peak of 178,000. Another 91,000 made their way to Hong Kong in 1980, not including the numerous others who slipped through the social statistics. Also see note 10.

10 Before 1980, under a 'touch-base' policy, illegal immigrants were allowed to stay on once they managed to reach the inner cities. The policy was abolished in 1980. See Siu, 1986; also, Zhou Yongxin, 'Hong Kong faces population explosion', *The Nineties*, Nov. 1980: 23-26. Also see *Hong Kong Government Information Services*, Hong Kong 1981, HK: Government Printing.

11 But in fact figures on employment and wages did not show significant correlation with the numbers of new immigrants. See CUHK Student Union, 1982.

12 See CUHK Sociological Dept, 1980 for a compilation of newspapers' editorials on the issue.

13 The first wave came around 1949, which became the major building-block of the Hong Kong population. The second wave came in the famine years in the late 1950s. Another wave consisted of mainlanders who escaped the social chaos of the Cultural Revolution in the 1960s. Compared with all these earlier immigrants, the newcomers in the 1970s bore the most distinct cultural differences.

14 Cinema was then the major entertainment medium. Local terrestrial television was not launched until 1967.

15 98 per cent of the people of Hong Kong speak Cantonese.

16 'Mainlander' is a neutral term which refers to Chinese immigrants in general. Obviously, the term does not embody the negative sentiments prevalent at that time. In daily conversation, 'mainlander' is more often rendered as 'mainland-boy', which carries a hint of contempt. But it still lacks the specificity of referring to the suddenly emerged social group. Before the serial was released, there was perhaps a more peculiar term 'The Big Circle Gang', which referred to the Chinese immigrants who committed serious crimes in Hong Kong. But apparently, the term was connected with violent gangs and could not apply to all who came from China in the 1970s.

17   In the dialogue, which is in Cantonese, 'brother' is not explicitly stated but is implied in the sentence.

18   Interestingly, the mother is also a black sheep of the family (see note 21).

19   Membership categorisation analysis (MCA) has been applied to relatively static conversation. It has been used to explore the already prevalent cultural patterns. The GBU case shows that MCA can be more fruitful if we add to the analysis the concept of 'categorisation struggles'. MCA can also be related to social changes to see how new categorisations are formed and established categorisations fade in times of rapid social change.

20   For instance, we see Wai working diligently in #12:12, which is immediately followed by another scene with Ah Chian dozing off in his office (#12:13).

21   Although it is the mother who causes greater havoc — she is a gambler who owes money to loan sharks - she earns redemption once she has given up gambling and is readmitted into the bosom of the family (Cheng, 1990). But Ah Chian is the black sheep through and through. He is rejected as a Ching family member (#42:17) and is blamed for dragging the family into disgrace (#76:27).

22   Besides, there are about ten other scenes where Ah Chian is alone or seen in the passing. I must admit that the counting is categorically crude and not very exact. I believe, however, the one-sided domination as shown in the figures is clear and sufficient to highlight the power relation between Ah Chian and other characters.

23   A name given to mainland criminals (see note 16).

24   Ben-Rafael builds a typology of socio-linguistic groups; for him, usurpation is a social process; here I borrow his concept and apply it to describe a textual configuration.

25   See above: 'The Threat of the Newcomers'.

26   For job-hunting, from 38 per cent it increased to 57.5 per cent; for salary from 27.7 per cent to 44.5 per cent; for the prospect of a job promotion from 23.3 to 50.4 per cent; and for making friends with locals 20.7 per cent to 38 per cent. See Lingnan College, 1985.

27   January 1995.

28   The interview was a class project of a methodological course on phenomenology at the Chinese University of HK. The name of the interviewer was Zhu. The interview was conducted in 1991.

29   Sennett and Cobb (1993) note that there are internal conflicts in the hearts and minds of people from different social classes. Similarly, the domination of Ah Chian is also expressed on the emotional level. Sennett and Cobb explain the hidden injuries in terms of class analysis, here the emphasis is more on identity differences, though the domination of social groups is often articulated with class domination.

30   This ritual side of the medium is toned down when the medium loses its novelty in the 1980s and the 1990s.

31   Adapted from Richard Johnson, quoted in Larrain, 1994:163.

32   The extraordinary ability of the GBU case to transpose textual domination into the social realm should be seen to be related to the cultural charisma of the newly established television medium in the 1970s.

33   Most new immigrants of the 1970s were of rural origin, while in contrast, a high percentage of those who came earlier had some skills in various trades,

many had industrial capital, and only 3.8 per cent were of rural origin. See Li Ming-kun, quoted in Siu, 1986:2.

34 In an interesting anthropological report, Chan tells the story of a large group of Chinese immigrants who came to Hong Kong some 30 years ago. They were construction workers and maintained close in-group networks for three decades. They showed no interest in integrating into Hong Kong society; most of them viewed their traditional lineage as their primary reference of personal identity. See Chan, M., 1993.

5 Re-imagining Hong Kong identity

1 Shot in black and white, this television advertisement of Hong Kong Bank aestheticises the survival spirit of old-time Hongkongers and won the Top Ten television ads in 1996. This is one of the first of an on-going series of ads on the theme of Hong Kong's social history. These ads have been very popular on Hong Kong television screens in recent years.

2 The Chinese title *Dashidai* literally means 'great times'. The serial's title is translated into English by TVB as *The Greed of Man*. Here I use the English title *Great Times* because this translation better captures the connotations that the Chinese title carries.

3 The same television station that produced GBU in 1979. TVB is the most-watched terrestrial television station in Hong Kong. Its drama serials, which dominate the prime-time hours, attract the widest attention and have become a major cultural force which consolidates the indigenous cultural identity of the Hong Kong audience.

4 It is literally entitled *Hong Kong Legend* in Chinese. TVB's official English title for the programme is *Hong Kong Epic Heritage*.

5 Audiences expressed their interpretation in radio phone-in programmes and in the readers' letters columns of popular magazines at the time the serial was released (see analysis in main text).

6 In this and the next chapter, character analysis is used to examine the ideology of the dramas in question. Throughout the history of television, successful dramas, especially melodramatic serials, have been most remembered for their impressive characters. Character is the central dramatic device to win audience identification. They are held to mediate a range of television effects, through processes such as imitation, identification, role modelling, and para-social interaction (Livingstone, 1990). These processes provide the symbolic resources for constructing or validating felt identities (Traudt and Lont, 1987). I shall also attend to stereotypes (Derry, 1985; Williams, T., 1992), character's narrative function (Propp, 1968), and other socio-economic classifications. These analytical dimensions can help us see how discourse is unobtrusively constructed around characters and character relations.

7 Discursive scenes are defined as scenes charged with emotion and explicit discourse. The detailed analysis of discursive scenes can allow us to highlight the visual elements within the *mise-en-scène* and the reasoning within dialogues that forms the basis of the discursive arguments put forward in these scenes.

8 The building of the Daya Bay nuclear plant caused a series of Sino-Hong Kong disputes. Despite strong opposition from the people of Hong Kong,

China insisted on building the plant at Daya Bay, which is within Chinese territory but very near to Hong Kong. Since then, the nuclear plant has been a symbol of China's political and psychological threat to Hong Kong.

9 Structuralists such as Ferdinand de Saussure and Claude Lévi-Strauss assert that binary opposition is the fundamental operation of the human mind in meaning production. The structuralist's project of discovering deep binary oppositions that are stable across histories has been rightly criticised in the post-structuralist literature as being too essentialist and mechanical. Oppositions are not fixed and unchangeable, yet they are relatively stable relationships and open to analysis. In this and the next chapter, I shall identify in the melodramatic serials those opposing relations within the narrative and between characters or a group of characters. I shall try to see how positive and negative valorisations of these binary oppositions affirm or negate identity categories or discursive arguments and reasoning. I am using it not in the essentialist sense of deep structural meaning; but rather, binary opposition is regarded as a commonly used way of sense-making.

10 The executive producer of GT said that the inspiration of this suicide-cum-homicide scene came from the open firing on protesting students in the June Fourth crackdown.

11 *Next Magazine*, 4 December 1992: 18.

12 In 1994, college students were asked to send the questionnaires to relatives and friends. Those who had watched the serial were invited to fill in the questionnaires. Fifty-six per cent of the respondents had watched more than half of the episodes of GM and 114 completed questionnaires were collected.

13 The distribution of the respondents in this survey was quite homogeneous:

Ages of respondents		Education of respondents	
18-24	99	Primary	5
25-34	6	Secondary	19
35-44	4	Tertiary	90
45-54	3		
55 and over	2	N=114	

14 Also see a counter-argument in Lui, 1997.

15 Since I was invited as the presenter of the programme, I was able to document the production process, which is presented in detail elsewhere. See Ma, 1998.

16 Lee Siu Fung, head of a corporation, specialised in pottery.

17 Regarding the phone-in programmes of RTHK and Commercial Radio, I was invited to one of the programmes to talk to the audiences after the first episode was aired.

18 E.g. C. K. Lau, 'The politically correct past', *South China Morning Post*, 25 August 1996. L. M. Ho, 'Reading false and poisonous ideology on television', *Sing Tao Yat Pao*, 19 August 1996.

19 L. M. Ho, 'Reading false and poisonous ideology on television', *Sing Tao Yat Pao*, 19 August 1996.

20 We successfully interviewed a random sample of 769 people, with a success rate of 51 per cent, from 12 to 23 August 1996. See Ma and Fung, 1997.

21 These are ethical, friendly, civilised, humble, optimistic, self-disciplined, sympathetic, enduring, ambitious, easy to adapt, clever, realistic, outspoken, expressing social concern, patriotic, and Westernised. See Ma and Fung, 1997.

22 Most media workers in the electronic media are local Hongkongers.

6 Public voices/private anxieties

1 See appendix 3 on methodology for a discussion of the social practice dimension of televisual discourse.

2 Concerning the public impressions of new immigrants, the statistical information from various social surveys (see chapter 4) conducted in the late 1970s and early 1980s by and large converged with those depicted in the electronic and print media. For a collection of media comments, see CUHK Sociology Dept, 1980.

3 Radio Television Hong Kong (RTHK) produces television programmes that are released on borrowed air-time on the commercial television channels. RTHK is officially a government broadcaster and relies on government funding. However, the television section, particularly the drama unit, has been operating autonomously with minimal government interference. The programming is similar to that of other public television. Since the mid-1980s, the government has been working on a corporatisation project to turn RTHK into a public broadcaster. The project suffered from prolonged political procrastination and was discarded (see Chan, K. C., 1990; Lee, 1992).

4 Television organisational context refers to the organisational setting in which television contents are selected and developed under controlling and evaluative processes and finally produced into television programmes to meet the goal of the television organisation.

5 See note 3 above.

6 Idea research for BLR started in December 1991 and the programme was released from 8 August 1992 to 3 October 1992, on Saturday prime-time, TVB Jade (as RTHK does not have a broadcasting channel of its own); idea research for GT started in Jan. 1992; the programme was released from 5 October to 27 November 1992, on weekday prime-time, TVB Jade.

7 It carries a public image similar to that of the British realist soaps, which stress the importance of drawing on different kinds of experiences based on the lives of 'ordinary' people (see Geraghty, 1995).

8 Single-play series are those drama series that have a common theme but each episode carries independent characters and stories, while the continued serial has one single story that continues through all the episodes of the serial. The effects of different genre on the ideological character of the texts will be examined in the next chapter.

9 *Stormy Weather* scored 27 rating points. The average rating of BLR is 22.8 rating points.

10 Lyric and choric dramas have been given different labels in the past. Dramas reflecting the mainstream ideology are labelled as mass/popular/commercial dramas or hegemonic television. While dramas with negotiatory or oppositional discourses are called 'emancipatory television' (Kellner,

1987), 'radical text' (Kaplan, 1983), 'oppositional television' (Himmelstein, 1984), 'quality drama' and 'liberal drama' (Feuer, 1987), or generally as 'elite drama' and 'serious drama'. These terms are used in the high vs. low culture debate and are loaded with value judgements. Popular dramas are often accused of being monolithic and expressing a single set of values that is marketed to an undifferentiated audience. Advocates call for the production of television dramas to be ideologically progressive and to challenge the establishment of the advanced capitalist society (Kellner, 1987). They ask for opposition to the domination of commercial television (Himmelstein, 1984). However, these positions are often elitist; they explain the ideological differences of these two types of drama in terms of high and low artistic taste or the hegemonic control of the capitalists. In contrast, the terms lyric and choric drama are far more neutral labels which enable us to avoid some of the polemics in the high-vs.-low culture debate.

11   See another case study of media divergence in Curran (1990a).

7   The production of television culture

1   The analytical strategies follow the frameworks of Czarniawska-Joerges (1992) and Jankowski and Wester (1992). Also see Intintoli (1985) for a critical review of ethnographic methods for media production.

2   Schema is defined as a coherent set of premises that works as a cognitive frame for 'satisficing' decisions within an organisation. In other words, when participants choose between convenient options at hand, the cognitive schema automatically provides the taken for granted premises to screen off undesirable options. Cognitive schema is considered by the New Institutional School (see Powell and DiMaggio, 1991) as an important co-ordinating device of organisations.

3   The building of the Daya Bay nuclear plant caused a series of Sino-Hong Kong disputes. The nuclear plant was then a symbol of political and psychological threat to Hong Kong.

4   The so-called 'story selling meeting'.

5   See Ma, 1992, for a historical analysis of the dual role played by RTHK. See also Ma, 1996.

6   Ratings for the first six weeks stayed slightly above 30 points, than went up to 40 in week seven and week eight. This had something to do with a programme of the rival station ATV. Ratings were up in week seven, after the competitive serial with the same time-slot on ATV ended its last episode.

7   Producers of the RTHK drama unit consider the assignment of hour-length dramas more prestigious than half-hour dramas. Some are eager to get the one-hour assignment.

8   For example, dramas that are scheduled for hot spots such as year end or that are used to compete with production of rival stations.

9   All his productions have high ratings. His best-received dramas are among the best-ranked programmes of TVB.

10   Since the mid-1980s, editorial independence has been the major proclaimed rationale behind the prolonged project to corporatise RTHK.

8 Rethinking television culture

1 For instance, theories of the strong behavioural effects of the mass media share with the dominant ideology thesis the assumption of a manipulatory media. Curran *et al.* (1982) argue that Marxist and pluralist traditions are not as opposite as is usually supposed.
2 For example, Fiske (1993, 1994) has responded to the criticisms and made some revisions in his recent works. Also see Hardt, 1997.
3 For an introduction of the concept, see Jenkins, 1992; for critical evaluation and connection with communication studies, see Garnham and Williams, 1986, and Garnham, 1993.

Appendix 3: On methodology: analysing televisual discourse

1 Detextualisation refers to the reduction of the complex textual system of television to audience activities alone (Allen, 1993).
2 For instance, content analysis emphasises the manifest content and strictly distinguishes between objective analysis and interpretation of latent meaning. Semantics is usually concerned with the internal textual contexts and relations. Structuralists are most interested in the linguistic context and external factors refereed to or derived from the text (Lindkvist, 1981).
3 Discourse theory has emerged as a new discipline since the early 1970s, which saw for the first time the publication of monographs and collections explicitly dealing with systematic discourse analysis as an independent research within and across several disciplines. It grows primarily from the study of language, and then incorporates the field of semiology and structuralism (see MacDonell, 1986), and social and political theories (Corsaro, 1985; van Dijk, 1994). Discourse theory has been applied to the analysis of various kinds of spoken and written texts (see van Dijk, 1985a, 1985b, 1985c, 1985d) and more recently to media texts (see Graddol and Boyd-Barrett, 1994).
4 See the four-volume *Handbook of Discourse Analysis* edited by van Dijk (1985a, 1985b, 1985c, 1985d) for a review of the diverse disciplinary perspectives from which discourse theories are formulated. Also see Coulthard and Montgomery, 1981.
5 Also see Fairclough, 1995.
6 Here I borrow from Murdock's four elements of discursive formations (1989b:235), with some reformulations to fit the aim of this project.
7 See Thompson, 1990, for a discussion of processes of symbolic valorisation.
8 For the tension between discourse and context, see Schegloff, 1991.
9 Discourse constitutes social objects and social subjects (see Fairclough, 1992).
10 Power is discursive; it is asserted by discourse, and to a certain extent, is itself inside discourse.
11 There is no daytime soap in Hong Kong.
12 They have multiple plots and a continuous storyline and are broadcast every weekday evening.
13 In the 1970s, they usually achieved audience figures of 60 per cent and sometimes the final episodes could have more than 70 per cent. The format

of drama series, which are very popular in Anglo-American television, do not share the popularity of the melodramatic serials in Hong Kong.

14 There are usually two one-hour melodramatic serials and one half-hour situation comedy serial scheduled for every evening.

15 The commercial media-giant 'Globo' in Brazil exports its *telenovelas* to well over 100 countries all over the world (Frey-Vor, 1990a).

16 See for instance a recent book edited by Allen (1995) which contains research on soap operas around the world.

Bibliography

Abbas, A. (1997) *Hong Kong: Culture and the Politics of Disappearance*, London: University of Minnesota Press.

Abercrombie, N. *et al.* (1984) *The Dominant Ideology Thesis*, London: Allen & Unwin.

Abercrombie, N. *et al.* (1990) *Dominant Ideologies*, London: Allen & Unwin.

Abercrombie, N. *et al.* (1992) 'Popular representation: recasting realism', in S. Lash *et al.* (eds) *Modernity and Identity*, Oxford: Blackwell.

Agassi, J. (1969) 'Social structure and social stratification in Hong Kong', in I. C. Jarvie (ed.) *Hong Kong: A Society in Transition*, London: Routledge & Kegan Paul.

Agassi, J. and Jarvie, I. C. (1969) 'A study in westernization', in I. C. Jarvie (ed.) *Hong Kong: A Society in Transition*, London: Routledge & Kegan Paul.

Alexander, J. C. (ed.) (1988) *Durkheimian Sociology: Cultural Studies*, Cambridge: Cambridge University Press.

Allen, R. C. (1983) 'On reading soaps: a semiotic primer', in A. Kaplan (ed.) *Regarding Television: Critical Approaches*, Frederick, Md.: University Publications of America.

Allen, R. C. (1985) *Speaking of Soap Operas*, Chapel Hill/London: University of North Carolina Press.

Allen, R. C. (1992) 'Audience-oriented criticism and television', in R. C. Allen (ed.) *Channels of Discourse, Reassembled*, London: Routledge.

Allen, R. C. (1993) 'Is this the party to whom I am speaking? The role of address in media textuality and reception', *Journal of Communication and Culture* 2(2):49–70.

Allen, R. C. (ed.) (1995) *To Be Continued: Soap Operas around the World*, London: Routledge.

Almond, G. and Verba, S. (1965) *The Civic Culture*, Boston: Little Brown.

Althusser, L. (1971) 'Ideology and ideological state apparatuses', in L. Althusser, *Lenin and Philosophy*, London: New Left Books.

Althusser, L. (1972) *For Marx*, Harmondsworth: Penguin.

Alvarado, M. (1978) *Hazell: The Making of a TV Series*, London: British Film Institute.

Anderson, B. (1983) *Imagined Communities: Reflections on the Origin and Spread of Nationalism*, London: Verso.

Ang, I. (1985) *Watching Dallas*, London: Methuen.

Ang, I. (1990) 'Culture and communication', *European Journal of Communications* 5:2–30.

Ang, I. (1991) *Desperately Seeking the Audience*, London: Routledge.

Ang, I. (1994) 'Understanding TV audiencehood', in H. Newcomb (ed.) *TV: The Critical View* (5th edn), New York: Oxford University Press.

Ang, I. (1996) *Living Room Wars: Rethinking Media Audiences for a Postmodern World*, London: Routledge.

Aronowitz, S. (1992) *The Politics of Identity: Class, Culture, Social Movements*, New York: Routledge.

Ash, R. F. and Kueh, Y. Y. (1993) 'Economic integration within greater China: Trade and investment flows between China, Hong Kong, and Taiwan', *The China Quarterly* 136:711–745.

Attallah, P. (1984) 'The unworthy discourse: Situation comedy in television', in W. D. Rowland and B. Watkins (eds) *Interpreting Television: Current Research Perspectives*, California: Sage.

Bagdikian, B. H. (1990) *The Media Monopoly*, Boston: Beacon Press.

Baker, H. (1983) 'Life in the cities: The emergence of Hong Kong man', *The China Quarterly* 95:469–479.

Barbalet, J. M. (1993) 'Citizenship in the modern west', in B. S. Turner (ed.) *Citizenship and Social Theory*, London: Sage.

Barker, D. (1994) 'Television production techniques as communication', in H. Newcomb (ed.) *TV: The Critical View* (5th edn), New York: Oxford University Press.

Barker, D. and Timberg, B. M. (1992) 'Encounter with the television image: Thirty years of encoding research', *Communication Year Book*, 15:209–238.

Barker, M. (1990) 'Review of Fiske: Reading the popular and understanding popular culture', *Magazine of Cultural Studies* 1:39–40.

Barkin, S. and Gurevitch, M. (1987) 'Out of work and on the air', *Critical Studies in Mass Communication* 4:1–20.

Barthes, R. (1975) *The Pleasure of the Text*, New York: Hill & Wang.

Barwise, P. and Ehrenberg, A. (1988) *Television and Its Audience*, London: Sage.

Baudrillard, J. (1988) *Selected Writings*, Cambridge: Polity.

Bee, J. (1989) 'First citizen of the semiotic democracy?', *Cultural Studies* 3(3):353–359.

Ben-Rafael, E. (1994) *Language, Identity, and Social Division: the Case of Israel*, Oxford: Clarendon Press.

Bennett, T. (1982) 'Theories of the media, theories of society', in M. Gurevitch *et al.* (eds) *Media, Society and Culture*, London: Routledge.

Bennett, T. (1987) 'Texts in history: The determinations of readings and their texts', in D. Attridge *et al.* (eds) *Post-Structuralism and the Question of History*, Cambridge: Cambridge University Press.

Bennett T. and Woollacott, J. (1987) *Bond and Beyond: The Political Career of a Popular Hero*, London: Macmillan.

Berger, P. L. and Luckmann, T. (1966) *The Social Construction of Reality*, London: Allen Lane.

Best, S. and Kellner, D. (1991) *Postmodern Theory: Critical Interrogations*, London: Macmillan.

Blumber, J. B. (ed.) (1992) *TV and the Public Interest*, London: Sage.

Blumber, J. G. *et al.* (1986) *Research on the Range and Quality of Broadcasting Services*, London: HMSO, for the Peacock Committee on Financing the BBC.

Bondebjerg, I. (1992) 'Intertextuality and metafiction: Genre and narration in the television fiction of Dennis Potter', in M. Skovmand and K. C. Schroder (eds) *Media Cultures: Reappraising Transnational Media*, London: Routledge.

Bourdieu, P. (1977) *Outline of a Theory of Practice*, Cambridge: Cambridge University Press.

Bourdieu, P. (1984) *Distinction: A Social Critique of the Judgement of Taste*, London: Routledge & Kegan Paul.

Brandt, G. W. (ed.) (1991) *British Television Drama*, Cambridge: Cambridge University Press.

Brandt, G. W. (ed.) (1993) *British Television Drama in the 1980s*, Cambridge: Cambridge University Press.

Brett, D. (1996) *The Construction of Heritage*, Ireland: Cork University Press.

Brooks, P. (1976) *The Melodramatic Imagination*, New Haven: Yale University Press.

Brown, M. E. (1994) *Soap Opera and Woman's Talk: The Pleasure of Resistance*, California: Sage.

Browne, N. (1994) 'Society and subjectivity: on the political economy of Chinese melodrama', in N. Browne *et al.* (eds) *New Chinese Cinemas*, Cambridge: Cambridge University Press.

Brunsdon, C. (1983) 'Crossroads: notes on soap opera', in E. A. Kaplan (ed.) *Regarding Television*, LA: American Film Institute.

Brunsdon, C. (1995) 'The role of soap opera in the development of feminist television scholarship', in R. C. Allen (ed.) *To Be Continued: Soap Operas around the World*, London: Routledge.

Budd, B. *et al.* (1990) 'The affirmative character of American cultural studies', *Critical Studies in Mass Communication* 7(2):169–184.

Budd, M. and Steinman, C. (1989) 'Television, cultural studies, and the "Blind Spot" debate in critical communication research', in G. Burns and R. J. Thompson (eds), *Television Studies: Textual Analysis*, New York: Praeger.

Burns, G. and Thompson, R. J. (eds) (1989) *Television Studies: Textual Analysis*, New York: Praeger.

Buxton, R. (1994) 'After it happened . . . : The battle to present AIDS', in H. Newcomb (ed.) *TV: The Critical View* (5th edn), New York: Oxford University Press.

Calhoun, C. (ed.) (1994) *Social Theory and the Politics of Identity*, Oxford: Blackwell.

Campbell, D. C. and Campbell, J. B. (1978) 'Public television as a public good', *Journal of Communication* 28(1):52–63.

Cannadine, D. (1983) 'The context, performance and meaning of ritual: The British monarchy and the invention of tradition', in E. Hobsbawm and T. Ranger (eds) *The Invention of Tradition*, Cambridge: Cambridge University Press.

Cantor, M. G. (1971) *The Hollywood TV Producer: His Work and His Audience*, New York: Basic Books.

Cantor, M. G. and Cantor, J. M. (1992) *Prime-Time Television: Content and Control* (2nd edn), Newbury Park: Sage.

Cantor, M. and Pingree, S. (1983) *The Soap Opera*, Beverly Hills: Sage.

Carey, J. W. (1989) *Communication as Culture: Essays on Media and Society*, Boston: Unwin Hyman.

Carey, J. W. (1995) 'Abolishing the old spirit world', *Critical Studies in Mass Communication* 12:62–71.

Carragee, K. (1990) 'Interpretative media study', *Critical Studies in Mass Communication* 7(2): 81–96.

Cassata, M. and Skill, T. (1983) *Life on Daytime Television*, Norwood, NJ: Ablex.

Chan, H. M. (1994) 'Culture and identity', in D. H. McMillen and S. W. Man (eds) *The Other Hong Kong Report*, Hong Kong: Chinese University of Hong Kong.

Chan, J. M. (1992) 'Mass media and socio-political formation in Hong Kong, 1949–1992', *Asian Journal of Communication* 2(3):106–129.

Chan, J. M. (1996) 'Television in greater China: structure, exports, and market formation', in J. Sinclair *et al.* (eds) *New Patterns in Global Television: Peripheral Vision*, New York: Oxford University Press.

Chan, J. M. (1997) 'Media internationalization in Hong Kong: Patterns, factors, and tensions', in G. A. Postiglione and J. T. H. Tang (eds) *Hong Kong's Reunion with China: The Global Dimensions*, New York: M. E. Sharpe.

Chan, J. M. and Lee, C. C. (1991) *Mass Media and Political Transition: The Hong Kong Press in China's Orbit*, New York: Guilford Press.

Chan, J. M. and Lee, P. S. N. (1990) 'Mass communication: consumption and evaluation', in S. K. Lau *et al.* (eds), *Indicators of Social Development, Hong Kong 1990*, Hong Kong: Chinese University of Hong Kong.

Chan, J. M. and Lee, P. S. N. (1992) 'Communication indicators in Hong Kong: Conceptual issues, findings and implications', in S. K. Lau *et al.* (eds) *The Development of Social Indicators Research in Chinese Societies*, Hong Kong: Chinese University of Hong Kong.

Chan, J. M. and Ma, E. K. W. (1996) 'Asian television: Global trends and local processes', *Gazette* 58: 45–60.

Chan, J. M. *et al.* (1992) 'Fighting against the odds: Hong Kong journalists in transition', *Gazette* 50:1–20.

Chan, J. M. *et al.* (1996) *Hong Kong Journalists in Transition*, Hong Kong: Hong Kong Institute of Asia-Pacific Studies, The Chinese University of Hong Kong.

Chan, J. M. *et al.* (1997) 'Back to the future: A retrospect and prospects for the Hong Kong mass media', in J. Y. S. Cheng (ed.) *The Other Hong Kong Report 1997*, Hong Kong: The Chinese University of Hong Kong.

Chan, K. C. (1990) 'Mass media and communication', in Richard Wong and Joseph Cheng (eds) *The Other Hong Kong Report 1990*, Hong Kong: Chinese University Press.

Chan, K. C. (1991) 'Mass media and communication', in Y. W. Sung and M. K. Lee (eds) *The Other Hong Kong Report 1991*, Hong Kong: Chinese University Press.

Chan, K. C. and Choi, P. K. (1989) 'Mass media and communication', in T. L. Tsim and Bernard H.L. Luk (eds), *The Other Hong Kong Report 1989*, Hong Kong: Chinese University Press.

Chan, M. (1993) 'Chinese emigrant construction workers in Hong Kong', *The Hong Kong Anthropologist*, 6:9–20.

Chaney, D. (1986) 'The symbolic form of ritual in mass communication', in P. Golding *et al.* (eds) *Communicating Politics*, New York: Holmes and Meier.

Cheng, J. Y. S. (ed.) (1984) *Hong Kong in Search of a Future*, Hong Kong: Oxford University Press.

Cheng Yu (1990) 'Uninvited guests', *The China Factor in Hong Kong Cinema*, Hong Kong: Urban Council.

Cheng, Y. M. (1996) 'Culture and lifestyles', in M. Nyaw and S. Li (eds) *The Other Hong Kong Report 1996*, Hong Kong: The Chinese University of Hong Kong Press.

Cheung, A. B. L. (1988) 'The political impact of the Hong Kong new middle class', in A. B. L. Cheung *et al.* (eds) *Class Analysis and Hong Kong*, Hong Kong: Twilight Books (in Chinese).

Cheung A. B. L. and Louie, K. S. (1991) *Social Conflicts in Hong Kong*, Hong Kong: Hong Kong Institute of Asia-Pacific Studies.

Chiu, F. Y. L. (1996) 'Politics and the body social in colonial Hong Kong', *Positions* 4(2):187–215.

Choi, P. K. (1990a) 'Popular culture', in R. Wong and J. Cheng (eds), *The Other Hong Kong Report 1990*, Hong Kong: Chinese University of Hong Kong Press.

Choi, P. K. (1990b) 'From dependence to self-sufficiency: The rise of the indigenous culture of Hong Kong, 1945–1989', *Asian Culture* 14:161–177.

Choi, P. K. (1991) 'Hong Kong education', in J. Y. S. Cheng (ed.) *A New Hong Kong Era*, Hong Kong: Breakthrough (in Chinese).

Chun, A. (1996) 'Discourses of identity in the changing spaces of public culture in Taiwan, Hong Kong and Singapore', Theory, *Culture & Society* 13(1): 51–75.

Clarke, A. and Clarke, J. (1982) 'Highlights and action relays: Ideology, sport and the media', in J. Hargreaves (ed.) *Sport, Culture and Ideology*, London: Routledge.

Cohen, A. P. (1985) *The Symbolic Construction of Community*, London: Routledge.

Collins, Randall (1988) *The Durkheimian Tradition in Conflict Sociology*, in J. C. Alexander (ed.) *Durkheimian Sociology: Cultural Studies*, Cambridge: Cambridge University Press.

Collins, Richard (1990) *Culture, Communication and National Identity: The Case of Canadian Television*, Toronto: University of Toronto Press.

Collins, Richard *et al.* (eds) (1986) *Media, Culture & Society*, London: Sage.

Comstock, G. A. (1989) *The Evolution of American Television*, Newbury Park: Sage.

Condit, C. (1989) 'The rhetorical limits of polysemy', *Critical Studies in Mass Communication* 6(2):103–122.

Connerton, P. (1989) *How Societies Remember*, Cambridge: Cambridge University Press.

Connor, S. (1989) *Postmodernist Culture*, Oxford: Blackwell.

Corcoran, F. (1987) 'Television as ideological apparatus: The power and the pleasure', in Horace Newcomb (ed.), *Television: The Critical View* (4th edn), New York: Oxford University Press.

Corner, J. (1991) *Meaning, Genre and Context*, in J. Curran and M. Gurevitch (eds) *Mass Media and Society*, London: Edward Arnold.

Corner, J. (1995) *Television Form and Public Address*, London: Edward Arnold.

Corner, J. and Harvey, S. (eds) (1992) *Enterprise and Heritage: Cross Currents of National Culture*, London: Routledge.

Corsaro, W. A. (1985) 'Sociological approaches to discourse analysis', in T. van Dijk (ed.) *Handbook of Discourse Analysis* (vol. 1), London: Academic Press.

Coulthard, M. and Montgomery, M. (eds) (1981) *Studies in Discourse Analysis*, London: Routledge.

Crane, D. (1976) 'Reward systems in art, science, and religion', *American Behavioral Scientist* 19(6):719–734.

Crane, D. (1992) *The Production of Culture*, California: Sage.

Crane, D. (1994) (ed.) *The Sociology of Culture*, Oxford: Blackwell.

Crowley, D. and Mitchell, D. (1994) 'Communication in a post-mass media world', in D. Crowley and D. Mitchell (eds) *Communication Theory Today*, Cambridge: Polity.

Cruz, J. and Lewis, J. (ed.) (1994) *Viewing, Reading, Listening*, Boulder, Col.: Westview Press.

CUHK Sociological Department (1980) *Immigration: Hong Kong, The Facts*, Hong Kong: CUHK Library.

CUHK Student Union (1982) *New Immigrants*, Hong Kong: CUHK Student Union.

Curran, J. (1982) 'Communications, power and social order', in M. Gurevitch *et al.* (eds), *Media, Society and Culture*, London: Routledge.

Curran, J. (1986) 'The impact of advertising on the British mass media', in R. Collins *et al.* (eds) *Media, Culture & Society*, London: Sage.

Curran, J. (1990a) 'Culturalists' perspectives of news organisations: A reappraisal and a case study', in M. Ferguson (ed.) *Public Communication: The New Imperatives*, London: Sage.

Curran, J. (1990b) 'The new revisionism in mass communication research', *European Journal of Communications* 5:2–3.

Curran, J. (1991a) 'Rethinking the media as a public sphere', in P. Dahlgren and C. Sparks (eds) *Communication and Citizenship*, London: Routledge.

Curran, J. (1991b) 'Mass media and democracy: a reappraisal', in J. Curran and M. Gurevitch (eds) *Mass Media and Society*, London: Edward Arnold.

Curran, J. (1996a) 'Rethinking mass communications', in J. Curran *et al.*(eds) *Cultural Studies and Communications*, London: Edward Arnold.

Curran, J. (1996b) 'The new revisionism in mass communication research: A reappraisal', in J. Curran *et al.* (eds) *Cultural Studies and Communications*, London: Edward Arnold.

Curran, J. and Gurevitch, M. (1991) *Mass Media and Society*, London: Edward Arnold.

Curran, J. and Seaton, J. (1991) *Power without Responsibility*, London: Routledge.

Curran, J. *et al.* (eds) (1977) *Mass Communication and Society*, London: Edward Arnold.

Curran, J. *et al.* (1982) 'The study of the media: Theoretical approaches', in M. Gurevitch *et al.* (eds) *Media, Society and Culture*, London: Routledge.

Curran, J. *et al.* (eds) (1987) *Impacts and Influences*, London: Methuen.

Curran, J. *et al.* (eds) (1996) *Cultural Studies and Communications*, London: Edward Arnold.

Czarniawska-Joerges, B. (1992) *Exploring Complex Organisations: A Cultural Perspective*, California: Sage.

Dayan, D. and Katz, E. (1992) *Media Events: The Live Broadcasting of History*, Cambridge: Harvard University Press.

DeGolyer, M. E. (1993) 'A collision of cultures: systemic conflict in HK's future with China', in D. H. McMillen and M. E. DeGolyer (eds), *One Culture, Many Systems: Politics in the Reunification of China*, Hong Kong: Chinese University of Hong Kong Press.

Denzin, N. (1970) *The Research Act in Sociology*, London: Butterworth.

Derry, C. (1985) 'TV soap opera: Incest, bigamy, and fatal disease', in S. Kaminsky and J. Mahan (eds) *American TV Genres*, Chicago: Nelson-Hall.

DiMaggio, P. J. (1977) 'Market structure, the creative process, and popular culture', *Journal of Popular Culture* 11:426–452.

DiMaggio, P. J. and Powell, W. W. (1991) 'The iron cage revisited: Institutional isomorphism and collective rationality in organizational fields', in W. W. Powell and P. J. DiMaggio (eds), *The New Institutionalism in Organization Analysis*, Chicago: The Chicago University Press.

Douglas, M. (1966) *Purity and Danger*, Harmondsworth: Penguin.

Drummond, P. *et al.* (eds) (1993) *National Identity and Europe: The Television Revolution*, London: British Film Institute.

Dyer, R. (1973) *Light Entertainment*, London: British Film Institute.

Dyer, R. *et al.* (eds) (1981) *Coronation Street*, London: British Film Institute.

Eagleton, T. (1991) *Ideology: An Introduction*, London: Verso.

Eco, U. (1972) 'Towards a semiotic inquiry into the TV message' in J. Corner and J. Hawthorn (eds) (1980), *Communication Studies: An Introductory Reader*, London: Edward Arnold.

Eldridge, J. (1993) 'Whose illusion? Whose reality? Some problems of theory and method in mass media research', in J. Eldridge (ed.), *Getting the Message: News, Truth and Power*, London: Routledge.

Elias, N. and Scotson, J. L. (1994) *The Established and the Outsiders*, London: Sage.

Elliott, P. (1972) *The Making of a Television Series: A Case Study in the Sociology of Culture*, London: Constable.

Elliott, P. (1977) 'Media organizations and occupations: an overview', in J. Curran (ed.), *Mass Communication and Society*, London: Open University.

Ellis, J. (1992) *Visible Fictions*, London: Routledge.

Ettema, J. S. (1982) 'The organizational context of creativity: a case study from public television', in J. S. Ettema and D. C. Whitney (eds), *Individuals in Mass Media Organizations: Creativity and Constraint*, California: Sage.

Ettema, J. S. and Whitney, D. C. (eds) (1982) *Individuals in Mass Media Organizations: Creativity and Constraint*, California: Sage.

European Communities, Commission of (1984) *Television without Frontiers*, Brussels: EC.

Evans, W. (1990) 'The interpretative turn in media research', *Critical Studies in Mass Communication* 7(2):147–168.

Fairclough, N. (1992) *Discourse and Social Change*, Cambridge: Polity.

Fairclough, N. (1995) *Media Discourse*, London: Edward Arnold.

Femia, J. V. (1981) *Gramsci's Political Thought: Hegemony, Consciousness and the Revolutionary Process*, Oxford: Clarendon.

Fentress, J. and Wickham, C. (1992) *Social Memory*, Oxford: Blackwell.

Ferguson, M. and Golding, P. (1997) 'Cultural studies and changing times: An introduction', in M. Ferguson and P. Golding (eds) *Cultural Studies in Question*, London: Sage.

Feuer, J. (1987) 'The MTM Style', in Horace Newcomb (ed.), *Television: The Critical View* (4th edn), New York: Oxford University Press.

Feuer, J. (1992) 'Genre study and television', in R. C. Allen (ed.), *Channels of Discourse Reassembled*, London: Routledge.

Feuer, J. *et al.* (1984) *MTM: Quality Television*, London: British Film Institute.

Fiske, J. (1984) 'Popularity and ideology: A structural reading of Dr. Who', in W. D. Rowland and B. Watkins (eds), *Interpreting Television: Current Research Perspectives*, California: Sage.

Fiske, J. (1986) 'TV: polysemy and popularity', *Critical Studies in Mass Communication* 3(4):391–407.

Fiske, J. (1987) *Television Culture*, New York: Routledge.

Fiske, J. (1989a) *Understanding Popular Culture*, London: Routledge.

Fiske, J. (1989b) *Reading the Popular*, London: Routledge.

Fiske, J. (1991) 'Postmodernism and television', in J. Curran and M. Gurevitch (eds) *Mass Media and Society*, London: Edward Arnold.

Fiske, J. (1993) *Power Plays. Power Works*, New York: Verso.

Fiske, J. (1994) *Media Matters*, Minnesota: University of Minnesota Press.

Fok, K. C. (1990) *Lecture on Hong Kong History*, Hong Kong: Commercial Press.

Foucault, M. (1972) *The Archaeology of Knowledge*, London: Tavistock.

Foucault, M. (1979) *Discipline and Punish*, Harmondsworth: Penguin.

Foucault, M. (1981) *History of Sexuality*, Harmondsworth: Penguin.

Frey-Vor, G. (1990a) 'Soap opera', *Communication Research Trends* 10(1):1–16.

Frey-Vor, G. (1990b) 'More on soaps', *Communication Research Trends* 10(2):1–12.

Furedi, F. (1992) *Mythical Past, Elusive Future: History and Society in an Anxious Age*, London: Sage.

Gallagher, M. (1982) 'Negotiation of control in media organisations and occupations', in M. Gurevitch *et al.* (eds) *Media, Society and Culture*, London: Routledge.

Gans, H. J. (1974) *Popular Culture and High Culture*, New York: Basic Books.

Garcia, S. (1993) 'Europe's fragmented identities and the frontiers of citizenship', in S. Garcia (ed.) *European Identity and the Search for Legitimacy*, London: Pinter.

Garnham, N. (1983) 'Towards a theory of cultural materialism', *Journal of Communication* 33(3): 314–329.

Garnham, N. (1990) *Capitalism and Communication: Global Culture and the Economics of Information*, London: Sage.

Garnham, N. (1993) 'Bourdieu, the cultural arbitrary, and television', in C. Calhoun *et al.* (eds), *Bourdieu: Critical Perspectives*, Cambridge: Polity Press.

Garnham, N. (1995) 'Political economy and cultural studies: reconciliation or divorce?', *Critical Studies in Mass Communication* 12:62–71.

Garnham, N. (1997) 'Political economy and the practice of cultural studies', in M. Ferguson and P. Golding (eds) *Cultural Studies in Question*, London: Sage.

Garnham, N. and Williams, R. (1986) *Pierre Bourdieu and the Sociology of Culture: An Introduction*, in R. Collins *et al.* (eds) *Media, Culture and Society*, London: Sage.

Gellner, E. (1983) *Nations and Nationalism*, Oxford: Blackwell.

Geraghty, C. (1981) 'The continuous serial – a definition', in R. Dyer *et al.* (eds) *Coronation Street*, London: British Film Institute.

Geraghty, C. (1991) *Woman and Soap Opera*, Cambridge: Polity.

Geraghty, C. (1995) 'Social issues and realist soaps: A study of British soaps in the 1980s/1990s', in R. C. Allen (ed.) *To Be Continued: Soap Operas around the World*, London: Routledge.

Gerbner, G. (1973) 'Cultural indicators – the third voice', in G. Gerbner *et al.* (eds) *Communications Technology and Social Policy*, New York: Wiley.

Gerbner, G. *et al.* (1980) 'The mainstreaming of America', *Journal of Communication* 30:10–27.

Gillespie, P. (1995) *Sacred Serials, Devotional Viewing, and Domestic Worship*, in R. C. Allen (ed.) *To Be Continued: Soap Operas around the World*, London: Routledge.

Gitlin, T. (1983) *Inside Prime Time*, New York: Pantheon.

Gitlin, T. (1987) 'Prime time ideology: the hegemonic process in television entertainment', in H. Newcomb (ed.), *Television: The Critical View* (4th edn), New York: Oxford University Press.

Gitlin, T. (1997) 'The anti-political populism of cultural studies', in M. Ferguson and P. Golding (eds) *Cultural Studies in Question*, London: Sage.

Glasgow University Media Group (1976) *Bad News*, London: Routledge.

Goffman, E. (1959) *The Presentation of Self in Everyday Life*, New York: Doubleday.

Gold, T. (1993) 'Go with your feelings: Hong Kong and Taiwan popular culture in greater China', *The China Quarterly* 136:907–925.

Golding, P. (1981) 'The missing dimensions – news media and the management of social change', in E. Katz and T. Szecsko (eds), *Mass Media and Social Change*, London: Sage.

Golding, P. (1990) 'Political communication and citizenship', in M. Ferguson (ed.) *Public Communication: the New Imperatives*, London: Sage.

Golding, P. and Murdock, G. (1991) 'Culture, communication and political economy', in J. Curran and M. Gurevitch (eds) *Mass Media and Society*, London: Edward Arnold.

Graddol, D. (1994) 'What is a text?', in D. Graddol and O. Boyd-Barrett (eds) *Media Texts: Authors and Readers*, Clevedon: Open University.

Graddol, D. and Boyd-Barrett, O. (eds) (1994) *Media Texts: Authors and Readers*, Clevedon: Open University.

Gramsci, A. (1971) *Selection from the Prison Notebook*, New York: International Publishers.

Gripsrud, J. (1995) *The Dynasty Years: Hollywood TV and Critical Media Studies*, London: Routledge.

Grossberg, L. (1995) 'Cultural studies vs. political economy: Is anybody else bored with this debate?', *Critical Studies in Mass Communication* 12:62–71.

Gurevitch, M. *et al.* (eds) (1982) *Media, Society and Culture*, London: Routledge.

Hagedorn, R. (1995) 'Doubtless to Be Continued: A Brief History of Serial Narrative', in R. C. Allen (ed.) *To Be Continued: Soap Operas around the World*, London: Routledge.

Hagendoorn, L. (1993) 'Ethnic categorisation and outgroup exclusion: cultural values and social stereotypes', *Ethnic and Racial Studies* 16(1):26–51.

Hall, S. (1973) *Encoding and Decoding in the TV Discourse*, Birmingham: Centre of Contemporary Cultural Studies.

Hall, S. (1981) 'Recent developments in theories of language and ideology: Critical notes', in S. Hall *et al.* (eds) *Culture, Media, Language*, London: Hutchinson.

Hall, S. (1982) 'The rediscovery of "ideology": return of the repressed in media studies', in M. Gurevitch *et al.* (eds) *Media, Society and Culture*, London: Routledge.

Hall, S. (1985) 'Signification, representation, ideology: Althusser and the post-structuralist debates', *Critical Studies in Mass Communication* 2(2):91–114.

Hall, S. (1986a) 'Gramsci's relevance for the study of race and ethnicity', *Journal of Communication Inquiry* 10(2):5–27.

Hall, S. (1986b) 'The problem of ideology – Marxism without guarantees', *Journal of Communication Inquiry* 10(2):28–44.

Hall, S. (1988) *The Hard Road to Renewal*, London: Verso.

Hall, S. (1989) 'Ideology and communication theory', in B. Dervin *et al.* (eds), *Rethinking Communication* (vol. 2), London: Sage.

Hall, S. (1990) 'Cultural identity and diaspora', in J. Rutherford (ed.), *Identity: Community, Culture, Difference*, London: Lawrence & Wishart.

Hall, S. (1992) 'The question of cultural identity', in S. Hall *et al.* (eds) *Modernity and Its Future*, London: Polity.

Hall, S. (1996) 'The problem of ideology: Marxism without guarantees', in D. Morley and K. H. Chen (eds) *Stuart Hall: Critical Dialogues in Cultural Studies*, London: Routledge.

Hall, S. and du Gay, P. (eds) (1996) *Questions of Cultural Identities*, London: Sage.

Hall, S. *et al.* (1978) *Policing the Crisis*, London: Macmillan.

Hallin, D. C. (1993) *We Keep America on Top of the World: TV Journalism and the Public Sphere*, London and New York: Routledge.

Hamelink, C. (1983) *Cultural Autonomy in Global Communications*, New York: Longman.

Hardt, H. (1992) *Critical Communication Studies*, London: Routledge.

Hardt, H. (1997) 'British cultural studies and the return of the "critical" in American mass communications research: Accommodation or radical change?', in D. Morley and K. H. Chen (eds) *Stuart Hall: Critical Dialogues in Cultural Studies*, London: Routledge.

Hartley, J. (1992) *Tele-ology: Studies in Television*, London: Routledge.

Heath, S. (1981) *Questions of Cinema*, London: Macmillan.

Heck, M. C. (1981) 'The ideological dimension of media', in S. Hall *et al.* (eds) *Culture, Media, Language*, London: Hutchinson.

Heidt, E. U. (1987) *Mass Media, Cultural Tradition, and National Identity: The Cases of Singapore and Its TV Programmes*, Saarbrucken, Germany: Verlag Breitenbach Publishers.

Herman, E. S. and Chomsky, N. (1988) *Manufacturing Consent: The Political Economy of the Mass Media*, New York: Pantheon.

Hill, S. (1990) 'Britain: The dominant ideology thesis after a decade', in N. Abercrombie *et al.* (eds) *Dominant Ideologies*, London: Allen & Unwin.

Himmelstein, H. (1984) *Television Myth and the American Mind*, New York: Praeger.

Hirst, P. and Woolley, P. (1982) *Social Relations and Human Attributes*, London: Tavistock.

HKU Student Union (1980) *Research on Mainland Immigrants*, Hong Kong: HKU Student Union.

Hobsbawm, E. (1983) *Introduction: Inventing Traditions*, in E. Hobsbawm and T. Ranger (eds) *The Invention of Tradition*, Cambridge: Cambridge University Press.

Hobsbawm, E. (1992) *Nations and Nationalism since 1780: Programme, Myth, Reality*, Cambridge: Cambridge University Press.

Hobsbawm, E. and Ranger, T. (eds) (1983) *The Invention of Tradition*, Cambridge: Cambridge University Press.

Hobson, D. (1982) *Crossroads: The Drama of a Soap Opera*, London: Longman.

Hodge, R. and Kress, G. (1988) *Social Semiotics*, Cambridge: Polity.

Hoffmann, S. (1993) 'Europe's identity crisis', *Daedalus* 93(4):75–91.

Hoffmann, S. (1994) 'Europe's Identity Crisis Revisited', *Daedalus* 123(2):1–23.

Hook, B. (1983) 'The government of Hong Kong: Changes within tradition', *The China Quarterly* 95:491–511.

Hook, B. (1993) 'Political change in Hong Kong', *The China Quarterly* 136:840–863.

Hoskins, C. *et al.* (1989) 'US television programmes in the international market: Unfair pricing', *Journal of Communication* 39(2):55–75.

Hoynes, W. (1994) *Public TV for Sale*, Boulder, Col.: Westview.

Hurd, G. (1981) 'The TV presentation of the police', in T. Bennett *et al.* (eds) *Popular TV and Film*, London: British Film Institute.

Intintoli, M. (1985) 'Ethnography and media production', *Communication* 8(2):245–263.

Jameson, F. (1991) *Postmodernism, or, the Cultural Logic of Late Capitalism*, London: Verso.

Jankowski, N. W. and Wester, F. (1991) 'The qualitative tradition in social science inquiry: contributions to mass communication research', in K. B. Jensen and N. W. Jankowski (eds), *A Handbook of Qualitative Methodologies for Mass Communication Research*, London: Routledge.

Janowitz, M. (1960) *The Professional Soldier*, New York: Free Press.

Jarvie, I. C. (1977) *Windows on Hong Kong*, Hong Kong: University of Hong Kong, Centre of Asian Studies.

Jenkins, R. (1992) *Pierre Bourdieu*, London: Routledge.

Jenkins, R. (1994) 'Rethinking ethnicity: identity, categorisation and power', *Ethnic and Racial Studies* 17(2):197–223.

Jenks, C. (ed.) (1993) *Cultural Reproduction*, London: Routledge.

Jensen, K. B. (1992) 'The politics of polysemy: TV news, everyday consciousness and political action', in P. Scannell *et al.* (eds) *Culture and Power*, London: Sage.

Jhally, S. and Lewis, J. (1992) *Enlightened Racism*, Boulder, Col.: Westview.

Jordon, M. (1981) 'Realism and convention', in R. Dyer *et al.* (eds) *Coronation Street*, London: British Film Institute.

Kammen, M. (1993) *Mystic Chords of Memory: The Transformation of Tradition in American Culture*, New York: Vintage.

Kaplan, A. (ed.) (1983) *Regarding Television: Critical Approaches*, Frederick, Md: University Publications of America.

Karthigesu, R. (1988) 'Television as a tool for nation-building in the Third World', in P. Drummond and R. Paterson (eds), *Television and Its Audience*, London: British Film Institute.

Katz, E. and Wedell, G. (1977) *Broadcasting in the Third World*, Cambridge, Mass.: Harvard University Press.

Kellner, D. (1987) 'TV, ideology, and emancipatory popular culture', in Horace Newcomb (ed.), *Television: The Critical View* (4th edn), New York: Oxford University Press.

Kellner, D. (1992) 'Popular culture and the construction of postmodern identities', in S. Lash and J. Friedman (eds) *Modernity and Identity*, Oxford: Blackwell.

Kellner, D. (1995) *Media Culture*, London and New York: Routledge.

Kellner, D. (1997) 'Overcoming the divide: Cultural studies and political economy', in M. Ferguson and P. Golding (eds) *Cultural Studies in Question*, London: Sage.

King, A. (1975) 'Administrative absorption of politics in Hong Kong: Emphasis on the grassroots level', *Asian Survey* 15(5):422–439.

King, A. (1985) 'The Hong Kong talks and Hong Kong politics', *Issues and Studies* 22(6):52–75.

Kress, G. (1985) 'Ideological structures in discourse', in T. van Dijk (ed.) *Handbook of Discourse Analysis* (vol. 3), London: Academic Press.

Kreutzner, G. and Seiter, E. (1991) 'Not all soaps are created equal: towards a cross cultural criticism of TV serials', *Screen* 32(2):154–172.

Kuan, H. C. and Lau, S. K. (1988) *Mass Media and Politics in Hong Kong*, Hong Kong: Institute of Social Studies, Chinese University of Hong Kong.

Kung, J. and Yueai, Z. (1984) 'Hong Kong cinema and television in the 1970s', *A Study of Hong Kong Cinema in the 1970s*, Hong Kong: Urban Council.

Kwan, Y. K. (1990) 'Hong Kong television: a historical perspective', *Seminar on the Role of Public TV Broadcasting in the 1990s*, Hong Kong: RTHK.

Lam, K. C. and Liu, P. W. (1993) *Are Immigrants Assimilating Better Now than a Decade Ago? The Case of Hong Kong*, Hong Kong: Hong Kong Institute of Asia-Pacific Studies, Chinese University of Hong Kong.

Lane, K. P. (1990) *Sovereignty and the Status Quo: The Historical Roots of China's Hong Kong Policy*, Boulder, Col.: Westview.

Larrain, J. (1994) *Ideology and Cultural Identity*, Cambridge: Polity.

Lash, S. (1993) 'Pierre Bourdieu: cultural economy and social change', in C. Calhoun *et al.* (eds) *Bourdieu: Critical Perspectives*, Cambridge: Polity Press.

Lau, S. K. (1982) *The Society and Politics in Hong Kong*, Hong Kong: Chinese University of Hong Kong Press.

Lau, S. K. (1990) *Decolonization without Independence and the Poverty of Political Leaders in Hong Kong*, Hong Kong: Hong Kong Institute of Asia-Pacific Studies, Chinese University of Hong Kong.

Lau, S. K. (1997) '"Hong Konger" or "Chinese"?: The identity of Hong Kong Chinese 1985–1995', *Twenty-First Century Bimonthly* 41: 43–58 (in Chinese).

Lau, S. K. and Kuan, H. C. (1988) *The Ethos of the Hong Kong Chinese*, Hong Kong: Chinese University of Hong Kong Press.

Lau, S. K. and Kuan, H. C. (1991) *Public Attitude toward Laissez Faire in Hong Kong*, Hong Kong: Hong Kong Institute of Asia-Pacific Studies, Chinese University of Hong Kong.

Lau, S. K. and Wan, P. S. (1987) *A Preliminary Report on Social Indicators Research in Hong Kong*, Hong Kong: Centre for Hong Kong Studies, Chinese University of Hong Kong.

Lau, S. K. *et al.* (1991) 'Political attitudes', in S. K. Lau *et al.* (eds), *Indicators of Social Development: Hong Kong 1988*, Hong Kong: Institute of Asia-Pacific Studies, Chinese University of Hong Kong.

Law, K. (1984) 'The Shaolin Temple of the new Hong Kong cinema', *A Study of Hong Kong Cinema in the 1970s*, Hong Kong: Urban Council.

Law, K. (1986) 'Archetype and variations', *Cantonese Melodrama: 1950–1969*, Hong Kong: Urban Council.

Lee, C. C. (1997) 'Media structure and regime change in Hong Kong', in M. K.

Chan (ed.) *The Challenge of Hong Kong's Reintegration with China*, Hong Kong: Hong Kong University Press.

Lee, M. C. (1982) 'Emergent patterns of social conflicts in Hong Kong society', in J. Y. S. Cheng (ed.) *Hong Kong in the 1980s*, Hong Kong: Summerson.

Lee, P. S. N. (1991) 'The absorption and indigenization of foreign media cultures: a study on a cultural meeting point of the east and west: Hong Kong', *Asian Journal of Communication* 1(2):52–72.

Lee, P. S. N. (1992) 'Media and communications', in J. Y. S. Cheng and P. C. K. Kwong (eds) *The Other Hong Kong Report 1992*, Hong Kong: Chinese University of Hong Kong Press.

Lent, J. A. (1982) 'ASEAN mass communications and cultural submission', *Media, Culture and Society* 4:171–189.

Leung, B. K. P. (1994) 'Class and class formation in Hong Kong studies', in S. K. Lau *et al.* (eds), *Inequalities and Development: Social Stratification in Chinese Societies*, Hong Kong: Hong Kong Institute of Asia-Pacific Studies, Chinese University of Hong Kong.

Leung, B. K. P. (1996) *Perspectives on Hong Kong Society*, Hong Kong: Oxford University Press.

Leung, G. L. K. (1993) 'The evolution of Hong Kong as a regional movie production and export centre', M.Phil Thesis. Hong Kong: Chinese University of Hong Kong.

Leung, G. L. K. and Chan, J. M. (1997) 'The Hong Kong cinema and its overseas market: a historical review, 1950–1995', in *Fifty Years of Electric Shadows*, Hong Kong: The Urban Council of Hong Kong.

Leung, K. W. Y. and Chan, M. M. (eds) (1995) *Media Law: A New Introduction*, Hong Kong: Commercial Press (in Chinese).

Lewis, J. (1991) *Ideological Octopus*, London: Routledge.

Liang Tao (1992) *Origin of Hong Kong Street Names*, Hong Kong: Urban Council (in Chinese).

Liebes, T. and Katz, E. (1988) 'Dallas and genesis: primordiality and seriality in popular culture', in J. Carey (ed.), *Media, Myths and Narratives*, Newbury Park, Cal.: Sage.

Liebes, T. and Katz, E. (1990) *The Export of Meaning: Cross-Cultural Readings of Dallas*, New York: Oxford University Press.

Lincoln, B. (1989) *Discourse and the Construction of Society: Comparative Studies of Myth, Ritual, and Classification*, Oxford: Oxford University Press.

Lindkvist, K. (1981) 'Approaches to textual analysis', in K. E. Rosengren (ed.) *Advances in Content Analysis*, London: Sage.

Lindlof, T. (1988) 'Media audiences as interpretative communities', in J. Anderson (ed.), *Communication Year Book* 11 Newbury Park, Cal.: Sage, pp 81–107.

Lingnan College (1985) *Report on the Social and Economic Adaptation of the Chinese New Arrivals in Hong Kong*, Hong Kong: Lingnan College.

Livingstone, S. M. (1990) *Making Sense of Television*, Oxford: Pergamon Press.

Livingstone, S. M. (1992) 'The resourceful reader: interpreting TV character and narrative', in S. A. Deetz (ed.), *Communication Year Book* 15, Newbury Park, Cal.: Sage.

Lo, W. N. (ed.) (1983) *Hong Kong Blues*, Hong Kong: Wah Fung Books (in Chinese).

Lodziak, C. (1986) *The Power of Television: A Critical Appraisal*, London: Frances Pinter.

Lopez, A. M. (1995) 'Our welcomed guests: telenovelas in Latin America', in R. C. Allen (ed.) *To Be Continued: Soap Operas around the World*, London: Routledge.

Lopez-Pumarejo, T. A. (1991) 'Transnational television in national TV production: The case of Brazil', unpublished PhD thesis, University of Minnesota.

Lozano, E. and Singhal, A. (1993) 'Melodramatic television serials: mythical narratives for education', *Communications* 18(1):115–126.

Lui, T. L. (1988a) 'Home at HK', *Changes in Hong Kong Society through Cinema*, Hong Kong: Urban Council.

Lui, T. L. (1988b) 'Hong Kong new middle class: characteristics and prospects', in A. B. L. Cheung *et al.* (eds) *Class Analysis and Hong Kong*, Hong Kong: Twilight Books (in Chinese).

Lui, T. L. (1997) 'The Hong Kong new middle class on the eve of 1997', in J. Y. S. Cheng (ed.) *The Other Hong Kong Report 1997*, Hong Kong: The Chinese University of Hong Kong.

Luk, B. H. K. (1989) 'Chinese culture in the Hong Kong curriculum: heritage and colonialism', unpublished paper presented at CIES (Comparative and International Education Society) Annual Meeting, Boston, 30 March–2 April, 1989.

Luk, B. H. K. (1995) 'Hong Kong history and Hong Kong culture', in E. Sinn (ed.) *Culture and Society in Hong Kong*, Hong Kong: The Centre of Asian Studies, The University of Hong Kong (in Chinese).

Lull, J. (1990) *China Turned On*, London: Routledge.

Lum, C. M. K. (1996) *In Search of a Voice: Karaoke and the Construction of Identity in Chinese America*, New Jersey: Lawrence Erlbaum Associates.

Ma, E. K. W. (1992) *Hong Kong Television in Transition*, Hong Kong: Sub-Culture (in Chinese).

Ma, E. K. W. (1995) 'The production of television ideologies: A comparative study of public and commercial to dramas', *Gazette* 55:39–54.

Ma, E. K. W. (1996) 'Television', in S. M. Li and M. K. Nyaw (eds) *The Other Hong Kong Report 1996*, Hong Kong: The Chinese University Press.

Ma, E. K. W. (1998) 'Re-inventing Hong Kong: Memory, identity and television', *International Journal of Cultural Studies* 1(3):329–349.

Ma, E. K. W. and Fung, A. Y. H. (1997) 'Mediated re-sinicisation and nationalisation of the Hong Kong Identity', paper presented at the International Communication Association Annual Meeting, May 1997.

McAllister, M. P. (1996) *The Commercialization of American Culture: New Advertising, Control and Democracy*, Newbury Park, Cal.: Sage.

MacCabe, C. (1976) 'Theory of film: principles of realism and pleasures', *Screen* 17:7–27.

McDaniel, D. O. (1994) *Broadcasting in the Malay World*, New Jersey: Ablex Publishing Corporation.

MacDonald, M. (1993) 'The construction of difference: an anthropological approach to stereotypes', in M. MacDonald (ed.) *Inside European Identities*, Oxford: Berg.

MacDonell, D. (1986) *Theories of Discourse: In Introduction*, Oxford: Blackwell.

McLennan, G. (1989) *Marxism, Pluralism and Beyond*, Cambridge: Polity.

McLeod, J. M. *et al.* (1991) 'On understanding and misunderstanding of media effects', in J. Curran and M. Gurevitch (eds) *Mass Media and Society*, London: Edward Arnold.

McQuail, D. (1991) 'Media performance assessment in the public interest: principles and methods', *Communication Year Book* 14:111–145.

Manley, J. F. (1983) 'Neo-pluralism: a class analysis of pluralism I and pluralism II', *American Political Science Review* 77(2):368–383.

Mann, M. (1973) *Consciousness and Action among the Western Working Class*, London: Macmillan.

Martin-Barbero, J. (1988) 'Communication from culture: The crisis of the national and the emergence of the popular', *Media, Culture and Society* 10(4):447–466.

Martin-Barbero, J. (1993) *Communication, Culture and Hegemony: From the Media to Mediations*, London: Sage.

Martin-Barbero, J. (1995) 'Memory and form in the Latin American soap opera', in R. C. Allen (ed.) *To Be Continued: Soap Operas around the World*, London: Routledge.

Massey, D. (1991) 'A global sense of place', *Marxism Today*, June.

Mazziotti, N. (1993) 'Soap opera', *Communication Research Trends* 13(4):2–6.

Meeham, E. R. (1986) 'Conceptualising culture as commodity: The problem of TV', *Critical Studies of Mass Communication* 3:448–457.

Miliband, R. (1969) *The State in Capitalist Society*, New York: Basic Books.

Miliband, R. (1989) *Divided Societies: Class Struggle in Contemporary Capitalism*, Oxford: Clarendon Press.

Miners, N. (1991) *The Government and Politics of Hong Kong*, Hong Kong: Oxford University Press.

Morley, D. (1980) *The Nationwide Audience: Structure and Decoding*, London: British Film Institute.

Morley, D. (1993) *Television, Audiences, and Cultural Studies*, London: Routledge.

Morley, D. (1996a) 'Populism, revisionism and the "new" audience research', in J. Curran *et al.* (eds) *Cultural Studies and Communications*, London: Edward Arnold.

Morley, D. (1996b) 'EurAm, modernity, reason and alterity: Or, postmodernism, the highest stage of cultural imperialism?', in D. Morley and K. H. Chen (eds) *Stuart Hall: Critical Dialogues in Cultural Studies*, London: Routledge.

Morley, D. and Chen, K. H. (1996) (eds) *Stuart Hall: Critical Dialogues in Cultural Studies*, London: Routledge.

Morley, D. and Robins, K. (1993) *Spaces of Identities*, London: Routledge.

Murdock, G. (1982) 'Large corporations and the control of the communications industries', in M. Gurevitch *et al.* (eds) *Media, Society and Culture*, London: Routledge.

Murdock, G. (1989a) 'Cultural studies: Missing links', *Critical Studies in Mass Communication*, 12:436–440.

Murdock, G. (1989b) 'Critical inquiry and audience activity', in L. Grossberg *et al.* (eds), *Rethinking Communication* (vol. 2), Newbury Park, Cal.: Sage.

Murdock, G. (1990) 'Redrawing the map of the communications industries: Concentration and ownership in the era of privatisation', in M. Ferguson (ed.) *Public Communication: The New Imperatives*, London: Sage.

Murdock, G. (1992) 'Citizens, consumers, and public culture', in M. Skovmand *et al.* (eds) *Media Cultures: Re-appraising Transnational Media*, London: Routledge.

Murdock, G. (1995) 'Across the great divide: Cultural analysis and the condition of democracy', *Critical Studies in Mass Communication* 12:62–71.

Murdock, G. (1997) 'Base notes: The conditions of cultural practice', in M. Ferguson and P. Golding (eds) *Cultural Studies in Question*, London: Sage.

Newcomb, H. (1991) 'Media institutions: The creation of television drama', in K. B. Jensen and N. W. Jankowski (eds), *A Handbook of Qualitative Methodologies for Mass Communication Research*, London: Routledge.

Newcomb, H. (ed.) (1994) *TV: The Critical View* (5th edn), New York: Oxford University Press.

Newcomb, H. and Alley, R. S. (1983) *The Producer's Medium: Conversations with Creators of American TV*, New York: Oxford University Press.

Newcomb, H. and Hirsch, P. M. (1984) 'Television as a cultural forum', in W. D. Rowland and B. Watkins (eds), *Interpreting Television: Current Research Perspectives*, Newbury Park, Cal.: Sage.

Ochs, E. (1979) 'Transcription as theory', in E. Ochs *et al.* (eds), *Development Pragmatics*, New York: Academic Press.

Oltean, T. (1993) 'Series and seriality in media culture', *European Journal of Communication* 8:5–31.

Perrow, C. (1986) *Complex Organization: A Critical Essay*, New York: McGraw Hill.

Peterson, R. A. (1982) 'Five constraints on the production of culture: Law, technology, market, organizational structure and occupational careers', *Journal of Popular Culture* 6(2):143–153.

Peterson, R. A. (1994) 'Cultural studies through the production perspective: Progress and prospects', in D. Crane (ed.) *The Sociology of Culture*, Oxford: Blackwell.

Petrie, D. and Willis, J. (eds) (1995) *Television and the Household*, London: British Film Institute.

Philo, G. (1990) *Seeing is Believing*, London: Routledge.

Picht, R. (1993) 'Distributed identities: Social and cultural mutations in contemporary Europe', in S. Garcia (ed.) *European Identity and the Search for Legitimacy*, London: Pinter.

Pomery, C. (1988) 'Hong Kong', in M. Alvarado (ed.), *Video World Wide: An International Study*, London: UNESCO.

Powell, W. W. and DiMaggio, P. J. (eds) (1991) *The New Institutionalism in Organizational Analysis*, Chicago: University of Chicago Press.

Preston, P. W. (1997) *Political/Cultural Identity: Citizens and Notions in a Global Era*, London: Sage.

Propp, V. (1968) *The Morphology of Folktale*, Austin: University of Texas Press.

Radway, J. (1984) *Reading the Romance*, Chapel Hill: University of North Carolina Press.

Ragin, C. (1989) *The Comparative Method: Moving beyond Qualitative and Quantitative Strategies*, Berkeley, California: University of California Press.

Reeves, G. (1993) *Communications and the Third World*, London: Routledge.

Robins, K. (1996) 'Interrupting identities', in P. du Gay and S. Hall (eds) *Questions of Cultural Identity*, London: Sage.

Rogers, E. M. and Antola, L. (1985) 'Telenovelas: a Latin American success story', *Journal of Communication* 35(4):24–35.

Rootes, M. (1981) 'The dominant ideology thesis and its critics', *Sociology* 15(3):436–444.

Rosengren, K. E. (ed.) (1981) *Advances in Content Analysis*, Beverly Hills: Sage.

Rothman, S. (ed.) (1992) *The Mass Media in Liberal Democratic Societies*, New York: PWPA Books.

Rothman S. *et al.* (1991) *Elites in Conflict: Social Change in America Today*, Greenwood: Praeger.

Rothman, S. *et al.* (1992) *Television's America*, in S. Rothman (ed.), *The Mass Media in Liberal Democratic Societies*, New York: PWPA Books.

Rowland, W. and Watkins, B. (eds) (1984) *Interpreting Television: Current Research Perspectives*, Beverly Hills: Sage.

Ryan, B. (1991) *Making Capital from Culture: The Corporate Form of Capitalist Cultural Production*, Berlin New York: de Gruyter.

Sacks, H. (1992a) *Lectures on Conversation* (vol. 1), Oxford: Blackwell.

Sacks, H. (1992b) *Lectures on Conversation* (vol. 2), Oxford: Blackwell.

Samuel, R. (ed.) (1989a) *Patriotism: The Making and Unmaking of British National Identity (Vol. 1): History and Politics*, London: Routledge.

Samuel, R. (ed.) (1989b) *Patriotism: The Making and Unmaking of British National Identity (Vol. 3): National Fictions*, London: Routledge.

Samuel, R. and Thompson, P. (eds) (1990) *The Myth We Live By*, London: Routledge.

Sassoon, A. S. (1987) *Gramsci's Political*, Minneapolis: University of Minnesota Press.

Saussure, F. de (1959) [1916] *Course in General Linguistics*, London: Peter Owen.

Scannell, P. (1992a) 'Public service broadcasting and modern public life', in P. Scannell *et al.* (eds) *Culture and Power*, London: Sage.

Scannell, P. (1992b) 'Introduction', in P. Scannell *et al.* (eds) *Culture and Power*, London: Sage.

Scannell, P. (1996) *Radio, Television and Modern Life*, Oxford: Blackwell.

Scheff, T. (1994) 'Emotions and Identity', in C. Calhoun (ed.) *Social Theory and the Politics of Identity*, Oxford: Blackwell.

Schegloff, E. A. (1991) 'Reflections on talk and social structure', in D. Boden and D. Zimmerman (eds), *Talk and Social Structure*, Cambridge: Polity.

Schiller, H. I. (1989) *Culture Inc.: The Corporate Takeover of Public Expression*, Oxford: Oxford University Press.

Schiller, H. I. (1992) *Mass Communication and American Empire* (2nd edn), Boulder, Col.: Westview.

Schlesinger, P. (1990) 'Rethinking the sociology of journalism', in M. Ferguson (ed.) *Public Communication: The New Imperatives*, London: Sage.

Schlesinger, P. (1991) *Media, State and Nation: Political Violence and Collective Identities*, London: Sage.

Schlesinger, P. (1993) 'Wishful thinking: Cultural politics, media, and collective identities in Europe', *Journal of Communication* 43(2):6–17.

Schlesinger, P. (1994) 'Europe's contradictory communicative space', *Daedalus* 123(2):25–52.

Schlesinger, P. *et al.* (1983) *Televising Terrorism*, London: Comedia.

Schudson, M. (1991) 'The sociology of news production revisited', in J. Curran and M. Gurevitch (eds) *Mass Media and Society*, London: Edward Arnold.

Schudson, M. (1994) 'Culture and the integration of national societies', in D. Crane (ed.) *The Sociology of Culture*, Oxford: Blackwell.

Scott, W. R. (1987) *Organizations: Rational, Natural, and Open Systems*, Englewood Cliffs, NJ: Prentice-Hall.

Seiter, E. *et al.* (eds) (1989) *Remote Control*, London: Routledge.

Sek Kei (1988) 'The social psychology of Hong Kong cinema', *Changes in Hong Kong Society through Cinema*, Hong Kong: Urban Council.

Sek, K. (1997) 'Hong Kong cinema from June 4 to 1997', in *Fifty Years of Electric Shadows*, Hong Kong: Urban Council.

Self, D. (1984) *TV Drama: An Introduction*, London: Macmillan.

Sennett, R. and Cobb, J. (1993) *The Hidden Injuries of Class*, London: Faber & Faber.

Sheehan, H. (1987) *Irish Television Drama*, Dublin: Radio Telefis Eireann.

Shen, J. (1972) *The Law and Mass Media in Hong Kong*, Hong Kong: Mass Communication Centre, Chinese University of Hong Kong.

Silverman, D. (1993a) 'Unfixing the subject: Viewing bad timing', in C. Jenks (ed.) *Cultural Reproduction*, London: Routledge.

Silverman, D. (1993b) *Interpreting Qualitative Data*, London: Sage.

Silverstone, R. (1981) *The Message of Television: Myth and Narrative in Contemporary Culture*, London: Heinemann.

Silverstone, R. (1988) 'Television myth and culture', in J. Carey (ed.) *Media, Myths and Narratives*, Beverly Hills, Cal.: Sage.

Silverstone, R. (1994) *Television and Everyday Life*, London: Routledge.

Simon, R. (1991) *Gramsci's Political Thought: An Introduction*, London: Lawrence & Wishart.

Singhal, A. and Rogers, E. (1988) 'Television soap operas for development in India', *Gazette* 41:109–126.

Siu, H. S. (1986) 'Immigrants and social ethos: Hong Kong in the 1980s', *The Journal of the Hong Kong Branch of the Royal Asiatic Society* 26:1–16.

Siu, H. S. (1993) 'Cultural identity and the politics of difference in South China', *Daedalus* (Spring):19–43.

Siu, H. S. (1996) 'Remade in Hong Kong: Weaving into the Chinese cultural tapestry', in T. T. Lin and D. Faure (eds) *Unity and Diversity: Local Cultures and Identities*, Hong Kong: Hong Kong University Press.

Slack, J. D. (1996) 'The theory and method of articulation in cultural studies', in D. Morley and K. H. Chen (eds) *Stuart Hall: Critical Dialogues in Cultural Studies*, London: Routledge.

Smith, A. D. (1991) *National Identity*, Harmondsworth: Penguin.

So, A. Y. and Kwitko, L. (1990) 'The new middle class and the democratic movement in Hong Kong', *Journal of Contemporary Asia* 20(3):384–398.

Sreberny-Mohammadi, A. (1991) 'The global and the local in international communications', in J. Curran and M. Gurevitch (eds) *Mass Media and Society*, London: Edward Arnold.

Stevenson, N. (1995) *Understanding Media Cultures*, London: Sage.

Sumser, J. (1992) 'Not just any Tom, Dick or Harry: the grammar of names in TV drama', *Media, Culture and Society* 14:605–622.

Sung, Y. W. (1992) *Non-institutional Economic Integration via Cultural Affinity*, Hong Kong: Hong Kong Institute of Asia-Pacific Studies, Chinese University of Hong Kong.

Sutton, S. (1982) *The Largest Theatre in the World: 30 Years of TV Drama*, London: BBC.

Sweeting, A. E. (1992) 'Hong Kong education within historical processes', in G. A. Postiglione (ed.), *Education and Society in Hong Kong*, Hong Kong: University of Hong Kong Press.

Swidler, A. *et al.* (1986) 'Format and formula in prime-time TV', in S. Ball-Rokeach (ed.) *Media, Audience, and Social Structure*, Newbury Park: Sage.

Swingewood, A. (1977) *The Myth of Mass Culture*, London: Macmillan.

Tang, J. T. H. (1994) 'From empire defense to imperial retreat', *Modern Asian Studies* 28(2):317–337.

Taylor, E. (1989) *Prime-Time Families: TV Culture in Postwar America*, Berkeley: University of California Press.

Teo, S. (1997) *Hong Kong Cinema: The Extra Dimensions*, London: British Film Institute.

Tetzlaff, D. (1992) 'Popular culture and social control in late capitalism', in P. Scannell *et al.* (eds) *Culture and Power*, London: Sage.

Thompson, J. B. (1990) *Ideology and Modern Culture*, Cambridge: Polity.

Thompson, J. B. (1994) 'Social theory and the media', in D. Crowley and D. Mitchell (eds) *Communication Theory Today*, Cambridge: Polity.

Thorburn, D. (1976) 'Television melodrama', in D. Cater and R. Adler (eds) *Television as a Cultural Force*, New York: Praeger.

Tomlinson, J. (1991) *Cultural Imperialism*, London: Pinter Publishers.

Traube, E. G. (1992) *Dreaming Identities*, Boulder, Col.: Westview.

Traudt, P. J. and Lont, C. M. (1987) 'Media-logic in use: the family as locus of study', in T. R. Lindlof (ed.), *Natural Audiences*, New Jersey: Ablex Publishing.

Tsang, S. K. (1993) 'Income distribution', in P. K. Choi and L. S. Ho (eds), *The Other Hong Kong Report 1993*, Hong Kong: Chinese University of Hong Kong Press.

Tsang, W. K. (1992) *The Class Structure in Hong Kong*, Hong Kong: Hong Kong Institute of Asia-Pacific Studies, Chinese University of Hong Kong.

Tsang, W. K. (1993) *Education and Early Socioeconomic Status Attainment in Hong Kong*, Hong Kong: Hong Kong Institute of Asia-Pacific Studies, Chinese University of Hong Kong.

Tsang, W. K. (1994) 'Consolidation of a class structure: Changes in the class structure of Hong Kong', in S. K. Lau *et al.* (eds) *Inequalities and Development: Social Stratification in Chinese Societies*, Hong Kong: Hong Kong Institute of Asia-Pacific Studies, Chinese University of Hong Kong.

Tu, W. M. (1991) 'Cultural China: The periphery as the center', *Daedalus* 120(2):1–31.

Tuchman, G. (ed.) (1974) *The TV Establishment*, Englewood Cliffs, NJ: Prentice Hall.

Tuchman, G. (1978a) *Making News: A Study in the Construction of Reality*, New York: Free Press.

Tuchman, G. (ed.) (1978b) *Hearth and Home: Images of Women in the Mass Media*, New York: Oxford University Press.

Tulloch, J. (1990) *Television Drama: Agency, Audience, and Myth*, London: Routledge.

Tulloch, J. and Alvarado, M. (1983) *Doctor Who: The Unfolding Text*, London: Macmillan.

Tulloch, J. and Moran, A. (1986) *A Country Practice: Quality Soap*, Sydney: Currency Press.

Tunstall, J. (1991) 'A media industry perspective', *Communication Year Book* 14:163–186.

Tunstall, J. (1993) *Television Producers*, London: Routledge.

Turner, B. S. (1990) 'Conclusion: Peroration on ideology', in N. Abercrombie *et al.* (eds) *Dominant Ideologies*, London: Allen & Unwin.

Turner, M. (1988) *Made in Hong Kong*, Hong Kong: Urban Council.

Turow, J. (1984) *Media Industry: The Production of News and Entertainment*, New York: Longman.

Umphlett, W. L. (1983) *Mythmakers of the American Dream: The Nostalgic Vision in Popular Culture*, New York London: Cornwall Books.

van Dijk, T. (1977) *Text and Context*, London: Longman.

van Dijk, T. (1983) 'Discourse analysis: Its development and application to the structure of news', *Journal of Communications* 33(1):20–43.

van Dijk, T. (ed.) (1985a) 'Disciplines of discourse', *Handbook of Discourse Analysis* (vol. 1), London: Academic Press.

van Dijk, T. (ed.) (1985b) 'Dimensions of discourse', *Handbook of Discourse Analysis* (vol. 2), London: Academic Press.

van Dijk, T. (ed.) (1985c) 'Discourse and dialogue', *Handbook of Discourse Analysis* (vol. 3), London: Academic Press.

van Dijk, T. (ed.) (1985d) 'Discourse analysis in society', *Handbook of Discourse Analysis* (vol. 4), London: Academic Press.

van Dijk, T. (1994) 'Discourse analysis as social analysis', *Discourse and Society* 5(2):163–164.

Walsh, D. (1993) 'The role of ideology in cultural reproduction', in C. Jenks (ed.) *Cultural Reproduction*, London: Routledge.

Wang, G. W. (1991) 'Among non-Chinese', *Daedalus* 120(2):135–157.

Wang, G. W. (1993) 'Greater China and the Chinese overseas', *The China Quarterly* 136:926–948.

Wang, G. W. (1994) 'Among non-Chinese', in W. M. Tu (ed.) *The Living Tree: The Changing Meaning of Being Chinese Today*, Stanford: Stanford University Press.

Wang, M. L. (1991) 'Who is dominating whose ideology?', *Asian Journal of Communication* 2(1):51–70.

Whale, J. (1980) *The Politics of the Media*, London: Fontana.

Wheen, F. (1985) *Television*, London: Century.

White, M. (1992) 'Ideological analysis and television', in R. C. Allen (ed.), *Channels of Discourse, Reassembled*, London: Routledge.

White, R. A. (1983) 'Mass communication and culture: transition to a new paradigm', *Journal of Communication*, 33: 279–301.

White, R. A. (1994) 'Audience interpretation of media: emerging perspectives', *Communication Research Trends*, 14(3): 3–32.

Williams, B. (1994) 'North to the future', in H. Newcomb (ed.), *TV: The Critical View* (5th edn), New York: Oxford University Press.

Williams, R. (1990) *Television: Technology and Cultural Form*, ed. E. Williams, London: Routledge.

Williams, T. (1992) *It's Time for My Story*, London: Praeger.

Wong, S. L. (1988) *Emigrant Entrepreneurs: Shanghai Industrialists in Hong Kong*, Hong Kong: Oxford University Press.

Wong, T. W. P. (1988) 'Class and social analysis', in B. L. Cheung *et al.* (eds), *Class Analysis and Hong Kong*, Hong Kong: Twilight Books (in Chinese).

Wong, T. W. P. (1991) 'Inequality, stratification and mobility', in S. K. Lau *et al.* (eds), *Indicators of Social Development: Hong Kong 1988*, Hong Kong: Hong Kong Institute of Asia-Pacific Studies, Chinese University of Hong Kong.

Wong, T. W. P. and Lui, T. L. (1993) *Morality, Class and the Hong Kong Way of Life*, Hong Kong: Hong Kong Institute of Asia-Pacific studies, Chinese University of Hong Kong.

Wong, W. C. *et al.* (1997) *Hong Kong Un-Imagined: History, Culture and the Future*, Taiwan: Rye Field.

Yao, S. (1994) 'The predicament of modernity: Mass media and the making of the West in Southeast Asia', *Asian Journal of Communication* 4(1):33–51.

Yee, A. H. (1992) *A People Misruled: Hong Kong and the Chinese Stepping Stone Syndrome*, Hong Kong: AIP Press.

Young, J. D. (1994) 'The building years: Maintaining a China–Hong Kong–Britain equilibrium, 1950–71', in M. K. Chan (ed.) *Precarious Balance:*

Hong Kong between China and Britain, Hong Kong: University of Hong Kong Press.

Yung, D.Y. Y. (1991) *Mainlanders in Hong Kong Films of the 1980s*, M.Phil Thesis, Chinese University of Hong Kong.

Index